REPRESENTING UNCERTAIN KNOWLEDGE

An Artificial Intelligence Approach

Paul Krause
Dominic Clark

Imperial Cancer Research Fund
London

intellect

OXFORD, ENGLAND

First Published in 1993 by
Kluwer Academic Publishers
P.O. Box 17, 3300 AA Dordrecht, The Netherlands.

Sold and distributed in the U.S.A. and Canada by
Kluwer Academic Publishers
101 Philip Drive, Norwell, MA 02061, U.S.A.

First published in Paperback in 1993 by
Intellect Books
Suite 2, 108/110 London Road, Oxford OX3 9AW

Consulting editor: Masoud Yazdani
Copy editor: Andrew Healey
Cover design: Mark Lewis

Part of the proceeds of this book will go to support the *Surrey Wildlife Trust*, a
member of the RSNC Wildlife Trusts Partnership.

British Library Cataloguing in Publication Data

Krause, Paul J.
  Representing Uncertain Knowledge:
  Artificial Intelligence Approach
  I. Title II. Clark, Dominic A.
  006.3

    ISBN 1-871516-17-X

Library of Congress Cataloging-in-Publication Data available

    ISBN 0-7923-2433-1

Printed and bound in Great Britain by Cromwell Press, Wiltshire.

Preface

The representation of uncertainty is a central issue in Artificial Intelligence (AI) and is being addressed in many different ways. Each approach has its proponents, and each has had its detractors. However, there is now an increasing move towards the belief that an eclectic approach is required to represent and reason under the many facets of uncertainty. We believe that the time is ripe for a wide ranging, yet accessible, survey of the main formalisms.

In this book, we offer a broad perspective on uncertainty and approaches to managing uncertainty. Rather than provide a daunting mass of technical detail, we have focused on the foundations and intuitions behind the various schools. The aim has been to present in one volume an overview of the major issues and decisions to be made in representing uncertain knowledge. We identify the central role of managing uncertainty to AI and Expert Systems, and provide a comprehensive introduction to the different aspects of uncertainty. We then describe the rationales, advantages and limitations of the major approaches that have been taken, using illustrative examples. The book ends with a review of the lessons learned and current research directions in the field.

The intended readership will include researchers and practitioners involved in the design and implementation of Decision Support Systems, Expert Systems, other Knowledge-Based Systems and in Cognitive Science. This book will also be a valuable text for students of Computer Science, Cognitive Science, Psychology and Engineering with an interest in AI or Decision Support Systems. They will find here:

- A comprehensive review, with an extensive bibliography, of a field that is central to AI.
- A survey of the major knowledge engineering and computational implications for the different techniques in terms of their respective requirements, merits and limitations.
- Detailed worked examples and descriptions of applications.

Dedication

From Dominic

To Erica and Tristan.

From Paul

To my father, who would have enjoyed seeing this.

Acknowledgements

Writing this book has been a tremendous learning experience for us both. Several colleagues have read and commented on various chapters. Of course, they cannot have corrected all our failings, but great efforts were made by; Philippe Besnard, Frank Klawonn, Rudolf Kruse and David Spiegelhalter. Our deepest thanks go to them. Additionally, several chapters were proof read and given "sanity checks" by colleagues at work. Especial thanks go to Saki Hajnal, who has the sharpest eyes, Colin Gordon, Simon Parsons and Peter Hammond (the last two of whom proof read the whole book).

Our understanding of the subject has benefited greatly from our involvement with the ESPRIT Basic Research Action DRUMS. Our thanks go to all those who were involved in this project. It would perhaps be unjust to single out names for mention in case we missed anyone out. So our deepest thanks go to Philippe Smets who ran the whole show, and we hope that he will pass on our thanks to all the others.

Nearer home, further insight and understanding have been gained from talks with Simon Ambler, Paddy Byers (who reinvented default logic one afternoon; sadly to find it had been done before!), Mike Clarke, Morten Elvang-Gøransson, and Nic Wilson. We would also like to thank the reviewer for valued comments.

We must thank our Editor, Masoud Yazdani, for his patient encouragement during the preparation of this manuscript.

An especially big thank you goes to the Imperial Cancer Research Fund for employing us, and to SERC and ESPRIT for additional support over the last five years or more.

DAC would like to thank all the members of his family for their support, patience and encouragement. Dylan Jones also provided valued support and encouragement in the early stages of his career in uncertainty.

Finally, for allowing us time and facilities to work on this book, we must thank our respective ICRF heads of departments; Chris Rawlings (DAC) and John Fox (PJK and formerly DAC). Especially to the latter who generated so many ideas, introducing one of us (PJK) to uncertainty for the first time and initiated a line of research involving us both that has led to the important developments outlined in Chapter 7.

Contents

Chapter 4   Epistemic Probability: the Dempster-Shafer theory of evidence

Chapter 5   Reasoning with Imprecise and Vague Data

Chapter 6   Non-monotonic Logic

Chapter 7   Argumentation

Chapter 8   Overview

1
The Nature of Uncertainty

I am inviting the reader to imagine... that there is a space of possible theories about probability that has been rather constant from 1660 to the present... perhaps an understanding of our space and its preconditions can liberate us from the cycle of probability theories that has trapped us for so long. (Hacking, 1975).

1.1   Introduction

Uncertainty pervades life and can arise from many sources. It is present in most tasks that require intelligent behaviour, such as planning, reasoning, problem solving, decision making, classification and many others dealing with real world entities and data. Consequently, the management of uncertainty is central to the development of computer based systems that can successfully execute these tasks. This, in turn, depends upon the adoption of uncertainty management techniques that are appropriate for the particular task in hand.

1.1.1   Background.

The technology of Expert Systems and its parent discipline, Artificial Intelligence (AI), has attracted much attention in recent years. In part, this is because of the high level of problem solving performance that has been achieved by some programs (Reddy, 1988), and in part because of the breadth of scientific and commercial domains in which the technology is potentially applicable.

Throughout this book, we shall refer to a number of specific Expert Systems to illustrate the ideas presented, as the technology of Expert Systems has hitherto been the most successful area of commercial AI exploitation.

Several definitions of the term "Expert System" have been proposed which differ in their emphases. Some emphasise Expert Systems as computer simulations of human expertise while others stress expert level performance, usually operationalised as accuracy (see Shafer, 1987). Whilst these are both aspects of Expert System technology, Expert Systems can, in general, be distinguished from conventional computer programs by five characteristics (identified by Buchanan and Smith, 1988) with particular applications differing in the degree to which each characteristic is represented. These five characteristics are:

- The use of symbolic as well as mathematical reasoning.
- The use of domain specific heuristic knowledge (as well as algorithmic knowledge).
- Expert level performance.
- Facilities to explain the reasoning strategy and justification of inferences.
- Flexibility for modification and extension.

While some of these characteristics may be present in well designed conventional software, it is their combination that characterises and distinguishes Expert Systems from conventional software. Further, in contrast to the kinds of quantitative representation and evaluation that are the basis of statistical modelling techniques, it is the characterisation of Expert Systems by (1) the use of symbolic reasoning, and (2) heuristic methods for the representation and manipulation of information that mark Expert Systems as AI programs (Buchanan and Smith, 1988, p23) and distinguish them from purely statistical approaches. In this respect, Expert Systems may be said to draw more inspiration from models of human reasoning than do statistical models.

Although the idea of an Expert System began in AI, the tendency has been to term any system with expert capabilities as "expert". Consequently because quantitative uncertainty management techniques have proved useful in some systems with expert level capabilities, quantitative methods for reasoning about uncertainty have come to be associated with AI through their use in Expert Systems. As a result, Shafer has argued that: *"the field of artificial intelligence is now struggling to maintain its sense of identity."* It is this tension between symbolic and numerical methods that makes the issue of managing uncertainty a melting pot for AI.

The concern with uncertainty has resulted in the development of many techniques for uncertainty management and a vigorous debate about the appropriateness of particular techniques. The current state of this debate can be summarised by the observation of Lemmer and Kanal that: *"there continues to be no consensus concerning the 'best' approach to uncertainty for AI systems. Moreover there is no agreement on how to measure 'best'."* (Lemmer and Kanal, 1988, p. vi). In the course of this book through detailed descriptions of a number of techniques and their respective rationales, merits and shortcomings, we attempt to clarify why there is no single best approach. More substantively we try to provide the reader with a number of criteria that may be used to measure the efficacy of a given technique for a given uncertainty management problem.

1.1.2   The nature and sources of uncertainty.

As will be discussed in Chapter 2, traditional (i.e. probabilistic) approaches to uncertainty management have tended to focus upon viewing uncertainty either as a frequentistic measure of randomness or in terms of a subjective measure of confidence satisfying well circumscribed propositions. This emphasis is reflected in Cox's (1946) probabilistic axioms (Section 2.2) which include; clarity (propositions are clearly defined), unidimensionality (degrees of belief are represented by a single number on a continuum between truth and falsity) and completeness (every clear proposition can be assigned a degree of belief).

In contrast to Cox's axioms, however, even the most condensed dictionary definition of uncertainty provides testimony to the breadth and heterogeneity of the concepts subsumed by the term. These include: error; lack of confidence; imprecision; unreliability; variability; vagueness; ignorance; ambiguity.

As an illustration of how different aspects of uncertainty may co-occur in a given context, consider a hypothetical medical scenario in which written transcripts have been collected from a number of experts on the most appropriate dosage of a drug for a patient with a certain diagnosis (Table 1.1 overleaf).[1]

With the exception of the prescription of expert A, all the other statements contain some aspect of uncertainty relating to conflict or ignorance. Specifically: B and C are vague, B imprecise (or unspecific) and C fuzzy; D is a statement of subjective confidence containing uncertainty; E is ambiguous; F is inconsistent since the two disjuncts lead to different daily totals; G and H are incomplete since G does not provide frequency information and H does not specify an upper dosage limit; I appears to be based on a default rule or assumption of possibly questionable relevance;

---

1. Part of the inspiration for this example was provided by Michael Smithson.

J is anomalous in relation to the other responses, being an order of magnitude larger and may be an error; K and L are statements of ignorance, but with K suggesting that the ignorance is resolvable; while it would seem that M is completely irrelevant to the specific issue. Taken as a whole the set of responses can also be deemed to be inconsistent.

Expert	Prescribed Treatment
A	450mg, 3 times a day.
B	600mg-800mg, 3 times a day.
C	About 650mg 2-3 times a day.
D	Likely to be 500mg twice a day.
E	500mg or 800mg (*Handwriting unclear*), twice a day.
F	400mg 4 times a day or 200mg once a day.
G	500mg.
H	At least 500mg, twice a day.
I	The usual dose for this drug is 500mg, twice a day.
J	10g, twice a day.
K	Don't know, have to look it up.
L	No idea whatsoever.
M	13, Acacia Avenue.

Table 1.1   *Hypothetical assignments for a given patient.*

This set of responses both individually and collectively represents a broad range of aspects of uncertainty that may be encountered either in the development or application of Expert Systems. Furthermore, it also demonstrates that whereas some aspects of uncertainty apply to atomic propositions (vagueness, confidence and ambiguity), others such as inconsistency and incompleteness are set theoretic. That is, with the exception of self referential paradoxes, it is only really possible to think of inconsistency and incompleteness in terms of sets of propositions.

It should be borne in mind that the elicitation and representation of knowledge that is uncertain is not solely the preserve of AI research. In-

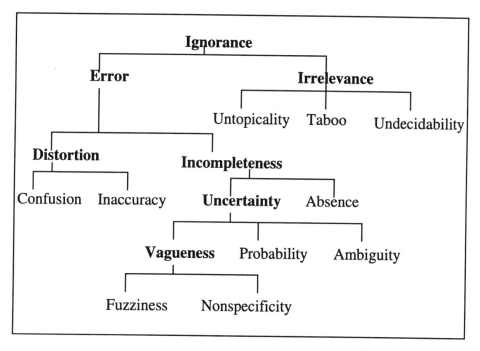

Fig 1.1   *Smithson's Typology of Uncertainty (1989).*

deed the elicitation of such knowledge was well known in the fields of so-
ciology, psychology, operations research and decision analysis long
before the advent of Expert Systems, and researchers in many disciplines
are familiar with the problems raised in the analysis of data such as that
in Table 1.1.

What makes elicitation of uncertain knowledge for Expert Systems
and AI especially interesting, however, is the requirement for formal rigour in representation that such systems impose and the concomitant exe-
cutable nature of the resulting representations encountered in both expert
and non-expert domains.

A number of authors have provided partial enumerations of the logical aspect or dimensions of uncertainty (Mamdani and Efstathiou, 1985;
Bonissone, 1987). However, Smithson (1989) has proposed a typology
which attempts to interrelate a set of concepts relating to uncertainty and
ignorance (Figure 1.1).

In this typology the overriding concept is ignorance. This is decomposed recursively firstly into irrelevance and error, then distortion and

incompleteness, absence and uncertainty and finally into vagueness, probability and ambiguity. The last distinction derives from Black (1937).

This typology goes some way towards the logical characterisation of uncertainty which Smithson puts to good use in his sociological treatise (Smithson, 1989). In this book he argues that Western science and philosophy places excessive emphasis on the categorisation of certain knowledge to the relative neglect of ignorance and uncertainty. However, for discussing AI approaches to uncertainty management, this typology is problematic in a number of respects. Specifically (1) it omits the concepts of inconsistency which underlies some of the formalisms discussed in this book, and (2) mistakenly, we argue, views uncertainty as a species of incompleteness. From an AI perspective, incompleteness is more specific than uncertainty since uncertain information is not necessarily incomplete (e.g. it may be complete but vague, ambiguous, anomalous etc., or described fully in terms of probability or possibility functions (see chapters 2 and 5)). Thus we argue that the hierarchical relationship between these concepts should be reversed and incompleteness viewed as a species of uncertainty.

1.1.3   An AI classification of uncertainty.

Clearly different typologies of uncertainty concepts serve different purposes. In this section we propose an alternative characterisation of uncertainty (Figure 1.2) aimed at classifying uncertainty in terms of those aspects which are most relevant to the development of AI applications and which therefore provides a focus for the formalisms discussed in this book. We will use this classification for discussing the representational aspects of the uncertainty management techniques described in the following chapters.

This typology retains a number of concepts from Smithson (1989) but is centred on the concept of uncertainty rather than that of ignorance. Within uncertainty the principal distinctions are, at the top level, between aspects of uncertainty that are unary, that is to say apply to individual propositions, and those aspects that are set theoretic and apply to sets of propositions. At the second level, the distinction is between ignorance (lack of knowledge) and conflict (conflicting knowledge). At the tertiary level of the typology, further distinctions are made.

Unary uncertainty based on ignorance is subdivided into indeterminate knowledge (or vagueness) of the extent of a proposition (subsuming non-specificity and fuzziness as in Smithson, above) and partial knowl-

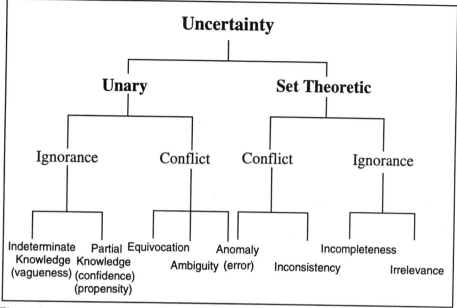

Fig 1.2   *Uncertainty Classification for AI systems.*

edge (confidence/propensity or probability), referring either to the subjective degree of belief in a proposition (confidence) or some measure of statistical propensity. Unary uncertainty based on conflict is divided into equivocation (in which a proposition may simultaneously be both supported and discredited), ambiguity (alternative non overlapping interpretations of the meaning of a proposition) and anomaly (discussed below, which includes error).

Within the set theoretic branch, uncertainty based on conflict is subdivided into inconsistency and anomaly. Inconsistency arises when a set of propositions cannot be simultaneously true. Anomaly refers to the situation when one of a set of propositions is irregular or incongruous with respect to other associated propositions, though not formally inconsistent. In this respect anomaly has both unary and set theoretic properties in so far as it arises when a particular proposition is incongruous with the other members of a set. It can therefore be claimed to be both a property of the set and the individual proposition. Error is viewed as a species of anomaly.

Set theoretic uncertainty based on ignorance is subdivided into incompleteness (in which the extension or actual examples of a set of relevant propositions has one or more missing elements) and irrelevancy (in which the intention or definition of the set of relevant items is unknown). This latter case might be viewed as a kind of meta-uncertainty since not only is the confidence or the specificity in the individual propositions uncertain, but the extension of the set of propositions itself is also uncertain. It is these properties of incompleteness that make Expert Systems "brittle". Overall, this typology preserves Black's distinction between vagueness, probability and ambiguity, while identifying the key areas of uncertainty for AI systems.

As this book will show, it is the acknowledgement of aspects of uncertainty other than probability (subjective or frequentistic) that has led to the development of other techniques for managing uncertainty in Artificial Intelligence.[2] Conversely it is the relative denial of interest in these other aspects of uncertainty that has been the demarcation of Bayesian and other schools of uncertainty management.

1.2   Representation and management of uncertainty

One important, though not the only, role of reasoning under uncertainty is to assist in decision making. Expert Systems and other AI systems need not necessarily be capable of making decisions per se, but they should be able to marshal, propagate and combine information that can potentially assist the user in a decision task. This might involve determining the set of possible decision options for a given task, determining which information is relevant to each decision option (and thereby which information can distinguish between them), determining which decision options are mutually exclusive and which are mutually compatible, and evaluate individual or combined sets of decision options along specified dimensions.

The uncertainty management debate and the typology of uncertainty presented above have highlighted a number of aspects of uncertainty relevant to the assessment of uncertainty management techniques. Bonissone (1987, revised in 1992), drawing upon the ideas of Quinlan (1983), has suggested a number of features, or desiderata, relevant to the selection of uncertainty management techniques. These draw upon representational and other factors (summarized in Table 1.2), relating to the assumptions of the methods, the explicitness of representation and cognitive factors. These are described in terms of the three levels of *representation, inference* and *control* (Table 1.2). Representation emphasises making explicit

---

2. Some experimental studies intended to establish the psychological validity of these concepts are discussed in chapters 7 and 8.

all the potentially relevant aspects of the data, inference represents closure and assumptions to be avoided, while control emphasises operations on the resulting data structures.

	Representation Layer
1	There should be an explicit representation of the amount of evidence for and against each hypothesis.
2	There should be an explicit representation of the information about the evidence, i.e. meta-information such as evidence source and credibility, logical dependencies etc.
3	The representation should allow the user to describe the uncertainty of any information at the available level of detail (i.e. allowing heterogeneous information granularity).
4	There should be an explicit representation of consistency, to detect potential conflicts and to identify factors contributing to conflict.
5	There should be an explicit representation of ignorance to allow non committal statements.
6	The representation should be natural to the user to facilitate graceful interaction and natural to the expert to permit elicitation of consistent weights for each rule.
	Inference Layer
7	Combination rules should not be based on global assumptions of evidence independence.
8	The combination rules should not assume the exhaustiveness and exclusiveness of the hypotheses.
9	The syntax and semantics of the representation should be closed under the rules of combination.
10	Propagation and summary functions should have clear semantics.
	Control Layer
11	There should be a clear distinction between a conflict in the information (violation of consistency) and ignorance about the information, so that conflicts may be removed by retracting one or more elements of the conflicting set of evidence and ignorance removed by the selection of a (retractable) default value.

Table 1.2 *Desiderata of Uncertainty Management (paraphrased from Bonissone, 1992).*

12	The traceability of the aggregation and propagation of uncertainty through the reasoning process must be available to resolve conflicts or contradictions, to explain the support of conclusions, and to perform meta reasoning for control.
13	Making pairwise comparisons of uncertainty should be feasible as these are required for decision making.
14	It should be possible to select the most appropriate combination rule by using a declarative form of control (i.e. a set of context dependent rules that specify the selection policy).

Table 1.2   *Desiderata of Uncertainty Management (paraphrased from Bonissone, 1992).*

In discussing these desiderata a number of factors should be borne in mind.

- Firstly, it should be emphasised that these desiderata are by no means universally accepted, nor completely met by any existing system.
- Secondly, that they are by no means complete nor perhaps necessary (see discussion below), although the set does answer some of the criticisms made of the earlier presentation of Bonissone (1987) (e.g. by Clark 1990a).
- Finally, however, what should be emphasised is (a) the relation between the desiderata in Table 1.2, and the typology in Figure 1.2, where it is clear that many of Bonissone's Desiderata relate to representational aspects of uncertainty management as made explicit by the typology (especially desiderata 3, 4, 5, 8 and 11), and (b) they do provide the reader and systems developer with a short-list of some of the things to consider in developing a system that must reason under uncertainty.

More generally, in determining which criteria to apply, it should be borne in mind that most Expert Systems are intended not to operate as autonomous agents but as intelligent assistants. Here the appropriate level of analysis for evaluation is not the performance of the Expert System in isolation but of the performance of the wider cognitive system embracing both the human decision maker and the Expert System. When this broader perspective is taken, it is clear that the ultimate criterion is improvement in the user's performance as a result of consultations with the Expert System. This will be affected by factors such as the intelligibility of the advice provided, in terms of the dimensions or aspects of uncertainty included and the manner in which this information is presented to the user, the ability to perform appropriate support tasks (such as critiquing users' proposals) in real time, and the nature of system dialogues. Furthermore, the system may need to represent and reason about whatever aspects of uncertainty are deemed pertinent by the user. Clearly people are unlikely to follow advice from Expert Systems if the latter cannot produce intelligible explanations of their advice (Teach and Shortliffe, 1981).

Therefore, as well as the factors relating to representation, inference and control as defined by Bonissone, it is also necessary to consider the pragmatics of system development and the run-time system *per se*. It is one thing to identify the formalism which, from an ideal perspective, has the appropriate representation factors for the reasoning task in hand, quite another actually to build a system that employs that formalism and see it operate satisfactorily. Indeed, it is frequently the pragmatics of system construction that determine which formalism(s) can even be considered (e.g. Chapter 7). With this in mind, our emphasis in this book will be on three principal factors. These are:

- representational adequacy (which subsumes many of the desiderata described above at each of Bonissone's three levels and is the major dimension along which the formalisms are generally compared);
- knowledge engineering considerations (both pragmatic and psychological); and
- computational considerations (both in terms of complexity and availability of software aids/shells).

These will all contribute to the ultimate success of a system and are used throughout the rest of this book for assessing uncertainty management techniques.

With respect to the second consideration of knowledge engineering, it is also worth looking at the relationship between AI approaches and those of other disciplines which impact upon AI techniques. In Figure 1.3 for example, we present an overview schema of the interrelationships between a number of disciplines as proposed by Henrion. Without going into the particular details of the semantics of the precise links, or their weights, what is clear is that work in AI and Expert Systems on the development of systems that can reason with uncertainty by no means exists in a vacuum. Rather, it has a set of inter-relations with a number of other disciplines. Throughout this book references will be made to results from these other disciplines in so far as they have implications for knowledge representation and elicitation issues in AI uncertainty management systems.

The following sections provide more details concerning the criteria which we will pursue.

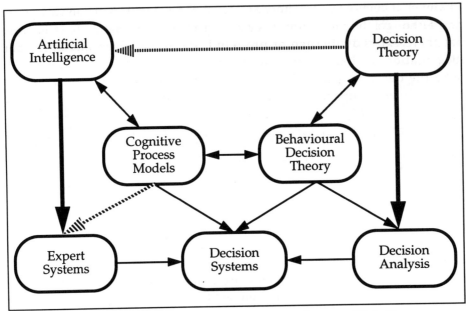

Fig 1.3   *A diagram of influences (adapted from Henrion, unpublished).*
Thicker lines indicate stronger influences.

1.2.1   Knowledge representation considerations.

As illustrated above, uncertainty embraces a wide variety of concepts. In
some circumstances, aspects of uncertainty present in a domain may not
be deemed relevant to the performance of a particular task. In reasoning
about the appropriate dosage and frequency of the drug for our hypothetical patient of Section 1.1.2, we may, for example, simply ignore the pre-
scriptions of a subset of the experts (e.g. B to L) since these are vague/
incomplete etc. and give the dosage prescribed by expert A. After all, he
is an expert. Alternatively we may ignore all but A, B and C and try and
combine these in some way to produce a consensus dosage. The important point is that by admitting only specific types of information we confine ourselves to reasoning only in terms of that information and ignore
other aspects of uncertainty.

As an illustration, suppose we decide to ignore all statements of ignorance in our preferred uncertainty management technique for a given
context since they contribute nothing towards the relative weighting of
alternatives. Suppose we ask 100 clinicians whether they prefer drug A or
B for a given patient. If 90 say A, 5 say B and 5 say 'don't know' then we
have strong support for A and the 'don't knows' need not be considered.

However, if one clinician chooses A and the other 99 say 'don't know', then although the net support for A is greater than that of B, it is clear that there exists a situation of profound ignorance which merits further investigation. Perhaps further information about the patient is needed to make the decision, perhaps the one clinician who said A is mistaken or out of date with current practice. In such a situation the lack of an explicit representation of ignorance will disguise it and therefore prevent reasoning about the ignorance *per se*. Similar arguments can be made in the context of the issue of brittleness of Expert Systems. Essentially, without an explicit representation of the broad range of uncertainty categories described above it is not possible for the system to know when the advice being sought is beyond its scope, or exceeds the implicit assumptions of the designer.

Other important aspects of representational adequacy are how uncertainty is to be used in the reasoning process, whether performance of the uncertainty management technique degrades gracefully as less of the relevant information becomes available, what happens if the assumptions of the uncertainty management technique are violated and what meta-level capability is necessary (Wyatt and Spiegelhalter, 1989; 1990).

Thus, from the perspective of knowledge representation, an uncertainty management system should be able to support all the uncertainty management tasks deemed relevant and necessary.

1.2.2   Knowledge engineering considerations.

In building Expert Systems the practicalities of knowledge engineering are a major constraint on the types of uncertainty management technique that may be implemented. Having decided, for example, on the basis of precision, that it is desirable to take a full Bayesian network approach to a given domain (see Chapter 2), the questions relating to (a) the construction of a qualitative network of all the relevant variables in the domain and (b) the elicitation of all relevant probabilities become germane. If the probabilities are to be elicited from human experts, can we be sure that they will be precise and accurate? If, because of the size of the domain, it is simply impossible to think in terms of either constructing an adequate qualitative network or eliciting all relevant probabilities, it may be necessary to adopt some other method that embodies weaker assumptions.

A second consideration relating to knowledge engineering concerns the completeness of the specification of a reasoning method. For example, Clark (1990a) noted that some of the more experimental symbolic methods of uncertainty management proposed by Cohen (1985) and Fox (1986a; 1986b), and which are discussed in Chapter 7, were formally underspecified (cf. Bonissone's desiderata relating to closure). The problem with these methods is that because they are not described axiomatically, it is not possible to determine all their properties, including whether they are complete and do what is intended. Note, however, that some symbolic methods are specified axiomatically, as we will discuss (Chapters 6 and 7).

1.2.3   Computational considerations.

In terms of the computational aspects of uncertainty management techniques, it is necessary to consider three main questions; (a) is off-the-shelf software available that implements the version of the uncertainty management technique of interest, (b) if not, is the method sufficiently well specified to allow it to be implemented and (c) either way, are the relevant propagation algorithms sufficiently fast to operate in real time on the proposed hardware configuration?

1.3   The structure of this book

The sections above have identified both the various aspects of uncertainty that are relevant to the development of knowledge based systems and the various factors by which the appropriateness of different uncertainty management techniques may be assessed. The next six chapters of this book describe the main streams of research in uncertainty management techniques that have been developed in the literature in the last few decades. Specifically, we will cover: Bayesian approaches; certainty factors; belief functions; fuzzy sets and possibility theory; non-monotonic logics; and argumentation approaches. In this respect it should be emphasised, however, that far from constituting uniform approaches to uncertainty management, the various formalisms are themselves pluralistic; there exist different variants of the same underlying theme. Thus there are different Bayesian schemes, differing belief function approaches, different version of possibilistic, non-monotonic and default logics and many other symbolic systems. The question of whether a particular uncertainty management technique is appropriate to a given uncertainty management task is, therefore, also to some extent dependent upon which variant of the formalism is being considered.

This book describes in detail at least one version of each of the principal techniques and indicates, where appropriate, variations of the underlying axioms which lead to different properties. Each technique is described in terms of its representational motivation and is illustrated by worked examples whose level of detail is a function of the maturity of the technique. Pointers are also given to more detailed descriptions in the literature and each technique is assessed in relation to the criteria of representational, computational and knowledge engineering considerations described above.

The final chapter provides a resumé of the motivations, advantages and limitations of each system in relation to the criteria set out above, identifies systems in use, gives pointers to other systems not directly discussed, provides some insight into how the formalisms map onto patterns of human reasoning and identifies a number of key issues relating to integration and factors which remain to be resolved.

2
Bayesian Probability

When I say 'S is probably P', I commit myself guardedly, tentatively or with reservations to the view that S is P, and (likewise guardedly) lend my authority to that view. (Toulmin, 1958).

2.1   Introduction

Of all the methods for handling uncertainty which are discussed in this book, probability theory has by far the longest tradition and is the best understood. For this reason it may be considered in the nature of a 'gold standard', for representing *some* aspects of uncertainty, against which more recent approaches may be measured. That is not to say that we subscribe to the view that probability theory is really all you need. Rather, that by giving a thorough description of its strengths and weaknesses we can provide a reference point for the discussion of some of the alternative formalisms.

The title of this chapter, Bayesian Probability, refers to a specific school of probabilists. At present this is the dominant school in the use of probability in AI. It takes a *subjective* view of probability as a measure of the degree of belief of an (ideal) person in an hypothesis. In addition it uses the Bayesian rule of conditioning (to be presented in Section 2.2.1) to determine the revised degree of belief in a hypothesis upon observation of some evidence. As a model of belief revision, current psychological experiments indicate that in general it is normative and not descriptive. That is, it *prescribes* an ideal method of establishing degrees of belief rather than *describes* how people actually evaluate belief themselves; in general, people are poor estimators of numerical values and do not perform complex arithmetic in their routine reasoning. As a descriptive framework within which many studies in behavioural decision theory have been conducted, there is little evidence that humans process uncertain information in a classical

Bayesian manner (see for example Kahneman et al, 1982). We will come back to this point in the discussion section. However, probability is not just about numbers. Modern Bayesian approaches also provide a way of formalising the notions of relevance and independence which people *do* use in their everyday reasoning. The correct structuring of the problem is as important as, if not more important than, the actual numerical coefficients used. We shall emphasise how these qualitative aspects can be incorporated into Bayesian reasoning.

2.2   Foundations

A sweeping and rather coarse grained generalisation is to categorise those who have worked on the foundations of probability theory into one of two camps; objectivists and subjectivists. Objectivists, R.A. Fisher having been perhaps the most notable, take the view that probability is about events we can count. They use a frequentistic definition of the probability of an event being the proportion of favourable events out of all possible events. For example, the probability of a coin landing heads up is the proportion of events in which a tossed coin will land heads up out of all possible coin tosses (for a sufficiently long sequence of repeated events). The subjective view, on the other hand, is that probability is a logic of degrees of belief. The probability of an hypothesis (that the coin will land heads up) is a measure of an, admittedly idealised, person's degree of belief in that hypothesis given the available evidence (that the coin is fair, in this example).

The subjective view can be given a rationality in terms of betting behaviour (von Neumann and Morgenstern, 1947; de Finetti, 1937). The degree of belief in an hypothesis is the amount a rational person should be prepared to wager expressed as a fraction of the winnings they would receive if the hypothesis is confirmed. For example, it would be reasonable to place and have accepted a bet of 50p against the possible receipt of £1.00 if a tossed coin should land heads up. Any change in this ratio from 1:2 would result in one party being guaranteed to lose money in the long run. The identification of a betting strategy which will guarantee one party losing money is referred to as a "Dutch Book". One justification of the usage of probability is that basing betting behaviour on probability will ensure that a Dutch Book cannot be made against you.

In their early days, electronic computers were perceived very much as number crunching machines. This was reflected in a dominance of the objectivist viewpoint in computer applications of probability theory in the 1950's. However, as the discussion of Expert Systems emphasised, Artificial Intelligence is not simply about numerical and statistical modelling. The view of probability as a subjective measure of belief, and probability theory as a framework for plausible reasoning is much nearer to the heart of AI. Consequently many of the strongest protagonists of the use of probability theory in AI are subjective Bayesians, and we will base the rest of this chapter within that framework.

We will take the following definition as a starting point:

The (conditional) probability of a proposition given particular evidence is a real number between zero and one, that is an entity's belief in that proposition, given the evidence. (Cheeseman, 1985).

Note there is not a notion of "absolute" probability. The degree of belief in a proposition or hypothesis is context sensitive; the belief that a coin will land heads up will change from 0.5 to 1 if it is discovered that the coin is double sided heads. We shall always be interested in the conditional probability $p(h \mid e)$ of a hypothesis h given the evidence e. Sometimes the evidence used or the context within which the problem is framed can be taken to remain unchanged throughout the discussion and explicit reference to it may be dropped, in which case we will just refer to the probability $p(h)$ of the hypothesis. But this should always be understood as an abbreviation. What is of interest to the AI community is that probability provides a coherent framework for revising the probability of, or rather, belief in a hypothesis as new evidence is identified.

A mathematical approach to the definition of probability theory is to provide a set of axioms defining the theory and then demonstrate that the desirable properties, and no undesirable ones, are logical consequences of the axioms. A common axiomatisation is that probability is a continuous monotonic function 'p' such that:

P1. $0 \leq p(h \mid e) \leq 1$

P2. $p(\text{True} \mid e) = 1$

P3. $p(h \mid e) + p(\neg h \mid e) = 1$

P4. $p(gh \mid e) = p(h \mid ge) . p(g \mid e)$

The rationale behind these axioms should be clear. P1 states that probability values should lie in the range [0,1]. P2 says that the probability of a true hypothesis is unity, P3 that either the hypothesis or its negation will be true. P4 is important and we will expand on it a little more later. It says that the probability of the conjunction of two hypotheses is the probability of the first hypothesis *given that the second hypothesis is true* multiplied by the probability of the second hypothesis.

P1 - P4 provide a mathematical, objective axiomatisation of probability. The formal connection with the subjective view of probability as a measure of belief was made by Cox (1946), Schrödinger (1947), Reichenbach (1949) and Tribus (1969) who showed that these axioms were a necessary consequence of a simple set of intuitive properties of measures of belief. This was a deliberate attempt to move away from the betting behaviour model of probability to one based solely on belief. These properties, as summarised in Horvitz, Heckerman and Langlotz (1986), are:

B1.   *Clarity*: Propositions should be well defined.

B2.   *Scalar continuity*: A single number is both necessary and sufficient for representing a degree of belief.

B3.   *Completeness*: A degree of belief can be assigned to any well defined proposition.

B4.   *Context dependency*: A belief assigned to a proposition can depend on the belief in other propositions.

B5.   *Hypothetical conditioning*: There exists some function that allows the belief in a conjunction of propositions to be calculated from the belief in one proposition and the belief in the other proposition given that the first proposition is true.

B6.   *Complementarity*: The belief in the negation of a proposition is a monotonically decreasing function of the belief in the proposition itself.

B7.   *Consistency*: There will be equal belief in propositions that are logically equivalent.

A corollary of this result is that if an uncertainty calculus is defined which satisfies a distinct set of axioms to those of probability theory, then it must also fail to satisfy at least one of the properties B1 - B7 as a measure of belief. As discussed in (Horvitz, Heckerman and Langlotz, 1986), this means we may use these properties as a framework for comparing different formalisms. We will refer back to this point in subsequent chapters. It should, of course, be emphasised that these properties are in no sense preordained. One may quite legitimately dispute the desirability or necessity of an uncertainty calculus satisfying certain of them.

2.2.1   Conditional probability and Bayesian updating.

In the previous section we presented a simple axiomatisation of probability theory, stated the justification for this in terms of its conformity to a number of simple properties, and discussed that actions taken on the basis of a probabilistic measure of belief were also "rational" from the point of view of betting behaviour.

We have also emphasised that the basic expressions in the Bayesian formalisation of probability theory are *conditional* probabilities. In making this statement we are beginning to address the contention that Bayesian reasoning is as much about structure as it is about numbers. To say that the probability of an hypothesis is conditional on one or more items is to identify the information *relevant* to the problem at hand. To say that the identification of an item of evidence *influences* the degree of belief in a hypothesis is to place a directionality on the relevance links between evidences and hypotheses. In fact the directionality placed on the links will depend on the way in which the problem is structured. The term *causal networks* has often been used for belief networks because a direction corresponding to causal influence can be the most meaningful. In some sense, measles 'causes' red spots, for example. In addition, assessing the probability of a symptom giv-

Fig 2.1   *Very simple influence network.*

en a cause can be an easier problem than assessing the probability of a cause given a symptom. In general, however, the ordering need not be based on causality. The point is to take any natural cognitive ordering which will enable a confident assessment of the associated probability to be made.

Note that to say that **p('red spots' | measles) = p** means that we can assign probability 'p' to 'red spots' if measles is observed *and only measles is observed*. If any further relevant evidence 'e' is observed, then we will be required to determine **p('red spots' | measles,e)**.

The Bayesian rule of conditioning, although easily derivable from axiom P4, is central to the subjective Bayesian conception of probabilistic reasoning. It provides a normative rule for updating the belief in a hypothesis in response to the observation of evidence. That is, the revised belief in a hypothesis 'h' on observing evidence 'e', p(h|e), is obtained by multiplying the prior belief in 'h', p(h), by the probability p(e|h) that 'e' will materialise if 'h' is true:

$$p(h|e) = \frac{p(e|h) \cdot p(h)}{p(e)} \qquad (2.1)$$

The revised belief p(h I e) is often referred to as the *posterior* probability, p(e), the prior probability of the evidence, acts as a normalisation coefficient (the degree of belief that accrues to a hypothesis on the basis of some evidence is clearly dependent on the prior frequency of occurrence of that evidence). So, in the previous example, it may be easiest to elicit the probability of red spots given measles. But, given this value, we can use Bayes' rule to reason from red spots as evidence to obtain the posterior probability of measles as a hypothesis (provided we know the prior probability for measles and for red spots).

Thus, the subjective Bayesian approach provides a framework for answering the query: "Given that I know 'e', what is my belief in 'h'?". We have so far been thinking only in terms of one or two related propositions. The power, and some of the difficulties, of this approach will become clearer when we consider larger networks of propositions.

2.2.2   Probability into rule-based systems won't go.

In formal logic, propositions may be combined using simple syntactic principles and the truth value of the resulting formula obtained as a simple function of the truth values of the sub-formulae. Thus we can obtain the truth value of $A \wedge B$ from the truth values of A and of B[1]. Probabilities, in contrast, cannot be *composed* in this way. If we know p(A) and p(B) we cannot, in general, combine these values in any simple way to obtain the probability p(A,B) of their conjunction. Referring back to P4 and ignoring the contextual evidence for the moment, we do have that:

$$p(A, B) = p(A|B) \cdot p(B)$$

It is only if p(A I B) = p(A) that we can obtain p(A,B) as a simple conjunction: p(A,B) = p(A).p(B). We will have p(A I B) = p(A) if it is the case that knowing B has no effect on our belief in A. That is, A and B are *marginally independent*.

In many rule-based Expert Systems, MYCIN (Shortliffe, 1976) and Prospector (Gashnig, 1982) being particularly notable examples, uncertainty values are associated with the rules and combined using simple syntactic principles as the rules are fired. That is, the way in which the values are combined in a formula just depends on the structure of the formula and the uncertainty values of its subformulae. This *extensional* or *syntactic* approach

---

1. Here and in the following we use capital letters (e.g. A) to denote variables which may be instantiated with an arbitrary proposition, and small letters to denote the actual instantiated states of the proposition (e.g. 'a' for A is true; '¬a' for A is false).

to uncertainty handling is computationally efficient. But unless strong independence assumptions can legitimately be made, it is semantically sloppy as illustrated in the previous paragraph. This contrasts with a fully *intensional* probabilistic approach, which is semantically coherent but in the general case computationally intractable. We recommend the first chapter of Pearl (1988) for a full discussion, but hope that the following will suffice to illustrate this point. The examples are taken from Pearl. Notwithstanding the following comments, there are circumstances where a rule-based approach is satisfactory and acceptable. Consequently, we will discuss one formalism, Mycin's certainty factors, in the next chapter as an approach to handling uncertainty in a rule-based system.

What gives rule-based systems their computational advantage is their *modularity*. By modularity is meant the only requirement for a rule "**if** A **then** B" to be fired is the presence of A in a database, no matter *how* it has been obtained and no matter *what else* is in that database. Suppose we have a simple Expert System for diagnosing weather conditions from observations about the state of the garden. It has been fairly intelligently designed, and the rule-base contains information about possible causes (such as the lawn becoming wet can be caused by rain), as well as possible effects (such as the neighbour's sprinkler being on will make the lawn wet). For example, it may contain a diagnostic rule such as:

> **if** wet lawn **then** rain (0.8)   *rule 1*

and a predictive rule such as:

> **if** sprinkler on **then** wet lawn (0.95)   *rule 2*

Suppose, now, 'wet lawn' is observed. Rain will be concluded, with a certainty of 0.8. But, if the database also contains 'sprinkler on' this explains 'wet lawn' and the belief in 'rain' should be reduced. That is, other information that is relevant to the problem should have been considered.

Suppose, on the other hand, the database only contains 'sprinkler on'. Then rule 2 will be fired to conclude 'wet lawn' (0.95). Once 'wet lawn' has been concluded, rule 1 will be fired to conclude 'rain' (0.76) (using a very naive multiplicative rule to chain probabilities). Thus, ignoring the fact that 'wet lawn' has been obtained as a prediction, and not as a fact requiring explanation, has led to a quite erroneous conclusion. If a naive forward chaining mechanism is used with this rule base, the distinction between diagnostic and predictive rules is confounded. Equally, if rain is observed, we cannot use rule 1 to *predict* 'wet lawn'. In order to make this prediction, a separate rule:

if rain **then** wet lawn   *rule 3*

will have to be added to the database. Then we are open to the possibility of circular reasoning, with 'rain' supporting 'wet lawn', 'wet lawn' supporting 'rain' (by rule 1) and so on.

The reasoning pattern in which a rule "A **implies** B" is used to increase the credibility of A if B is observed is known as *abduction*, as opposed to *deduction* for concluding B if A is observed. Such *bidirectional inferences* can be handled by probability. By exploiting Bayes' rule, we can make diagnostic as well as predictive inferences; reason from evidence to hypothesis as well as from hypothesis to evidence.

The second pattern of reasoning we have discussed (a change in the belief in a possible explanation if an alternative explanation is actually observed) should be modelled as follows. If 'wet lawn' is observed then 'rain' is supported. However, upon observing that the sprinkler was on, support for 'rain' should subsequently be decreased. This retraction of belief in a hypothesis by the discovery of an alternative explanation is known as *explaining away*. Again, this can be handled by framing the problem in a probabilistic framework. But note that this is a *plausible* inference pattern, it is not necessarily correct. It may have been raining as well.

A third difficulty with the rule-based approach is the problem of *correlated sources of evidence*. Evidences e_1 and e_2 may both add support to hypothesis h. But if they have both been derived from a common source the combined support they give to the hypothesis should not be as strong as that obtained were they independent evidences. Again, a rigorous probabilistic model can handle this correctly.

Although semantically clear, we have mentioned that the probabilistic approach can be computationally intractable. A naive representation of a problem in a probabilistic framework would require the elicitation of a probability distribution function defined over all the propositions of interest. For example, if we let A stand for 'wet lawn', B for 'rain' and C for 'sprinkler on', in order to model the above problem we would need to elicit $p(a,b,c)$, $p(a,\neg b,c)$, $p(a,\neg b,\neg c)$, $p(a,b,\neg c)$, $p(\neg a,b,c)$, $p(\neg a,\neg b,c)$, $p(\neg a,\neg b,\neg c)$, and $p(\neg a,b,\neg c)$. A problem involving n propositions, A_1, ..., A_n, will require the elicitation of 2^n such values. Calculating the marginal probability $p(A_i)$ that A_i is true will, for example, require summing over the 2^{n-1} values for which A_i is true. As well as being computationally intensive, such functions and calculations are not conceptually meaningful. We will discuss in the remainder of this chapter how the Bayesian approach enables the problem to be structured in a more conceptually meaningful way which will also enable 'beliefs' to be updated using just local calculations.

In summary. The modularity of rule-based systems makes them computationally efficient. But they require an extensive representation of the inferences which may be drawn from them. On the other hand, the intensional, or semantic, approach taken in a rigorous probabilistic model is computationally intensive. But it does enable deduction, abduction and explaining away to be modelled, and correlated sources of evidence to be handled correctly. As we will see in the next section, a careful structuring of the problem is required before probabilistic inference may be effectively computed.

2.3   Resolution by independence

In much of the preceding discussion we have focused on conditional probabilities and dependencies rather than joint probability distributions. The motivation behind the work of Pearl, Cheeseman, Spiegelhalter and others in producing network representations of probabilistic knowledge is to *"make intensional systems operational by making relevance relationships explicit"* (Pearl, 1988). By formalising and exploiting the conditions under which discrete sections of the network of propositions may be regarded as independent we may transform belief revision from an intractable global operation into a sequence of local operations. In addition, the problem of eliciting massive joint distribution tables is reduced to that of eliciting the conceptually much more meaningful conditional probabilities between semantically related propositions. To quote Pearl once more:

> In a sparsely connected world like ours, it is fairly clear that probabilistic knowledge, in both man and machine, should not be represented as entries of a giant joint distribution table, but rather by a network of low order probabilistic relationships between small clusters of semantically related propositions. (Pearl, 1986, p357).

Before continuing with the discussion on independence, we state here an important result which will be referred to frequently in the following. By repeated use of axiom P4 (Section 2.2) it is a straightforward exercise for the reader to verify that the following chain rule for probabilities holds. Let $p(A_1, A_2, ..., A_n)$ be a probability distribution over the propositions A_1, A_2, ..., A_n. Then

$$p(A_1, A_2, ..., A_n) =$$

$$p(A_n \mid A_{n-1}, ..., A_1) \cdot p(A_{n-1} \mid A_{n-2}, ..., A_1) \cdot .... \cdot p(A_2 \mid A_1) \cdot p(A_1) \qquad (2.2)$$

Now remember that two propositions are independent if knowing one to be true has no effect on our belief in the other. That is, A is independent of B, given C, if P(A | B, C) = P(A | C). We will now consider three different representations for a probability distribution over a set of propositions {A,B,C}. They each embody different conditional independence assumptions which are made explicit through graphical representations.

Returning first to the 'wet lawn' example of the previous section. Both rain and the sprinkler being on may cause the lawn to become wet. In this example, before the lawn is observed to be wet our belief in whether or not it has been raining, and whether or not the sprinkler is on are quite independent. However, once the lawn has been observed to be wet, the observation of the sprinkler being on may affect our belief in it raining (as a possible explanation of the wet lawn). This problem may be represented in graphical form by the directed graph shown in Figure 2.2.

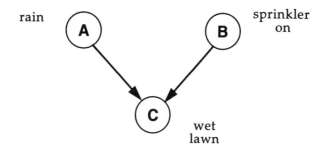

Fig 2.2   *Nodes A and B are conditionally dependent given C.*

Notice that the arrows from A = 'rain' and from B = 'sprinkler on' meet head to head at proposition C = 'wet lawn'.

A and B are marginally independent, but conditionally *dependent* given C. Application of the chain rule (eq. 2.2) to the probability distribution p(A,B,C) gives

p(A,B,C) = p(C | A,B).p(A | B).p(B)

Since A and B are marginally independent, we have p(A | B) = p(A), but are unable to reduce the expression p(C | A,B) any further. Thus, for this graph:

p(A,B,C) = p(C | A,B).p(A).p(B)

By way of contrast, consider the following scenario. Red spots and Koplik's spots are both symptoms of measles. In some sense, measles 'causes' red spots and Koplik's spots (which are small white spots found inside the mouth) and so this situation can be represented by the graphical structure of Figure 2.3.

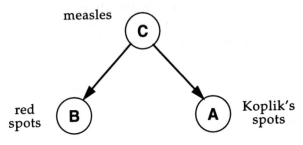

Fig 2.3   *A case where A and B are conditionally independent under condition C.*

Now the arrows to A = 'red spots' and to B = 'Koplik's spots' meet tail to tail at C = measles.

In contrast to the previous example, in this case, given that the patient is suffering from measles, the observation of red spots will have no influence at all on the belief that Koplik's spots will be observed. That is, A and B are conditionally independent given C. Applying the chain rule again:

$p(A,B,C) = p(A \mid B,C).p(B \mid C).p(C)$

But, since A and B are independent given C, $p(A \mid B,C) = p(A \mid C)$. That is:

$p(A,B,C) = p(A \mid C).p(B \mid C).p(C)$

As with the previous example, this equation seems to respect the intuitive independencies represented in the structure of the associated graph.

The third and final case we will consider is exemplified by the following. The disease A = 'kawasaki disease' is known to cause the pathological process C ='myocardial ischaemia'. This, in turn, has an associated symptom B = 'chest pain' (Figure 2.4).

In this case, the arrows meet head to tail at C. Now, the observation of B may lead to an increase in belief in C and subsequently of A. But, once C has been confirmed the observation of B can have no further influence on diagnosing A as the ultimate cause of C. So, as in the previous example, A and B are conditionally independent given C, and in this case:

$p(A,B,C) = p(B \mid A,C).p(C \mid A).p(A)$
$\qquad\quad = p(B \mid C).p(C \mid A).p(A)$

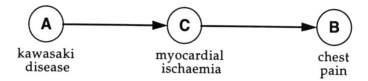

Fig 2.4   *Again, A and B are conditionally independent.*

The elicitation of a causal network, or *influence diagram*, as a directed acyclic graph seems a natural way of representing many types of belief relationship. We have commented on the apparent relationship between the graphical representation and the independence relationships in the probability representation. One of the results which is an important component of Pearl's work is that all the conditional independence relationships can be derived from a directed acyclic graph (Geiger and Pearl, 1988; Verma and Pearl, 1988) using a notion of 'd-separation'. The reader is referred to (Pearl, 1988) and (Neapolitan, 1990) for a detailed coverage of d-separation and the subsequent development of a fast algorithm for belief propagation in Bayesian networks. The motivation behind much of Pearl's work is to derive a procedure for updating Bayesian belief networks which captures the way people structure their problem solving. The resulting algorithm is perhaps not as widely applicable as that of Lauritzen and Spiegelhalter, which was developed by exploiting recent results in graph theory and the mathematical representations of probability distributions. As space is limited we can only discuss one algorithm and will continue with a discussion of the way in which the Lauritzen and Spiegelhalter algorithm exploits independencies to enable the rapid updating of belief networks.

We have shown how independence relationships may be exploited in simple problems to give a slightly more intuitive probabilistic representation than the naive probability distribution over the set of propositions. This approach can be extended quite naturally to produce a probability representation for larger problems which employ only probabilistic relationships between closely related propositions. Consider, for example, the network shown in Figure 2.5. By repeated use of the three independence relationships considered earlier, it should be quite easy to confirm that the following is a correct representation of the probability distribution for this network:

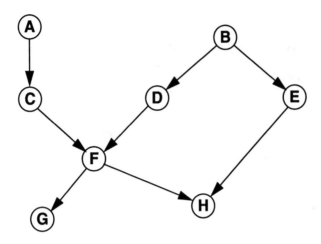

Fig 2.5   *A simple belief network.*

p(A,B,C,D,E,F,G,H)

= p(G | F).p(H | E,F).p(F | C,D).p(C | A).p(A).p(D | B).p(E | B).p(B)

= p(A).p(B).p(C | A).p(D | B).p(E | B).p(F | C,D).p(G | F).p(H | E,F)

(The second form is just a rearrangement of the first.)

Notice one important feature of this representation. We will call the nodes immediately preceding a given node in the graph the *parents* of that node. So, for example, C and D are the parents of F, F and E are the parents of H. We will also refer to the set of nodes which cannot be reached by a directed path from a given node as the *anterior* nodes to that node. For example, the nodes anterior to node F are {A,B,C,D,E}, those anterior to node B are {A,C}. Then the probability of each node in this graph is conditionally independent of its anterior nodes given its parent nodes. Thus, for example, p(F | A,B,C,D,E) = p(F | C,D).

The above equation can be expressed in a very simple general form. Let V be a set of nodes, and let parents(v) be the set of parent nodes for any v ∈ V. Then the second equality is just a specific instance of the general equation:

$$p(V) = \prod_{v \in V} p(v | \text{parents}(v)) \qquad (2.3)$$

In this section we have shown how notions of dependence and independence may be exploited in structuring a belief network. As a result, the probability distribution for a large set of propositions may be represented by a product of conditional probability relationships between small clusters of semantically related propositions. We will now consider a very simple example to demonstrate how evidence may be efficiently propagated through a belief network.

2.4   Belief propagation through local computation

This example is taken from (Spiegelhalter, 1986b) and is a simple demonstration of the belief update scheme which was first fully described in (Lauritzen and Spiegelhalter, 1988). A full scale application which uses this algorithm will be presented in the next section. This section is intended to be illustrative of the intuitions behind the algorithm, rather than to provide a rigorous description of it. The reader is referred to (Neapolitan, 1990) for a thorough analysis of propagation techniques in Bayesian networks.

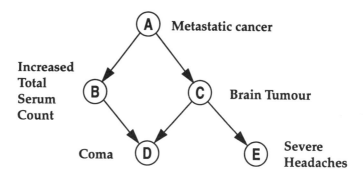

Fig 2.6   *Belief network for metastatic cancer example.*

It should be clear by now that the essence of this approach is to represent hypotheses and relations in the domain under consideration as a directed graph. This is illustrated for the following, deliberately restricted, piece of medical knowledge:

> *Metastatic cancer is a possible cause of a brain tumour, and is also an explanation for increased total serum [calcium] count. In turn, either of these could explain a patient falling into a coma. Severe headache is also possibly associated with a brain tumour.* (Spiegelhalter, 1986b).

The qualitative representation of this knowledge is shown in Figure 2.6. Here the nodes represent hypotheses and links indicate 'causal' or probability relationships. These do not have to derive from direct physiological reasoning but "any natural cognitive ordering that will ... allow reasonably confident probability assessments." (Spiegelhalter, 1986b, p49).

As in the last example in the previous section, the probability distribution may be decomposed into a product of conditional probabilities. Again, exploiting the independencies implicit in the graph, we have:

$$p(A,B,C,D,E) = p(E \mid C).p(D \mid B,C).p(B \mid A).p(C \mid A).p(A)$$

Hypothetical assignments for these probabilities, together with some explanation are shown in Table 2.1.

Attribute	Value	Explanation
$p(e \mid \neg c)$	.60	Headaches are common
$p(e \mid c)$	.80	but more common if tumour present.
$p(d \mid \neg b, \neg c)$	.05	Coma is rare,
$p(d \mid b, \neg c)$	.80	but common if
$p(d \mid \neg b, c)$	.80	either cause is present.
$p(d \mid b, c)$	.80	
$p(b \mid \neg a)$	.20	Increased calcium uncommon, but
$p(b \mid a)$	.80	common consequence of metastasis.
$p(c \mid \neg a)$	.05	Brain tumour rare and uncommon
$p(c \mid a)$	.20	consequence of metastasis.
$p(a)$	.20	Incidence in relevant clinic.

Table 2.1 *Hypothetical conditional probabilities for Figure 2.6 (adapted from Spiegelhalter 1986b).*

Now, we have emphasised that probabilistic reasoning need not be constrained by the directionality of the graphical representation. We may reason both forwards and backwards through the graph. Indeed, evidence may be received about any of the nodes in the graph and the consequences propagated throughout the graph. Thus, although the directed graph is appropriate for structuring the problem, we do not wish the propagation of evidence to be constrained by these directionalities. We need to convert the directed graph into an undirected graphical representation to allow complete flexibility in reasoning over the graph.

The basic idea is to decompose the graph into a sequence of clusters of nodes. These provide minimal subgraphs in which belief revision *must* be calculated as a global computation over the subgraph. However, if the average size of the clusters of nodes, known as *cliques*, is small then the computations over all nodes within any individual clique will not be too intensive. Belief revision may then propagate sequentially through the cliques. The probability distribution of one clique is revised. The influence of the change of probabilities of the nodes common to its neighbouring clique is then calculated for that clique. The effects of the revised distribution on this neighbour are then passed on to *its* neighbour, and so on.

In the case of our simple example, we may convert the directed/recursive model to an undirected graphical model by introducing a 'vacuous rule' linking nodes B and C (Wermuth and Lauritzen, 1983), and removing all arrows from the edges (Figure 2.7). In this simple example, the addition of one rule is all that is needed to enable the graphical model to be decomposed into a sequence of "cliques". The strict requirement is that the graph be "triangulated". This may be achieved by first "marrying" all parent nodes (to produce the "moral graph"), and then searching through the graph and adding links if necessary to ensure that there are no closed cycles of length greater than four nodes without an intersecting chord. The cliques are then maximal subsets of nodes in which each node in a clique is linked to all other nodes in the same clique.

In the example of Figure 2.7, the cliques are the sets of nodes: {A,B,C}, {B,C,D} and {C,E}. An important property which is a result of structuring the graph in this way is that we now have a decomposable graph with the Markov property. Viz: a variable is independent of all those nodes not adjacent to it, conditional on those that are adjacent to it. This is the property expressed by equation (2.3).

To illustrate what is meant by decomposable, the joint distribution may now be written:

p(A,B,C,D,E)

$$= p(E \mid C).p(D \mid B,C).p(C \mid A).p(B \mid A).p(A) \qquad \text{from equation (2.3).}$$

$$= \frac{p(C, E)}{p(C)} \cdot \frac{p(B, C, D)}{p(B, C)} \cdot p(A, B, C) \qquad \text{by conditional probability.}$$

This is simply the product of the marginal distributions on the cliques divided by the product of the distributions on their intersections. These values can be derived from the original assessments of Table 2.1. For example,   for   the   clique   {A,B,C},   the   relation   p(A,B,C)   =

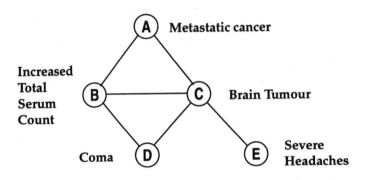

Fig 2.7   *Representation as an undirected graph.*

$p(C|A)\cdot p(B|A)\cdot p(A)$ used in the above derivation enables us to calculate from Table 2.1 that $p(a,b,c)=.032$, $p(\neg a,b,c)=.008$, $p(a,\neg b,c)=.008$, $p(\neg a,\neg b,c)=.032$, $p(a,b,\neg c)=.128$, $p(\neg a,b,\neg c)=.152$, $p(a,\neg b,\neg c)=.032$, and $p(\neg a,\neg b,\neg c)=.608$.

From these marginal distributions it is then possible to derive the prior probabilities of all the events specified (i.e. $p(b)=.32$, $p(c)=.08$, $p(d)=.32$, $p(e)=.616$). These are obtained by taking the probability distribution for a clique containing the node corresponding to the event of interest and summing over all the possible values for the other nodes in the clique. For example,

$$p(a) = p(a,b,c)+p(a,\neg b,c)+p(a,b,\neg c)+p(a,\neg b,\neg c)$$

$$= \sum_{\{A,B,C\}} p(a,B,C) \tag{2.4}$$

(Here we mean the sum over all possible states of the clique $\{A,B,C\}$ but with node A instantiated to true, 'a').

The impact of information on any node in the graph may now be propagated through the graph. To do this, we reconvert the graph, not so much into a directed graph, but into a directed 'hypertree' of cliques. First the nodes must be numbered. This is done as follows. The node whose evidence is observed is labelled as the first node. For example, suppose we wish to assess the effect of the observation of severe headaches on the probability of a patient lapsing into a coma. Then we would take node E as the starting point. The labelling is then continued by successively numbering the nodes attached to the maximum number of nodes that are already labelled. Ties may be broken at random. This is known as the 'maximum

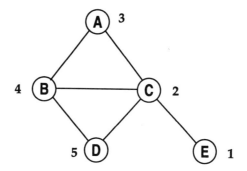

Fig 2.8   *A possible numbering using maximum cardinality search.*

cardinality search' and a possible numbering for the current problem is shown in Figure 2.8.

The cliques are then ranked according to the highest numbered node in each clique. This gives the sequence {C,E}, {A,B,C}, {B,C,D}. We now have a tree of clusters of nodes, or a hypertree (Figure 2.9).

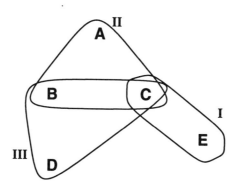

Fig 2.9   *Hypertree representation of the same knowledge.*

This sequence of cliques may now be recursively updated. If the current belief given the available evidence is indicated by an asterisk, p*, we have for clique I,

$$p^*(c) = p(c \mid e) = \frac{p(c, e)}{p(e)}$$

For clique II,

$$p^*(a,b,c) = p(a,b,c \mid e) \qquad \text{by definition.}$$
$$= p(a,b \mid c,e) \cdot p(c \mid e) \qquad \text{by conditioning.}$$
$$= p(a,b \mid c) \cdot p^*(c) \qquad \text{Markov property and definition of } p^*(c).$$
$$= p(a,b,c) \cdot \frac{p^*(c)}{p(c)} \qquad \text{definition of conditional probability.}$$

In turn, for clique III,

$$p^*(b,c,d) = p(b,c,d \mid e)$$
$$= p(d \mid b,c,e) \cdot p(b,c \mid e)$$
$$= p(b,c,d) \cdot \frac{p^*(b,c)}{p(b,c)}.$$

That is, the revised distribution for each successive clique is given by the original belief multiplied by the ratio of the revised belief to the original belief for those nodes on the intersection of the preceding clique.

Thus in turn, $p^*(c)$ can be obtained from clique I to enable the distribution on clique II to be revised; $p^*(b,c)$ may then be obtained from the revised distribution of clique II and the distribution for clique III revised. In this particular example, after conditioning on node E (severe headache is observed) the revised distribution for node III yields a revised marginal probability for the occurrence of coma as $p^*(d) = 0.333$. This differs very little from the prior of $p(d) = 0.32$, due mainly to the fact that headache has a high prior belief so its observation causes very little revision of belief. Much more significant changes will be observed in the more realistic demonstration of the following section.

This simple example has been used to illustrate the basic concepts underlying the Lauritzen-Spiegelhalter algorithm. The representation of the problem as a directed acyclic graph is a reasonably intuitive way of structuring the problem. It also simplifies the elicitation of the probability distribution by breaking it down into a product of conditional probabilities involving small numbers of semantically related propositions. To enable the propagation of evidence in any direction, this representation must then be transformed into one associated with an undirected graph, which may be decomposed into a sequence of 'cliques'. The influence on the probability distribution of a clique due to evidence from a neighbouring clique, may be easily calculated using local computations. In this way, evidence from any node may be propagated efficiently through the graph, provided the average clique size is reasonably small.

2.5   MUNIN - An application of probabilistic reasoning in electromyography

The theoretical developments in the propagation of probabilities through graphical structures has lead to the development of a number of applications based on these principles. One specific application in electromyography, MUNIN, has a very close association with the development of the Lauritzen and Spiegelhalter (L & S) algorithm and we will use it here to illustrate the theory in action.

Electromyography involves the diagnosis of muscle and nerve diseases through the analysis of bioelectrical signals from the affected muscle and nerve tissues. There are a number of possible observations which may be made, and MUNIN (for MUscle and Nerve Inference Network) was developed to assist in the diagnosis of the associated neuro-muscular disorder, given a set of findings (Andreassen et al, 1987; Jensen et al, 1987). The examples we will use are derived from a network modelling a single muscle which was used for illustrative purposes in the above reference. The final system comprises many such networks.

The model is essentially divided into three levels. The disease node represents the three possible neuro-muscular disorders (with associated gradations and/or different varieties of the disorders), together with the possible states "normal" and "other". The state "normal" means there is no evidence for the patient suffering from a disease with neuro-muscular symptoms, whilst the state "other" corresponds to support for a neuro-muscular disorder other than the three mentioned diseases. The disease node is linked to nodes representing possible pathophysiological conditions. These are the physical manifestations of the underlying diseases. For example, MU.LOSS represents the loss of motor units, where a motor unit consists of a grouping of several hundred muscle fibres enervated by a single nerve fibre. MU.LOSS then represents the percentage of nerve fibres which still survive and reach the muscle. These pathophysiological disorders are difficult or impossible to observe directly and non-invasively, but they can be deduced indirectly through the electromyographical tests.

The third layer of the model consists of the findings nodes for such tests. (The pathophysiological nodes may be linked to the findings nodes indirectly through intermediate nodes which integrate information from several of the findings nodes.) Figure 2.10 shows the MUNIN model for a single muscle, where the lengths of the horizontal bars indicate the probabilities of the various states of the nodes. At this stage the probabilities reflect the prior distribution for the network.

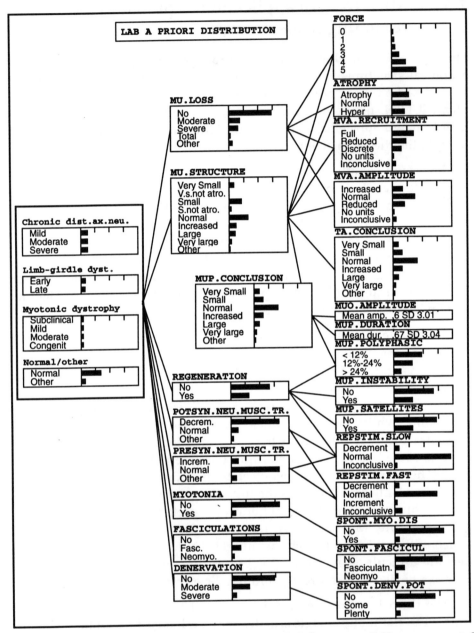

Fig 2.10   *The a priori probabilities for individual disease states (left) are propagated through the layer of pathophysiological nodes (middle) to the findings nodes (right). The length of the bar indicates the probability of the corresponding node state. (After Andreassen et al, 1987).*

Construction of the model required medical knowledge of the domain to be employed in three distinct tasks. First, the number and character of the nodes needed to be chosen. Note, for example, that very few of the nodes have binary states corresponding to yes/no answers. Secondly the 'causal' links had to be assigned between the various nodes. Then, finally, the prior and conditional probabilities had to be assessed for the disease states and the links between the node states respectively. Each of these is a non-trivial task and requires the development of effective elicitation and validation methods. An advantage of the probabilistic approach, as we will discuss in the next section, is that the numerical values may be critiqued and updated as case data passes through the system. However, although there are methods under development for the elicitation of the network structure (Heckerman, 1991), there has as yet only been a limited amount of success with the development of methods for systematically critiquing the graphical structure.

The assessment of the probabilities, even for a network as apparently simple as Figure 2.10, is a non-trivial task. For example, a complete specification of the conditional probability for the FORCE node, p(FORCE | MU.-LOSS, MU.STRUCTURE), requires the assessment of 6x5x9 = 270 probabilities to cover all combinations of the states of the three nodes. This emphasises the difficulties with trying to use objective estimates for the probabilities, as at least 10,000 cases would be needed to generate a reliable statistical estimate for the FORCE node. Instead of doing this, the MUNIN team used subjective estimates which were supported by an underlying 'deep knowledge model'. That is, the values were assessed with reference to a knowledge model derived from the current scientific understanding of the pathophysical processes involved (Andreassen et al, 1987).

With regard to the elicitation of the probabilities, it is worth emphasising one point. The network model will usually be used to assess the likelihood of certain disorders given evidence derived from certain findings, and related pathophysiological disorders. However, the relative influence of the various findings on the likelihoods of the possible diseases can be very hard for an expert to estimate. The frequency of occurrence of certain symptoms given specific disease states can, on the other hand, be much more intuitive to assess. For example, patients with no disorder (normal) are very likely to have no motor unit loss (MU.LOSS). Some of those suffering mild chronic axonal neuropathy will exhibit moderate MU.LOSS, while in moderate cases of neuropathy the majority of patients will suffer moderate loss. The majority of patients with severe cases will show severe signs of MU.LOSS (see Figure 2.11). As discussed in Section 2.2.1, the (implicit) use of Bayes' theorem enables the influence of the findings nodes to be propagated in the *reverse* direction if required in a diagnostic case. The problem can, and should, be framed in such a way as to simplify the elicitation of the prior and conditional probabilities as much as possible.

Having constructed the network and elicited the required probabilities, the findings for a specific case may be entered. The efficiency of the L & S algorithm enables the findings to be entered and their effects to be propagated through the network interactively. In Figure 2.12 the findings of a hypothetical case have been entered which results in high probabilities for the patient suffering from moderate or severe chronic axonal neuropathy (dashed lines indicate nodes which have been conditioned on). Notice also that the expected values for several of the so far unobserved findings nodes have also changed from Figure 2.10 (see for example, the expected values for "TA.CONCLUSION").

The network may also be used for hypothetical reasoning. In Figure 2.13 the system has been consulted for the expected findings given a moderate case of chronic axonal neuropathy.

Many of the nodes in the network contain a state labelled 'other'. A high probability assigned to 'other' in any of the nodes indicates that the system is either being asked to diagnose a disease it does not yet know about, or that it has been presented with conflicting evidence. There is thus some allowance made for the expression of conflict or ignorance, although

DISORDER	MU.LOSS					Σ
	no (%)	mod (%)	sev (%)	total (%)	other (%)	(%)
	91.9	5.0	1.0	0.1	2.0	100
Chronic axonal neuropathy:						
mild	60.0	33.0	4.0	1.0	2.0	100
moderate	16.0	64.0	16.0	2.0	2.0	100
severe	2.0	25.0	61.0	10.0	2.0	100
Other	33.0	30.0	30.0	5.0	2.0	100

Fig 2.11   *Conditional probabilities for the states of MU.LOSS.*

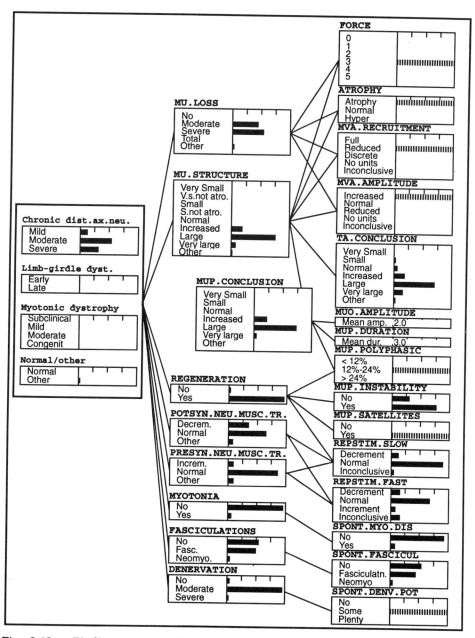

Fig 2.12   *Findings corresponding to a typical case of "moderate chronic axonal neur-opathy" have been entered. The broken horizontal 100% bars correspond to the entered findings. (After Andreassen et al, 1987).*

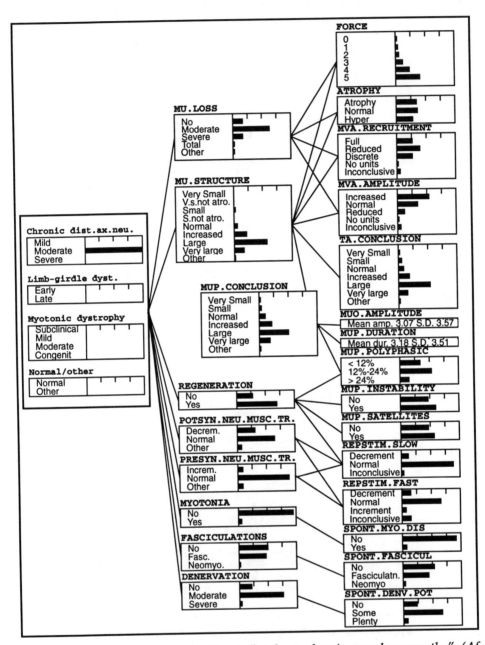

Fig 2.13   *Expectations corresponding to "moderate chronic axonal neuropathy". (After Andreassen et al, 1987).*

what to do about it is left to the initiative of the user. It is also worth mentioning that one of the possible conditions of ignorance is that the system is unable to handle multiple diseases.

The technology underlying MUNIN has been very rigorously developed over the latter part of the 1980's and is now available commercially in the Expert System shell HUGIN. However, this technology is still undergoing many refinements, one of which is to introduce a learning capability.

2.6   Learning from the children of Great Ormond Street

Expert Systems which employ some method of reasoning under uncertainty will often rely upon a large element of subjective knowledge. This will have been elicited from experts in the domain of application, whose judgement in turn will have been influenced by experience gained whilst practising their profession. Just as an expert may learn with experience, may it not be possible to build an Expert System which learns too? This is an emerging field of AI research, and a problem for which probabilistic systems do have a solution. Essentially, one can exploit "the ability of Bayesian probabilistic reasoning to become Bayesian statistical reasoning" (Spiegelhalter et al, 1989; Spiegelhalter and Cowell, 1991); as case data passes through the system, the information can be used to revise the parameters, the probabilities, of the Bayesian network. This is being exploited in a system for diagnosing congenital heart disease which is currently being developed (Spiegelhalter et al, 1991).

Congenital heart disease requires rapid and accurate diagnosis. Its effects can be immediately apparent at birth, resulting in cyanosis ('blue' babies) or heart failure (breathlessness). Any child with these symptoms will be suspected as suffering from congenital heart disease and will need to be transported immediately after birth to a specialist referral centre. The condition of the child may deteriorate very rapidly. Consequently, the referral centre will need to make a preliminary diagnosis over the telephone so that treatment can be started before the journey. A misdiagnosis at this stage could be life threatening, and so there is a great deal of interest in improving the reliability of the telephone diagnosis. This has stimulated the Great Ormond Street Hospital for Sick Children (a major referral centre for the South East of England) to become actively involved in the development of the probabilistic Expert System referred to above.

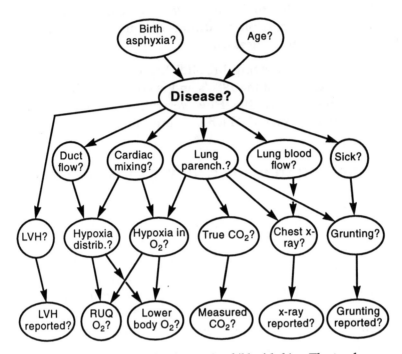

Fig 2.14   *Five layer model for the diagnosis of 'blue' babies. The top layer represents risk factors. The disease itself is manifest as a pathophysiological disturbance (third layer). These produce clinical features (fourth layer), which may differ from the reported clinical features (fifth layer). (After Spiegelhalter et al, 1991).*

This system is based on a five layer model (Figure 2.14). Two *risk factors* directly influence the likelihood of specific *diseases*. During diagnosis, reported *clinical features* may differ from *true clinical features* due to observer error. The true clinical features reflect specific *physiological disturbances*, which in turn are caused by the specific diseases of interest.

This graphical model was constructed in collaboration with consultant paediatric cardiologists at Great Ormond Street Hospital. The next step was to elicit the probabilities for the model. A large amount of case data was available, but still not enough to provide reliable estimates for all the required values. So, as with MUNIN, extensive tables of subjective probabilities had to be elicited. In many cases the experts were not prepared to commit to a point value, and so the probability was specified as a range of values. For example, it was believed that 80-90% of cases of lung disease would exhibit 'grunting'. If some simple assumptions about the interpretation of this interval are made, a fairly straightforward learning algorithm may be developed.

In the above example, the expert's opinion was that the proportion of cases of lung disease (ld) which they would expect to exhibit grunting (g) was between 80 and 90%. This has a mean value of 85%, so $p(g \mid ld)$ is taken to be 0.85. Subjective probability may be interpreted as an estimate of the frequency of occurrence obtained from an implicit population of cases underlying the expert's experience. The imprecision in the subjective probability then corresponds to a prior distribution over the domain of possible frequencies; the more precise estimates reflecting a larger implicit sample size.

It is straightforward to estimate the implicit population size. We make the assumption that the range either side of the mean value may be taken to represent one standard deviation, and that the expected value has a gaussian distribution about the mean. Then standard binomial theory for a binary state variable gives:

$$\sigma = \sqrt{\frac{p(1-p)}{n}}$$

Here, σ is standard deviation, p is the mean value and n is the implicit population size.

For the example of grunting given lung disease, this gives $n \approx 50$. The expert's opinion is then interpreted as though $p(g \mid ld) = 42.5/50$. Now it is simple to update this value as data passes through the system. Suppose a baby is now admitted to the hospital who turns out to have lung disease, but did not exhibit grunting. It may be said that 42.5 cases exhibit grunting (unchanged) out of a population of 51. That is, $p(g \mid ld) = 42.5/51 = 0.83$. This is a small change, but as real data accumulates the revised probabilities will converge towards the 'true' (objective) value.

This unfortunately is still not very satisfactory. The trouble is that if the expert's judgement was very much in error, it can take a long time for the revised estimates to stabilise at a final objective value. Although many of the probabilities elicited for the Great Ormond Street system were in good agreement with the later case data, it turned out that the above probability for grunting was not. Of sixteen babies with lung disease, only four exhibited grunting. Using the above learning technique, the revised value after these sixteen cases was $p(g \mid ld) = 46.5/66 = 0.7$; still a long way from the much lower value which seems to be suggested by the case data. Intuitively it would appear at this stage that the expert's prior belief had been wide-

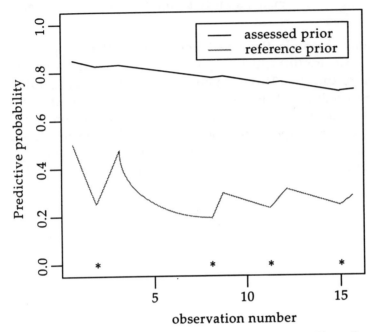

Fig 2.15   *Revisions of predictive probabilities that next case of lung disease be reported to grunt. Starting point for the top curve is assessed prior, that for the bottom curve is the reference prior. Asterisks mark positive observations. (After Spiegelhalter et al, 1991).*

ly in error and that more reliable results would be obtained if this value were rejected in favour of a more objective reference prior. Figure 2.15 shows the revisions of the expert's prior belief over the sixteen cases. It also shows the revisions that would have been made if the expert's judgement had been rejected in favour of the reference value of $p(g|ld) = 0.5$, with an implicit sample size of 1.

It is clear that in the case of grunting given lung disease the reference prior turned out to be the better value to take as a starting point for the learning algorithm. Significance tests have been developed which provide a measure of the discrepancy between the expert's assessment and the observed data (Spiegelhalter and Lauritzen, 1990; Spiegelhalter and Cowell, 1991). This provides a formal basis for the rapid rejection of the expert's prior assessment in favour of a reference value which would provide better predictions.

It is quite possible that modifications to the graphical structure of the model may have more influence on improving the reliability of the predictions than identifying inaccuracies in the numerical coefficients. Work is also under way to develop techniques for critiquing and systematically modifying the structure of the model.

2.7   Discussion

We began this chapter with the observation that probability theory has the longest history of all the formalisms discussed in this book; its place in the classification of uncertainty for the representation of partial knowledge as characterised by propensity, or subjective confidence, is clear (Figure 1.2). In many respects, therefore, probability theory is the yardstick against which the other formalisms should be compared. The following discussion is intended to provide the reader with a clear indication of the advantages and pitfalls of the probabilistic and, specifically, subjective Bayesian approach to uncertainty management in Artificial Intelligence. It will thus give some insight into the rationales for the alternative frameworks discussed in the remainder of this book.

The point to emphasise is that under a number of conditions the Bayesian calculus both imposes a strict discipline on knowledge engineering, and provides a useful tool for representing and updating subjective probabilities. As the examples shown above have illustrated, the use of Bayesian inference is clearly recommended if we are satisfied that:

(a) knowledge in the domain of interest can reasonably be assumed to satisfy the axioms specified by Cox (for example, that all the propositions are well defined, that a degree of belief can in principal and empirically be assigned to all atomic and conditional propositions);

(b) there is access to the appropriate sources (e.g. experts) from whom both a qualitative domain model *and* the relevant probabilities can be elicited;

(c) in the domain it is not necessary to reason explicitly with some of the non-probabilistic sources of uncertainty identified in Figure 1.2 (such as directly manipulating contradictions, vague propositions etc.);

(d) the domain is reasonably constrained in its size.

However, to the extent that these conditions are not met, applying the Bayesian scheme may impose some difficulties. As stated by Shafer and Pearl (1990, p2):

"Not all problems of uncertainty in AI lend themselves to probability."

2.7.1   Knowledge representation.

With respect to knowledge representation, it is clear from Cox's axioms (Section 2.2) that probability theory is centred on the notion of uncertainty as it applies to atomic or conditional propositions. Therefore, concepts such as ambiguity, inconsistency, incompleteness and irrelevance are not permitted, and are not formally part of the Bayesian model. More specifically, these aspects of uncertainty (inconsistency or contradiction) have to be engineered out of the problem domain in order to make the calculus usable. That is not to say that such concepts cannot be dealt with within a probabilistic framework, but that some additional features must be added to support these extensions.

As an example, consider the case of contradiction. In classical logic, contradictions are by definition always false. In Expert Systems, which may be built to capture heuristics rather than formal theories, apparent contradictions might occur from time to time. Suppose, for the sake of argument, that we have two rules/conditional statements which we wish to represent in a Bayesian net: p(pregnant | male) = 0, p(pregnant | positive scan) = 1. Furthermore, suppose we also make the dubious assumption of conditional independence between being male and the ultrascan result. Theoretically, we might now imagine that some input error in which a patient was both classified as male and having a positive scan might send the system into turmoil. In a rigorous probabilistic system, this would not be the case. The strictness of the Bayesian inference system in fact prevents such inconsistencies from ever occurring, since in the specification of marginal probabilities we must estimate each $p(A,B,C) = p(C | A,B).p(A | B).p(B)$. In other words, we would need to elicit p(pregnant | male, positive scan), which would clearly highlight the possible error. Thus the requirement for coherence prevents contradictions from ever occurring.

Weaker forms of contradiction (e.g. anomaly) are simply represented as low probability conjunctions and can be used as the basis of parameter revision as described in Section 2.6. Incompleteness and irrelevance are, however, potentially problems when constructing the qualitative model.

With respect to vagueness, Cheeseman (1986) has argued that statements such as John is tall or bald, which are dealt with explicitly in fuzzy sets and possibility theory as possibility distributions (see Chapter 5), can be represented as probability density functions. This is certainly a feasible suggestion where a population of the relevant observations are available, or the relevant probability density functions can be elicited from human experts. However, this is frequently not the case. The point about many situations, especially those for which possibility theory was devised, is that often the most we can reasonably say or infer is what the limits are whereby a proposition becomes tautological or self-contradictory, together with some assessment of the nature of the function that relates the two. Possibility functions are dealt with in more detail in Chapter 5.

2.7.1.1 Incompleteness: any more hypotheses?

When discussing incompleteness it is useful to distinguish a number of levels, as in Figure 1.2. Specifically we can have incompleteness with respect to individual parameters (e.g. specific values are missing), or with respect to individual propositions missing from a set (e.g. associated with a variable), or even more generally with respect to the sets of sets of variables (missing nodes/variables in the network).

Incompleteness of the first type can be dealt with by the use of entropy methods. Attempts to deal with missing propositions typically centre on the introduction of a node bearing the variable name "any other hypothesis" with possible values "yes" and "no" (as in Figures 2.10 to 2.12). However, this introduces more complications since it places a requirement upon users/data for probabilities such as the probability of none of the symptoms given any other hypothesis, and so on. For example, in Figure 2.10 the expert will be required to estimate values such as the probability of an inconclusive mva.recruitment given some "other" mu.structure.

2.7.2   Knowledge engineering.

Because so many areas of Decision Science are orchestrated around the use of subjective probabilities, many texts have described some of the problems associated with the elicitation of subjective probabilities (e.g. von Winterfeldt and Edwards, 1988). These include both simple biases such as sub- or super-additivity in the context of the assignment of probabilities to sets of mutually exclusive and exhaustive propositions, to more subtle biases such as base-rate neglect (the tendency to ignore base-rates or priors) in probabilistic updating, representativeness, anchoring (failure to update sufficiently probabilities with new evidence), availability, overconfidence (assigning subjective probabilities to events which are greater than their objective probabilities), the conjunction fallacy, over/underconfidence in calibration and many others. Indeed, almost the entire psychological literature of Behavioural Decision Theory is devoted to studies of the identification, comprehension and elimination of such biases.

In fact, many of the activities that produce these biases (e.g. propagating probabilities) are handled by the propagation algorithms and therefore are actually solved rather than problematic. Furthermore, biases relating to incoherence are made explicit and therefore potentially removed.

Generally, the generation of a Bayesian inference model involves two steps:

1. construction of the relevant qualitative inference network, and
2. elicitation of the relevant prior and conditional probabilities within this structure.

For the first step the kinds of biases likely to be problematic relate to salience, since this is effectively ignoring conditioning information which should be represented in the network. With respect to (2) the important point is calibration of probabilities. Essentially an individual is well calibrated if for all events X assigned a probability $p(X)=P$, a proportion P are found to be true. Learning techniques, such as those of Section 2.6, can be used to critique and revise possibly miscalibrated sources. However, this is dependent upon the establishment of objective case libraries.

A further point to note, of course, is the sheer number of probability assignments that are generally required. Let N_i be the number of states for each node i in a clique ($1 \leq i \leq n$), where n is the total number of nodes in that clique. Then a full specification of the probability distribution over the clique will require the elicitation of

$$\prod_{i=1}^{n} N_i$$

probability assignments. As mentioned in Section 2.5, this can be quite a large number, even for modest clique sizes. However, despite the large number of assignments required, the very strong coherence requirements will eliminate those biases that are associated with incoherence.

Three other points are also important.

Firstly, especially if the network is to be published, it should contain face validity. That is to say, it should appear to the user to represent meaningful relationships between the semantic entities it includes. It should not, for example, include directed links from one type of symptom to another, even if being associated with the same disease they have a strong statistical association; a realistic assessment of their conditional independencies is required (Section 2.3). No such requirement of ecological validity exists for the propagation algorithms themselves, however. This is a purely formal matter to which the individual user is not exposed.

Secondly, in constructing the qualitative representation, a distinction should be drawn between actual events and instruments/reports concerning those events. In Figure 2.14, for example, reports of symptoms (such as "grunting") are clearly separated from the confirmed symptoms. In the example given in Section 2.6, reports are typically taken over the phone from less specialist staff whose assessment of a specific symptom, such as grunting, may not match that of the expert paediatric cardiologists taking the call. Therefore the relationships between the reports and the actual symptoms, as defined by the expert, are represented as statistical associations. In fact, an initial analysis for the network in Figure 2.14 without the additional nodes representing reporting errors had a much lower predictive accuracy than the final model (Spiegelhalter, personal communication).

Finally, an important point has been made by de Dombal et al. (1992) in the context of one of the oldest and most established Bayesian advice systems used in the diagnosis of acute abdominal pain. He points out that one of the principal problems with Bayesian systems is ensuring that the user (in this case a physician) is able accurately to assess and act upon the significance of the computer's prediction. In the system reported in (de Dombal et al, 1992), instead of presenting raw probabilities to clinicians, the Bayesian posteriors were in fact employed along with other context specific information to classify patients according to three wide bands (50-70% prediction, 70-90% prediction and > 90% prediction). On the basis of this categorisation, a database of patient data was then searched for the outcomes of patients with similar predicted diagnoses in similar contexts. A summary of cases from this database is then presented to users, rather than the probabilities in isolation. Thus, rather than presenting a diagnostic prediction to the user, the system actually retrieves what happened to a large group of patients with similar clinical presentations, and presents overview data. In this respect the prior probabilities are used as a basis for classification. As a result of using this system, de Dombal et al. report there was an enormous improvement in the diagnostic accuracy of trainee physicians.

The pivotal point here concerns the pragmatics of Expert System use. Useful as they are as summary measures of evidence impact, and in propagation algorithms, it is the very abstractness of probabilistic assessments that potentially limits their acceptability. By making the cross reference with actual patient data the ecological validity can be restored.

2.7.3   Computational considerations.

The propagation algorithms which have been developed using the various graph-theoretic approaches have enabled rigorous probabilistic Expert Systems to be built which can be used interactively. However, although the influence diagram approach will often reduce the computational overhead relative to that required for updating an unstructured probability distribution, the computation time still rapidly becomes very large as the number of nodes and links is increased. In the limit, the complexity is exponential in the size of the largest clique. So this approach will only offer significant computational advantages for those problems where the graph can be decomposed into a number of relatively small cliques. Cooper (1990) provides a detailed account of the complexity of Bayesian propagation algorithms.

2.8   Conclusions

We have seen in this chapter a number of clear situations in which Bayesian network techniques can be used to assist in uncertainty management as a result of the recent work on developing efficient propagation algorithms. We have identified advantages and pitfalls of their use. Several commercial tools (e.g. HUGIN, the "shell" derived from MUNIN) are now available which can be used to build such systems.

It should be emphasised that work on Bayesian inference nets is fundamentally concerned with the structure of reasoning; not merely with the numerical coefficients themselves. In this respect throughout this book we will refer to a number of generalisations of the Bayesian approach which deal with coefficients other than probabilities (e.g. Shenoy and Shafer, 1990). There are, for example, some systems which employ essentially Bayesian methods to propagate non-numerical coefficients (e.g. MUM (Cohen, 1989)).

Equally, it should be emphasised that a critical difference between the use of probabilistic methods in AI and other domains is that the latter are traditionally predicated on the assumption that a probability structure already exists. This is not the case in many AI domains and consequently probability theorists are being forced to deal with the serious problems of model construction (e.g. Heckerman, 1991).

At the more general level, however, there is still the question of whether reducing information to purely numerical values does not somehow strip away potentially useful information which can be employed in reasoning under uncertainty. This is the view taken by many of the other approaches described in this book. For example, propositions may not always be well defined, as in "patient blood pressure is high" (contra property B1 of Section 2.2), or it may be unreasonable to attempt to apply degrees of belief to certain propositions (contra B3), we may simply not know. Chapters 4 and 5 discuss models for handling these aspects of imprecision and ignorance.

There may also be information available about the causes of the uncertainty, which can be exploited rather than just compiled into numbers. This is the foundation of more recent approaches to uncertainty management which are based on the ideas of endorsement or argumentation. These are presented in detail in Chapter 7. Here it is sufficient to mention that such approaches are predicated on the notion that the content of information rather than just its strength is germane to uncertainty management.

3
The Certainty Factor Model

3.1   Introduction

In this chapter we will discuss an approach to reasoning under uncertainty, the certainty factor (CF) formalism, which was intended for use with rule-based Expert Systems. It has been criticised on a number of grounds, as we shall see. However, it is an interesting example of a heuristic approach which attempts to weaken some of the axioms of probabilistic approaches and be computationally efficient. This approach was first employed in Mycin. Mycin was a pioneering rule-based Expert System designed to assist physicians in the antimicrobial treatment of patients with serious infections such as bacteremia and meningitis (Shortliffe, 1976; Buchanan and Shortliffe, 1984). It is sometimes considered a type of modified Bayesian system. However, it differs from Bayesian systems in a number of respects, most notably in its use of a mathematical calculus within a goal-driven rule-based inference procedure.

To illustrate the Mycin System, Figure 3.1 shows a typical rule which relates laboratory results to a diagnosis with an associated certainty factor:

If the stain of the organism is gram positive,
    and the morphology of the organism is coccus
    and the growth conformation of the organism is chains

Then there is suggestive evidence (0.7) that
    the identity of the organism is streptococcus.

Fig 3.1   *English Translation of a Mycin Rule (Shortliffe and Buchanan, 1975).*

3.1.1   Rationale.

The rationale for the development of the CF formalism derives in part from the attempt to overcome some of the perceived weaknesses of the so called "idiot bayes" approaches (Duda et al, 1979) which had been used in a number of systems, and in part from the attempt to model expert reasoning in bacteriology.

The term "idiot bayes" has been applied in retrospect, rather derogatorily, to a number of Bayesian systems in which, for reasons of expediency in system construction, a number of simplifying assumptions were made. This contrasts with the Bayesian systems described in the preceding chapter. Unfortunately it turned out that these assumptions were often inappropriate. Specifically, they were that:

- faults/hypotheses are mutually exclusive and exhaustive (denying the possibility of multiple simultaneous faults), and

- evidence is conditionally independent given each fault/hypothesis (knowing that a particular piece of evidence is true has no effect on our belief in the other evidence).

The CF formalism attempted to overcome the limitations of these assumptions by both:

- collecting evidence for and against different hypotheses in independent rules, such that an increase of belief in one hypothesis does not necessarily result in a decrease in belief in other hypotheses, and

- modularising the expression of conditional dependence in evidence/hypothesis relations in rules so that the addition or deletion of rules would not affect the dependency relationships between faults/hypotheses and evidence not explicitly mentioned in those rules.

3.1.2   Foundations.

The specific representational requirements of the CF formalism arise from experience during construction of the Mycin system. Here domain experts were asked to rate their confidence in the inference rules they produced on a numeric scale, normalised to values in the range $[0,1]$. However, these normalised values could not be treated as probabilities because they did not satisfy the additivity axiom (P3 in Section 2.2). That is, the probabilities of the set of mutually exclusive events did not sum to one. This was because evidence deemed partially to support an hypothesis was not also considered as partially conflicting with that hypothesis. In Figure 3.1, for example, the inference embodied by the rule has a confidence factor of 0.7, but the complementary inference (i.e. that the organism is not streptococcus) is not simultaneously supported to degree 0.3. That is, from a→b (0.7), it does not follow a→¬b (0.3). This models the observation that the expert bacteriologists tend to gather evidence for and evidence against hypotheses independently (Shortliffe and Buchanan, 1975). This is a very different conception of evidence integration to that employed in the Bayesian calculus. It anticipates developments in the Dempster-Shafer theory (Chapter 4) which allows (in a coherent way) an argument for an hypothesis to be agnostic with respect to the negation of that hypothesis.

The CF formalism makes explicit this distinction between supporting and conflicting information using the concepts of measures of belief (MB), [0,1], measures of disbelief (MD), [0,1], and composite Certainty Factors (CF), [-1,1]. All three are defined in terms of hypothesised mathematical relationships governed by prior and posterior probabilities of the propositions they describe.

In equations 3.1 and 3.2 (from Shortliffe and Buchanan, 1975), p(h) is the prior probability of an hypothesis, h, and p(h | e) is the posterior probability of that hypothesis given some evidence, e. If the observation of e favours a particular hypothesis, h, the proportional measure of increased belief, MB, is defined as the increase in the probability of the hypothesis provided by the observation of e, p(h | e) - p(h), divided by the current disbelief, 1 - p(h). Thus,

$$MB = (p(h \mid e) - p(h)) / (1 - p(h)) \qquad (3.1)$$

Similarly if the observation of e counts against an hypothesis, h, the proportionate increase in disbelief, MD, is equal to the decrease in belief, p(h) - p(h | e), divided by the current belief, p(h). Thus,

$$MD = (p(h) - p(h \mid e)) / p(h) \qquad (3.2)$$

Each rule in Mycin had either an associated MB or MD, depending upon whether the truth of the antecedents provided evidence for or against the consequents. In the case of the rule in Figure 3.1 the MB is 0.7.

As in the earlier Prospector system (Duda et al, 1979), both data and hypotheses are treated as uncertain, so that not only rules but hypotheses and input data also have an associated MB or MD. The overall certainty of an hypothesis (the CF) is determined by combining the values of MB and MD. The original combination function was:

$$CF = MB - MD \qquad (3.3)$$

One problem with this formulation, however, is that in some circumstances a single piece of negative evidence could outweigh the impact of several pieces of positive evidence, or vice versa (discussed in Section 3.4). In more recent applications, however, specifically EMYCIN (van Melle et al, 1984), an Expert System shell based on Mycin, the definition of CFs was changed (equation 3.4) to prevent this.

$$CF = (MB - MD) / 1 - min(MB,MD) \qquad (3.4)$$

Equations 3.3 and 3.4 differ only when both MB and MD are non-zero.

CFs are given the following interpretations:

- $CF = -1$:   complete certainty that a proposition is false
- $-1 < CF < 0$: decrease in belief
- $CF = 0$:   no change in belief
- $0 < CF < 1$: increase in belief
- $CF = 1$:   complete certainty that a proposition is true.

From equations 3.1 and 3.2, it is clear that unlike probabilistic frameworks in which the basic measures, probabilities, are intended as absolute measures of belief (albeit attached to conditional propositions), CFs are relative increases or decreases in belief. This difference in computational semantics can be simply illustrated (Adams, 1984). Suppose we have two mutually dependent events, h_1 and h_2, and some evidence, e, which increases the probability of each such that:

$p(h_1) = 0.2$ and $p(h_2) = 0.8$, while

$p(h_1 | e) = 0.8$ and $p(h_2 | e) = 0.9$.

Since the evidence favours both hypotheses, $MD = 0$ for both, and by equation 3.1 we have:

$CF(h_1) = MB(h_1) = (0.8 - 0.2)/0.8 = 0.75$

$CF(h_2) = MB(h_2) = (0.9 - 0.8)/0.2 = 0.5$.

Hence although the resulting CF of h_1 is greater than the CF of h_2, the posterior probabilities have the opposite ordering ($p(h_1 | e) < p(h_2 | e)$). This contrasts the relative increases or decreases in belief inherent in the CF system and the absolute probabilities of the Bayesian model.

3.2   Operation

Data input by users either spontaneously or in response to systems requests have an associated confidence factor (an MB or an MD). This gives the user a scale of -1 to +1 for expressing confidence in each observation, though usually this will be -1 or 1. This input data is combined with the uncertain rules in the system to make inferences by the use of three combination functions:

- an antecedent pooling function that determines the pooled CF of a set of rule antecedents,

- a serial rule combination function that propagates CFs to the consequents of rules, and

- a parallel combination function that combines the results from different rules when they relate to the same proposition.

The *antecedent pooling function* (our terminology) determines a pooled CF for the set of antecedents in a rule. Specifically, for a conjunctive set of premises, the pooled MB is the individual minimum MB, while the pooled MD is the individual maximum MD. For a disjunctive set of premises, the pooled MB is the maximum of the MBs and the pooled MD is the minimum of the MDs (Shortliffe and Buchanan, 1975). More generally, as with possibility combination functions (Chapter 5), the conjunction of CFs is the minimum, while the disjunction is the maximum. Thus for the rule in Figure 3.1, if the CFs (MBs) attached to the three premises were 1, 0.9 and 0.8, the pooled CF of the premises would be 0.8. Alternatively, if any of the CFs attached to these propositions were negative (i.e. the CF was actually an MD) then the resulting CF for the antecedents would be this negative value.

The *serial combination function* is used to combine the pooled CF of a set of antecedents with the CF of a rule to propagate a CF to the consequent of a rule when it fires (equation 3.5). If the pooled CF of the antecedents of a rule is positive, this states that when a rule is fired, the CF attached to the consequent of a rule is the product of the pooled CF of the antecedents and the CF of the rule itself. Otherwise it is zero. That is, when the antecedents of a rule are not believed then there is no propagation.

$$CF_{consequent} = CF_{antecedents} \cdot CF_{rule} \qquad CF_{antecedents} > 0 \qquad (3.5)$$
$$CF_{consequent} = 0, \qquad\qquad\qquad CF_{antecedents} \leq 0$$

In the case of Figure 3.1, if the $CF_{antecedents}$ is 0.8 and the CF_{rule} is 0.7, then the CF attached to the consequent ($CF_{streptococcus}$, i.e., that the identity of the organism is *streptococcus*) is 0.56. Note that if the $CF_{antecedents}$ is negative then there is no change in belief concerning the identity of the organism.

The *parallel combination function* is used to pool evidence from different rules to produce an overall CF for each proposition. New evidence is pooled with existing evidence in proportion to the outstanding uncertainty (equation 3.6):

$CF_1, CF_2 < 0$: $CF_{combine}(CF_1, CF_2) = CF_1 + CF_2(1 + CF_1)$.

$CF_1, CF_2 > 0$: $CF_{combine}(CF_1, CF_2) = CF_1 + CF_2(1 - CF_1)$.   (3.6)

Otherwise: $CF_{combine}(CF_1, CF_2) = (CF_1 + CF_2) / 1 - \min(|CF_1|, |CF_2|)$.

Following the example of Figure 3.1, we have $CF_{streptococcus} = 0.56$. Suppose a second rule provides evidence that $CF_{streptococcus} = 0.4$, then by equation 3.6, $CF_{combine} = 0.56 + 0.4 (1 - 0.44) = 0.74$. Note that the order in which information arrives has no impact on the final combined CF, but that the combination function *does* assume that the rules providing the evidence are independent (Buchanan and Shortliffe, 1984).

The importance of the third case of equation 3.6 (and analogously equation 3.4) should be emphasised. Essentially, treating CFs as the simple difference between MBs and MDs can lead to some paradoxes. For example, if there are a number of rules (sources of evidence) which all support some hypothesis, then the associated MB will approach 1 asymptotically. However, if a single negative source of evidence arrives with an MD of 0.8, the resulting CF will be < 0.2, despite the fact that there may be many more positive rules supporting the hypothesis to the same degree.

By contrast the definition in case 3 of equation 3.6 has a much subtler effect. Suppose we have two independent sources of evidence each providing an MB (CF) of 0.8. Then, by the parallel combination function, the final MB (or CF) = 0.96 (i.e. 0.8 + 0.8*(1-0.8)). Now suppose a single source of negative evidence arrives with an MD (or negative CF) of 0.8. Using the revised combination function $CF_{combine}(0.96, -0.8) = (0.96 - 0.8)/(1 - 0.8) = 0.8$. The result of using this combination function is that equal but opposite sources of evidence effectively cancel each other out on a piecemeal basis. Generally, however, for weaker evidence the result of the computation with the revised combination function is similar to that obtained by the original formulation; e.g. $CF_{combine}(0.55,-0.5) = 0.1$, whereas for the original combination function $CF_{combine}(0.55,-0.5) = 0.05$.

3.3   Simple worked example

The following worked example is based upon the presentation of Pearl (1988; 1992) and Heckerman (1992), and is intended to illustrate some of the utilities and failures of the CF formalism. We begin with a simple scenario.

Holmes at the office receives a call from Watson stating that he can hear the sound of a burglar alarm coming from the direction of Holmes' house. Holmes, preparing to rush home, recalls that Watson is known for practical joking and decides to call his other neighbour, Gibbons, who despite occasional drink problems is generally reliable.

A miniature rule-based system (Figure 3.2) to represent this scenario might look like the following:

r1: If Watson calls then Alarm (0.5)

r2: If Gibbons calls then Alarm (0.9)

r3: If Alarm then Burglary (0.99)

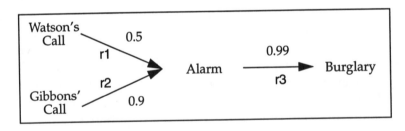

Fig 3.2   *Schematic representation of rules r1 to r3.*

Supposing now that Gibbons does confirm the alarm, it is straight forward to determine the CF of burglary. Specifically, applying the parallel combination function (eq. 3.6, case 2) to rules r1 and r2 we have $CF_{alarm} = 0.9 + 0.5(0.1) = 0.95$. Then applying the serial combination function (eq. 3.5, case 1) to r3 we have $CF_{burglary} = CF_{alarm} \cdot 0.99 = 0.94$.

In the case of this simple rule base it is not necessary to determine a pooled CF for any set of rule antecedents since each rule only has one antecedent. Furthermore, it is assumed that the input conditions relating to the calls have a CF of 1. Below, however, we describe some situations in which the apparent simplicity of the CF formalism breaks down.

3.4   Discussion

The attraction of the CF formalism is that it appears to provide a method for both formalising heuristic reasoning as rules and simultaneously allows uncertainty to be quantified and combined within a formal syntactically simple calculus. As a result, the CF formalism has been popular with Expert System designers. However, although Mycin was shown to demonstrate high diagnostic accuracy (Yu et al, 1979), it has been argued that this was not necessarily because of the way it handled uncertainty. The success of the Mycin system should certainly not be regarded as a validation of the CF formalism. Indeed in a sensitivity analysis conducted by the Mycin developers it was found that:

> *degradation of performance was only found when the number of intervals was changed to three ... The rules use CFs that can be modified by +/-0.2, showing that there are few deliberate (or necessary) interactions. The observed stability of therapy despite changing organisms lists probably results because a single drug will cover for many organisms, a property of the domain* (Buchanan and Shortliffe, 1984, p 219).

3.4.1   Computational considerations.

As mentioned in Chapter 2 (Section 2.2.2), the syntactic approach to uncertainty propagation adopted by the CF formalism is computationally efficient since it requires only a small number of local computations to be made. This is an apparent advance over some of the early Bayesian systems which dealt with huge conditional probability tables and is a major attraction for the use of an uncertainty handling technique such as the CF formalism. Such apparent efficiency is achieved as a result of the implicitly modular nature of the system rules and is thus predicated upon the viability of this assumption.

3.4.2   Knowledge engineering.

Using the certainty factor formalism for uncertainty management involves both:

    a.   eliciting the appropriate rules for generation of evidence for and against hypotheses, and

b.   eliciting the associated CFs.

Many problems arise in the context of rule base verification which are now well documented (see (Preece et al, 1992) for a review). Specifically it is necessary to verify that rule bases do not contain redundant rules (rules that are unusable, duplicated or subsumed by other rules), conflicting rules, circularities in the rule base, and that the rule base is complete according to some criteria of coverage. Furthermore, this process must be iterative with respect to revision of the rule base. In addition to these there are many problems specific to the CF formalism for uncertainty management.

In terms of knowledge elicitation, unlike studies of elicitation of probabilities, there are no studies in which CFs have been elicited from subjects. Consistent with the axioms of the CF formalism, however, some experimental studies concerned with mapping probabilities to verbal uncertainty expressions have suggested that the quantitative meanings given to terms such as "likely" may be dependent upon the subjective prior probability associated with that event (e.g.(Wallsten et al, 1986b), reviewed in (Clark, 1990b)). Such a finding would be in line with the interpretation of CFs under the CF formalism. However, it should be emphasised that this is only one single tentative finding.

If elicitation of CFs is viewed as being analogous to the elicitation of probabilities then an important point is made by Kahneman, Slovic and Tversky (1982). Given the choice, physicians are more confident and accurate in the estimation of probabilities of symptoms given diseases than in estimating the probability of a disease given a symptom as in the CF rules, since the latter requires the physician to take into account the prevalence (or base rate) of a given symptom in the population as a whole. As we have discussed, however, this is not a problem for Bayesian systems since the exact directionality of elicited probabilities is not a critical part of the formalism (Chapter 2). In effect it is possible to infer the relevant set of marginal probabilities from associations in either direction.

From an elicitation perspective, the lack of a requirement for additivity in CFs means that subjects' estimates are not formally so rigorously constrained. However, this loss of formal rigour, while allowing a greater latitude in estimates, also means the loss of formal tools for critiquing subjects' estimates. In other words it is not possible to provide tests of internal consistency between estimated CFs. These can only be checked and normalised by reference to external data sets.

3.4.2.1 Absolute and relative interpretations of CFs.

Section 3.1.2 provided a simple illustration of how CFs differ from probabilities (specifically posterior probabilities). Horvitz and Heckerman
(1986), have criticised this formulation on a number of accounts.

One criticism is that this notion of relative increase in belief is inconsistent with the elicitation procedure in which the specific prompt given
to physicians appears to be requesting posterior probabilities. That is,
"How confident?". This appears to be true. However, it should be borne
in mind that for equation 3.1 as p(h) tends towards 0, so the MB (or CF)
tends towards $p(h \mid e)$. Therefore, since CFs are fairly robust in sensitivity
analyses, if all the hypotheses have fairly low priors, which is typically
the case in medical domains, then there is no difficulty in approximating
CFs as posterior probabilities.

A further criticism made by Heckerman (1986) is that the original definition of CFs is inconsistent with the functions used in Mycin to combine
CFs. Specifically, that the original definition of the CFs prescribed non-
commutative combination of evidence. Although efforts were made to remove these inconsistencies, the resulting calculus still relied on global assumptions of conditional independence (Horvitz, Heckerman and
Langlotz, 1986).

3.4.3   Knowledge representation.

In terms of the uncertainty categories identified in Chapter 1, it is clear
that a potential advantage of separating measures of belief (MB) and disbelief (MD) is that it then becomes theoretically possible to distinguish
situations of ignorance about individual propositions (hypotheses/faults)
(where MB = MD = 0) from situations of conflict or equivocation where
MB = MD $\neq 0$), though this was not reported as a rationale for the CF formalism and does not appear to be utilized for meta-level control by the
backward chaining control strategy.

However, utilisation of such information can be envisaged in conflict
resolution, specifically, by looking for information that can potentially
discredit (reduce the CF associated with) the antecedents of the rules providing the conflicting evidence. So the formalism does suggest useful extensions.

With respect to incompleteness, like most other formalisms, the CF
formalism can deal with incompleteness, if identified, in the unary sense
of missing values. However, there are certainly no powerful techniques

analogous to maximum entropy methods for estimating the relevant CFs of rules for which no human or empirical estimate is available. With respect to the more pervasive set theoretic interpretation of incompleteness as might be manifested by large gaps in knowledge, the CF formalism essentially makes the closed world assumption (see Chapter 6 for a general discussion). That is, things it does not know about are assumed to be irrelevant, with the corollary that any subsequent knowledge can be appended to the rule base with no change to the existing rules. However, once again, any potential advantages of this approach are predicated upon the assumption of modularity that is the basis of the formalism.

3.4.4   Modularity and conditional dependency.

In discussing modularity and conditional independence, it is useful to recall the decomposition proposed by Pearl (1988) and discussed in Section 2.2.2. A logical rule such as "if A then B", is modular if B follows from A:

- regardless of how A is established (*detachment*), and
- regardless of what else is known (*locality*).

The CF formalism makes these assumptions of locality and detachment in its modular approach to uncertainty management.

In the simple example of Figure 3.2 above, the CF model works quite well because Burglary and Watson's/Gibbons' calls can be considered conditionally independent (see Section 2.3). That is, once we know that the alarm has sounded, knowing that a burglary has occurred has no effect on our belief of Watson's call, since his call is triggered only by the alarm and not by the burglary *per se*. Thus in assessing the $CF_{burglary}$ we need only consider CF_{alarm} and $CF_{alarm \rightarrow burglary}$ and do not need to worry about the source of the evidence for alarm. Furthermore, the example appears to be modular with respect to the addition of rules, since adding a rule of the form "if Smith (another reliable neighbour) calls then alarm (0.9)" appears entirely consistent with the other rules in the system.

There are at least two kinds of situation, however, where the modularity conditions break down (Heckerman and Horvitz 1988; Heckerman 1992) relating to multiple causation and correlated evidence, illustrated below.

As an embellishment to the simple scenario of Figure 3.2 consider the following:

Holmes recalls that in the alarm manual it mentions that the device is sensitive to

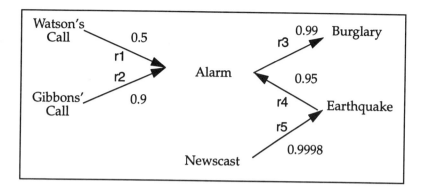

Fig 3.3   *Schematic representation of rules r1 to r5.*

earthquakes, which would provide an alternative explanation for the alarm. Furthermore he realizes that an earthquake would very likely be reported on a newscast.

Thus we ought to be able to add two further rules to our rule base in a modular fashion (Figure 3.3):

r4: if newscast of earthquake then earthquake (0.9998)

r5: if earthquake then alarm (0.95)

A major problem with this network of rules, however, is that it no longer captures all the important interactions among propositions. Specifically the current rule base allows Holmes to increase his belief in burglary if the alarm sounds regardless of the source of evidence for alarm. That is, hearing a newscast of an earthquake would now entitle Holmes to increase his belief in burglary, though in practice, this should now decrease since the alarm is explained by the earthquake. Therefore, the new rulebase is not modular and violates the principle of detachment. Essentially where there are multiple potential causes for some observation, the nature of the cause must be taken into account when propagating the associated belief.

At this point it would be tempting to add a further rule to try and repair the rulebase (Figure 3.4):

r6: if earthquake then burglary (-0.94).

Now if there is a newscast of earthquake (CF = 1), then there is an increase in belief of earthquake and alarm, and both an increase in belief for burglary (from alarm) and a decrease in belief in burglary (from earth-

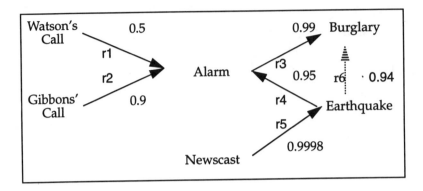

Fig 3.4   *Schematic representation of rules r1 to r6.*

quake) such that the total increase and decrease in belief of burglary cancel out. This seems to work at first sight except that:

- If either Watson or Gibbons now calls, the belief in alarm is increased further. This propagates to burglary such that if we have $CF_{burglary}$ = -0.94 (from earthquake) and $CF_{burglary}$ = 0.99 (from Alarm) then by the parallel combination function the resulting $CF_{burglary}$ is $CF_{combine}(0.99, -0.94) = 0.05/(1-0.94) = 0.83$. That is, there is still a resulting increase in belief in burglary even though, as stated earlier, the newscast should not affect belief in burglary. Essentially, whatever CF is applied to the fixing rule, it will only be appropriate in one situation. It thus violates the principle of locality since the precise CF assigned has to be dependent upon what else is known.

- A similar problem occurs if there is a newscast of earthquake in the confirmed absence of an alarm. This would allow Holmes to decrease his belief in burglary even though the newscast strictly has no bearing on his belief in burglary.

So, the fixing rule cannot be added without violating the principle of locality.

The problem here really stems from the confounding of what Pearl (1988) terms diagnostic (if symptoms then cause) and predictive (if cause then symptoms) rules within the same system (Section 2.2.2). Essentially both burglary and earthquake are potential causes of alarm. However, as the rules are written, r1, r2 and r3 are diagnostic, while r4 is predictive.

Continuing on the theme of conditional independence, the CF formalism also suffers from the problem of correlated evidence. We will use an example adapted from (Henrion, 1986). Suppose we receive three reports of a disaster (radio, TV and newspaper) each from a different correspondent, which in isolation provide evidence for the fact that thousands of people have died (Figure 3.5). Then the resulting belief that thousands of people have died is justifiably higher than it would be from any one source in isolation. That is, upon hearing reports 1, 2 and 3, by recursively applying the parallel combination function we have $CF_{1000s\ dead}$ = 0.9375.

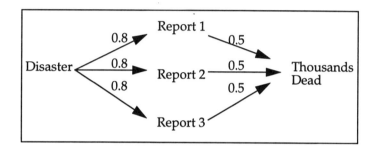

Fig 3.5   *Rule base for disaster scenario.*

However, if we subsequently discover that all the reports were actually based on a single observation of disaster then it is inappropriate to treat the three reports as independent. They are in fact highly correlated. Essentially, unlike the Bayesian systems discussed in Chapter 2 in which conditionally dependent hypotheses are arranged in cliques, the CF formalism provides no method for dealing with the problems discussed above except by:

- having all rules predictive or diagnostic, and
- chunking non-independent evidence in a set of rules, one to cater for each possible situation (i.e. if alarm and not newscast then burglary (0.95) etc.). For n antecedent boolean variables, this would require 2^n rules to cover all truth-conditional states.

Clearly, having all the rules predictive or diagnostic may not provide all the information needed by users. In addition, the clustering of non independent evidence is unsatisfactory for three reasons:

- it is untenable for large bodies of non-independent evidence since a separate rule would be required for each possible set of truth conditional states and must needlessly cluster propositions that are only remotely related[1];
- it is difficult to modify;
- it is computationally inefficient.

Thus, like the predicate calculus, the CF formalism has syntactic modularity. However, unlike the predicate calculus, the CF formalism lacks semantic modularity (Heckerman and Horvitz, 1988). The strength of association between the antecedents and consequents in non-categorical rules will change as a function of which other rules are added to or deleted from the knowledge base. This violates both the concepts of locality and detachment.

3.5   Conclusions

In Sections 3.4.1 to 3.4.3 the potential utility of the CF formalism for knowledge elicitation, representation and computational efficiency were discussed. These were identified as being dependent upon the assumption of semantic modularity of the rules and their CFs. However, in Section 3.4.5 it was demonstrated that this assumption is untenable in general and hence these advantages are apparent rather than real.

In defence of the CF formalism it should be stressed that it is not unusable, as demonstrated by Mycin. However, it does not provide the natural complement for dealing with uncertainty to the modular rule-based paradigm as originally intended. This is because of the non-modular operational requirements, discussed above, for all rules to be predictive or diagnostic and all non-independent evidence to be chunked in rules.

Many other criticisms of the CF formalism have also been made. Specifically, Heckerman (1992) argues that the CF formalism is actually worse than the idiot bayes model in some respects, since the parallel combination function assumes both conditional independence of evidence given each hypothesis *and* given the negation of each hypothesis. The "idiot bayes" model only assumes the former.

---

1. It is for this reason that a number of subsequent rule-based systems such as the OSM (described in (Clark et al. 1990) and Chapter 7) have incorporated general strategic rules which do not include case specific information.

An observation sometimes made as a criticism is that because Mycin made decisions about therapy, the MBs and MDs attached to rules were also used to represent utility considerations; for example, the potential cost of not diagnosing an infection with serious consequences. This was done by assigning higher CFs to rules with serious consequences. Thus the true semantics of CFs were more akin to measures of importance (i.e. confounding utility and uncertainty) than uncertainty in isolation. While this observation is true, there is nothing in the nature of the calculus that necessitates such misuse.

The concerns over the CF formalism were also shared by some of the developers of Mycin. They subsequently argued that a more appropriate technique for managing uncertainty in the application domain of Mycin would have been the Dempster-Shafer theory of evidence (Gordon and Shortliffe, 1984), discussed in Chapter 4. The CF formalism *has* proved popular with the developers of rule-based Expert Systems shells (e.g. Sage, and EMYCIN) and was also important for raising issues about the management of uncertainty not addressed in early "idiot bayes" systems. Nevertheless, the formal underpinnings of the system have been criticised to such an extent that it is now recognized more as a standard whose weaknesses must be overcome (see, for example, the discussion in Chapter 2), than as an effective method for uncertainty management.

4
Epistemic Probability: the Dempster-Shafer theory of evidence

The chance governed by an aleatory (random) *experiment may or may not coincide with our degrees of belief about the outcome of the experiment. If we know the chances, then we will surely adopt them as our degrees of belief. But if we do not know the chances, then it will be an extraordinary coincidence for our degrees of belief to be equal to them.* (Shafer, 1976).

4.1   Introduction

We mentioned in Chapter 2 the distinction between subjective and objective probability; two different interpretations of essentially the same mathematical formalism. This sharing of the use of the word 'probability' in the naming of both interpretations has led to an unfortunate confounding of two different concepts. The development of the mathematical formalism described in Chapter 2 has strong roots in the statistical analysis of games of chance. However, although Cox's axioms do provide a justification for the use of Bayesian probability as a measure of belief, it is not necessarily the case that a numerical measure of epistemic *belief* should be strictly governed by the frequentistic laws of *chance*. The Dempster-Shafer theory of evidence provides an alternative, more general, model for the assessment of numerical degrees of belief.

There are three important distinctions between the Dempster-Shafer theory and the Bayesian models of numerical degrees of belief. Firstly, the belief functions of Dempster-Shafer theory are set functions rather than point values. That is, belief may be assigned to sets of propositions without there being a necessary requirement to distribute belief with finer granularity among the individual propositions in the set. This allows for one form of an expression of ignorance; I may believe that a patient suffers from a form of arthritis, whilst being completely ignorant as to which of the set of possible forms of arthritis she is suffering from.

The second important distinction is the rejection of the law of additivity for belief in disjoint propositions or sets of propositions. In one form, the law of additivity states that the belief in a proposition and the belief in the negation of the same proposition should sum to one. This implies that the absence of belief in a proposition necessarily implies a corresponding belief in the negation of that proposition. This is rejected as too strong a constraint; I may only have weak evidence that supports the belief in the patient suffering from arthritis, but I may have no evidence at all to support the belief that the patient does not suffer from arthritis. Consequently, the Dempster-Shafer theory admits a second form of expression of ignorance; complete non-commitment to the truth of a proposition or its negation.

The third distinction is that the Dempster-Shafer theory has an operation (Dempster's rule of combination) for the pooling of evidence from a variety of sources. It would seem to be particularly appropriate when considering a hierarchy of hypotheses. Consider, for example, the diagnosis of a case of arthritis. Arthritis is a generic term for a variety of more specific conditions. We will use a simplified taxonomy (Figure 4.1) in which the name "arthritis" is given to a class of conditions represented by the set {osteoarthritis, rheumatoid arthritis, gout}. Suppose now that an argument is identified which supports the belief in a patient suffering from arthritis. A second argument may be identified which supports belief in osteoarthritis

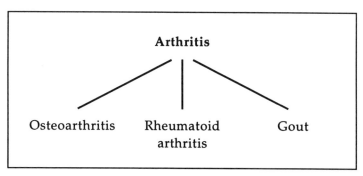

Fig 4.1   *Simplified subclass hierarchy for arthritis.*

(a specific form of arthritis). The degrees of belief arising from these two arguments may be pooled using the Dempster rule to give a combined measure of belief in osteoarthritis. As will be discussed in Section 4.3.3, this operation has two important features. Belief from the first argument may be transferred to the smaller hypothesis set supported by the second argument, and combined with that argument's belief. That is, as in this particular example, the pooling of evidence may result in a contraction in the hypothesis set from {osteoarthritis, rheumatoid arthritis, gout} to {osteoarthritis}, as well as a modification to the degree of belief assigned to the hypothesis set. This notion of pooling of evidence, or the aggregation of arguments, has foundations which predate the development of the Bayesian model of probability, and have no natural counterpart in that model.

Referring back to Section 2.2, the first two distinctions suggest that the Dempster-Shafer theory satisfies a weakened form of Cox's axioms (Cox, 1946). In particular, axioms B3, 'completeness', and B6, 'complementarity', are not satisfied; Dempster-Shafer belief may not necessarily be assigned to every proposition, and belief in the negation of a proposition is only weakly constrained by the belief in the proposition itself. The third distinction is of major importance in assessing the relative merits and suitability of the Dempster-Shafer theory for a particular problem. Use of the Bayesian model of Chapter 2 requires the framing of the problem in terms of a probability distribution function over all the propositions of interest. The exploitation of the dependencies between propositions eases the burden of the assessment of this distribution function by enabling its representation in terms of conditional probabilities between semantically related propositions. However, the use of the Bayesian model does effectively require a distinct and unique numerical belief value to be assigned to each of the possible events (assignment of truth values) in the network of propositions. This distribution function may then be revised as information becomes available by the process of conditioning on the observed nodes. The probabilities of the Dempster-Shafer model, however, are assigned as weights to the arguments for and against the propositions of interest. As arguments concerning the propositions of interest are identified, their respective associated 'epistemic probabilities' are then combined to give an overall probability based on the total evidence available.

We have introduced the terms 'chance', 'argument' and 'epistemic probability' in the preceding discussion. In a sense, these are key concepts in much of the motivation behind the development of the Dempster-Shafer theory of evidence. Consequently, we feel that a deeper understanding of this theory can be gained if its discussion is preceded by a historical introduction to the development of these concepts and the roots of the Dempster rule of combination. This will also emphasise some themes which will recur throughout the remainder of this book.

4.2   A short history of epistemic probability

4.2.1   Bernoulli and the appraisal of arguments.

Probability then is a likeness to be true. The very notation of the word signifying as much, and from its derivation may thus be defined: "Probabile est quod probari potest," i.e., a proposition for which there be arguments or proofs to make it pass or be received for true. (Locke, 1671).

As was discussed in Chapter 2, empirical studies of human reasoning to date tend to support the view that Bayesian probabilistic reasoning is prescriptive rather than descriptive as a model of human reasoning. Are there lessons that can be learned from a more descriptive model? In the absence of trustworthy numerical estimates of the frequency of occurrence of an outcome in a given situation, one will often find oneself weighing up the arguments pro and con to assess the likelihood of the outcome of interest. As has been discussed in Chapter 3, this intuitive approach is open to certain biases. Nevertheless, this view of probability as being based on the assessment of prior knowledge, *epistemic probability*, has a very different motivation to the frequentistic treatment of probability based on the analysis of games of chance. Epistemic probability need not be numerical; it is an attribute of opinion, and not of the mathematics of randomness or chance. The probability of a proposition does admit of degree, but this degree is a function of the number and weight of the arguments for and against that proposition. This epistemic view was the approach which Locke took in the draft essay quoted at the head of this section, and continued to maintain in his later *Essay Concerning Human Understanding* (Locke, 1690).

It is important to appreciate that the arguments referred to are not of the nature of logical demonstrative arguments which may be taken as proof of a thing if they are judged valid (on purely syntactic grounds). Rather, they are *contingent* arguments, and the way in which the probabilities derived from these arguments are combined to give a probability based on the total evidence may depend on the nature of this contingency. Jacob Bernoulli, in his *Ars Conjectandi* published in 1713, studied the combination of contingent arguments. *Ars Conjectandi* is perhaps best known for its statement of the famous, and important, law of large numbers for probabilities. However, as Shafer discusses in his very readable historical study of non-additive probabilities (Shafer, 1978), there is much in his work which was of significance to the development of epistemic probability. This aspect of Bernoulli's work is unfortunately now largely overlooked in favour of his contributions to the use of probabilities in the study of games of chance. Of particular significance is that certain of the kinds of argument he considered resulted in non-additive probabilities; that is, probabilities in which the degree to which an argument failed to support a proposition did not necessarily correspond to support for the negation of that proposition.

Consider, first, the following scenario. The Harley Street consultant Dr. Fortunatus is expecting his long standing patient Professor Letheian for an appointment at 11.00 am. The nurse rings through at 11.15 to say that the Professor still has not arrived. Dr. Fortunatus knows that the Professor is absent minded and it may be that he has forgotten about his appointment. It has also just been announced that the London rail termini have been closed due to a security alert, and if the Professor were coming in by train then he would certainly be delayed. On the other hand, the Professor may have been coming in by bus, in which case, the increase in road traffic caused by the security alert may have delayed the bus journey. Thus there are three arguments which concern Professor Letheian's lateness: absent-mindedness, closing down of the rail service, or increased road traffic. In the absence of further information, they are all contingent arguments, but the precise form of the contingency is different in each case. In Bernoulli's terms, the first argument exists necessarily, but proves contingently; it is known that Professor Letheian is absent-minded, but he may have been re-minded of the appointment and been delayed by some other event. The second argument exists contingently but proves necessarily; the Professor may or may not have intended to come by train but if he had he would certainly be delayed. The third argument both exists and proves contingently; the Professor may have been coming by bus, and if so the bus may have been delayed by increased traffic.

We thus have a classification of arguments according to the nature of their contingency. Put more succinctly, it may be contingent whether an argument arises, it may be contingent whether an argument proves, and either or both forms of contingency may apply to a specific argument. By perhaps simplifying the nature of what Bernoulli meant by argument it is possible to rephrase these distinctions in modern terms. To quote Shafer:

> If we think of an argument as consisting of premises and conclusion, then we surely come close to Bernoulli's meaning if we say that the argument exists contingently when the premises do not necessarily hold, and that

the argument proves contingently when the premises do not necessarily entail the conclusion. (Shafer, 1978)

Thus far, the modelling of arguments should not prove difficult for Bayesian probabilists. One can model uncertainty in the premises of an argument with prior probability, and uncertainty in the provability of a conclusion given the premises in terms of conditional probability. The departure from the modern conception of Bayesian probability comes in a further classification in terms of mixed and pure arguments.

Professor Letheian had made the appointment discussed above because he was beginning to suffer pain in one or two joints. Following a telephone conversation, Dr. Fortunatus believed that the Professor was either suffering from Rheumatoid Arthritis, Osteoarthritis or Gout. Referring back to the simplified taxonomy of arthritis (Figure 4.1), these are regarded as a mutually exclusive and exhaustive set of hypotheses. When the Professor finally arrived, Dr. Fortunatus decided to take an X-ray of the affected joints. Examination of the X-ray would potentially support one of the three possibilities whilst arguing against the remaining two. Evidence from the X-ray is thus of the nature of a mixed argument. Suppose that examination of the X-ray identifies the form of joint damage associated with Osteoarthritis. This is an argument for the hypothesis of Osteoarthritis. But it is also an argument against the negation of the hypothesis, i.e. Rheumatoid Arthritis or Gout.

Some years later, Professor Letheian was unfortunately taken into hospital with a suspected mild heart attack. He was complaining of breathlessness, and on arriving at the hospital also said he had a pain across his chest. A hasty telephone call to Dr. Fortunatus' surgery brought forth the information that the Professor was suffering from Osteoarthritis and that the chest pain might be due to a trapped nerve in one of the affected joints. In this context, the chest pain is a pure argument for his suffering from a heart attack. It supports the hypothesis of a heart attack, but if it turns out to be due to another cause, Osteoarthritis, this does not count against the hypothesis; he may still have suffered a heart attack. Pure arguments point only to the positive side of a hypothesis.

It is the concepts of pure arguments and arguments which exist contingently which lead to non-additive probabilities. A pure argument, as we have said, addresses only the positive side of a proposition. Equally, with an argument which exists contingently, in those cases where it does exist, it proves the thing. However, in those cases where it does not exist, it proves nothing at all. There is a close analogy here in the distinction between classical logic and intuitionistic logic. In classical logic a proposition P is, a priori, either true or it is false. That is, the law of the excluded middle (P ∨ ¬P) is always a theorem for any proposition P. Similarly in Bayesian probability, the event (P ∨ ¬P) is always certain to occur. That is, $p(P) + p(¬P) = p(P ∨ ¬P) = 1$. In intuitionistic logic (Brouwer, 1976) we cannot say anything at all about the truth value of P ∨ ¬P unless we can either construct a proof of P, or we can construct a proof of ¬P. However, we do have a notion of consistency so that P and ¬P may not be true simultaneously. Similarly, in epistemic probability, absence of support for the negation of an hypothesis, for example, need not be taken as conferring support on the hypothesis itself. We may have only a weak argument for a hypothesis and also only a weak argument for its negation, although we may not have confirmation for both. That is, in epistemic probability we have that, in general, $p(P) + p(¬P) ≤ 1$.

4.2.2   The combination of epistemic arguments.

Given that one argument concerning a hypothesis has a probability p_1, and a second argument concerning the same hypothesis has a probability p_2, what is the combined probability when this evidence is pooled? Bernoulli answered this question by giving a number of combination rules, the precise rule used in a given situation being dependent on the nature of the arguments concerned. One of these rules, that for combining arguments where some are pure and some are mixed, was later criticised by Lambert in his *Neues Organon* (Lambert, 1764). Lambert produced a generalisation of Bernoulli's rules which produced what he believed to be a more correct treatment in the case of combining pure and mixed arguments. We will base our discussion around Lambert's work.

Until the work initiated by Dempster and Shafer in the 1960's and 70's it would seem that Lambert was the last person to make a serious contribution to Bernoulli's ideas of non-additive epistemic probabilities (Shafer, 1978). His rule is a special case of the Dempster rule of combination, considering, as it does, only the combination of point value probabilities. Suppose we have an argument which has an associated probability p_1 for a given hypothesis, and q_1 against the hypothesis. In the general case, Lambert allows that $p_1+q_1 ≤ 1$. Suppose now a second argument is identified with associated probabilities p_2 and q_2 respectively for and against the same hypothesis (again p_2 and q_2 may sum to less than unity). Then, Lambert's rule states that the combined probability for the hypothesis is:

$$P_{12} = \frac{P_1 + P_2 - P_1 P_2 - P_1 q_2 - P_2 q_1}{1 - P_1 q_2 - P_2 q_1} \qquad (4.1)$$

whilst the probability against the hypothesis is:

$$q_{12} = \frac{q_1 + q_2 - q_1 q_2 - P_1 q_2 - P_2 q_1}{1 - P_1 q_2 - P_2 q_1} \qquad (4.2)$$

Note that Lambert's rule, as with Bernoulli's rule before him, is only valid for the combination of independent arguments.

In order to gain a picture of some of the properties of this rule, we will consider the extreme case of $q_1 = q_2 = 0$. This arises, as discussed above, in the case of pure arguments, or of arguments which exist contingently but prove necessarily. In this case, equations 4.1 and 4.2 respectively reduce to

$$P_{12} = P_1 + P_2 - P_1 P_2 = 1 - (1 - p_1)(1 - p_2). \qquad (4.3)$$

$$q_{12} = 0. \qquad (4.4)$$

One way of looking at this form of the rule is to consider that the number of cases in which the combination of arguments proves the hypothesis is equal to the sum of the number of cases in which each argument proves the hypothesis. But the number of cases in which both arguments simultaneously prove the hypothesis will be counted twice if we take a simple sum, so this number of cases should be subtracted once; $p_{12} = p_1 + p_2 - p_1 p_2$. Alternatively, one could view the rule as saying that the probability that both arguments will fail to prove the hypothesis is subtracted from unity to give the probability of the hypothesis; $p_{12} = 1 - (1 - p_1)(1 - p_2)$.

Extending the rule in its second form, consider the combination of n arguments each of which supports a hypothesis with a probability p. Then the combined probability is $1 - (1 - p)^n$. It is easy to see that as n increases this will tend to unity, no matter how small p may be. This only makes sense in the case of non-additive probabilities. One way of viewing this is to see it as n independent witnesses each providing a small fraction of the total evidence needed to be certain of a hypothesis.

This can be contrasted with a Bayesian rule for combining n probabilities, where, in this case, each probability p for the hypothesis has an associate probability (1-p) against the hypothesis. A Bayesian rule for combination is available (Shafer, 1978) provided some information is available, or assumptions made, about the prior belief in the hypothesis. If we assume a prior belief in the truth and the falsity of the hypothesis to each be equal to 1/2, than the Bayesian rule gives a probability:

$$\frac{p^n}{p^n + (1-p)^n}$$

for the hypothesis, and a probability:

$$\frac{(1-p)^n}{p^n + (1-p)^n}$$

against the hypothesis. In this case, if p is very low, then the probability for the hypothesis will tend to zero as n increases. Correspondingly, the probability against the hypothesis will tend to unity. Note the very different behaviours of the restricted form of Lambert's rule and the Bayesian rule. There is no a priori reason to suppose that either one is correct in any absolute sense. One must choose whichever behaviour seems most appropriate in a given context.

Much of this and the previous section has followed Shafer's very readable article "Non-Additive Probabilities in the Work of Bernoulli and Lambert" (Shafer, 1978). The reader is referred to this article for a more complete account of the early development of non-additive probabilities. We will now jump forward two hundred years to the development of the Dempster-Shafer theory of evidence. One interpretation of belief in the Dempster-Shafer theory is as non-additive epistemic probability. This is not the only view that may be taken, but this view does emphasise the similarities in the motivations behind the development of the theory of evidence and Bernoulli's analysis of arguments.

4.3   The Dempster-Shafer theory of evidence

4.3.1   Basic probability assignments.

We have already mentioned at the beginning of this chapter that the belief functions of the Dempster-Shafer theory are set functions. In a technical sense, the Dempster-Shafer (D-S) theory is built upon a Boolean Algebra of propositions. We will not dwell upon this, except to mention that this results in a correspondence between set operations (union, intersection, etc.) and logical operations (disjunction, conjunction, etc.). In the following, the word "proposition" will generally refer to a set of terms. For example, if we have A = {Rheumatoid Arthritis, Osteoarthritis, Gout}, we will refer to A as a proposition. The proposition A may be thought of as a disjunction of *elementary propositions*, those propositions corresponding to singleton sets.

Set union may then be interpreted as a disjunction of propositions, set intersection as conjunction, set inclusion as implication (A ⊆ B corresponding to A ⇒ B), and set complement ($\overline{A}$) as negation (¬A). The last of these may be looked upon as a form of *closed world assumption* (cwa); the universe of propositions is all there is to know, and if truth does not lie in a certain subset of the universe then it must lie in the complement of that subset. The use of cwa in the Dempster-Shafer theory is of some importance and will be referred to again in the discussion of the Dempster rule of combination.

Before discussing the notion of belief function, we must first introduce the notion of a *basic probability assignment* (bpa). The choice of name is somewhat contentious at present. We follow here the preference of (Shafer, 1976). There is a school of thought that "mass distribution" is a more appropriate term, e.g. (Kruse et al, 1991). However, here we wish to promote an interpretation of the word 'probability' which is not overly constrained by the modern preoccupation with probability as an attribute of chance rather than of argument.

A basic probability assignment is defined with respect to a *finite* universe of propositions Ω. It is usual for Ω to be referred to as the *frame of discernment*. The empty set, ∅, has an important logical interpretation in terms of the Boolean Algebra defined by Ω. ∅ may be thought of as the logical constant *false*. This is a proposition which cannot be believed, so would be expected to have zero probability assigned to it. At the other extreme, the proposition Ω, the *tautology*, is always true. This proposition represents the universe of propositions, and the truth must be somewhere in that universe. Hence the sum of the probabilities assigned to all subsets of Ω, all propositions which support Ω, must be unity. Correspondingly, a bpa is a function from the set of subsets, 2^Ω, of Ω to the unit interval [0,1] such that

   i. $m(\emptyset) = 0$.

   ii. $\sum_{A \subseteq \Omega} m(A) = 1$

Note first that the bpas are assigned to subsets of the frame of discernment, and not to point values as is usual in classical probability. The bpa acts as a measure of the support *exactly* assigned to specified sets of propositions whilst remaining ignorant about the precise division of support amongst strict subsets of those sets. Those sets which do have a non-zero bpa are referred to as *focal elements*. The union of the focal elements forms the *core* of the bpa.

A second point to note is that although the bpas must sum to unity, it is not necessarily the case that the probability of a proposition A and of its negation $\overline{A}$ sum to 1 (remember that a proposition corresponds to a subset of the frame of discernment, and its negation to the complement of that subset). For example, in the frame of discernment {Rheumatoid Arthritis, Osteoarthritis, Gout} suppose an argument for Osteoarthritis has an associated bpa of 0.6. That is, m({Osteoarthritis}) = 0.6. There may be no further evidence for or against Osteoarthritis or any other member of the frame of discernment. This state of ignorance can be modelled by assigning a bpa of 0.4 to the entire frame of discernment, i.e. m({Rheumatoid Arthritis, Osteoarthritis, Gout}) = 0.4. As we shall see later, this additional belief may be *transferred*, on receipt of further evidence, to any subset of the frame of discernment. In particular, the absence of belief in Osteoarthritis may turn out not to correspond to belief in its negation, but merely be due to a lack of awareness of further evidence which later transfers support to {Osteoarthritis}.

4.3.2   Measures of belief and plausibility.

The bpa is a measure of the support which is assigned precisely to a focal element. It is also a measure of support for any subset of the frame of discernment implied by that proposition. For example, if I have support for the belief that the patient is suffering from a form of Osteoarthritis, then I certainly have support, for example, for the patient suffering from one of {Rheumatoid Arthritis, Osteoarthritis, Gout}. There may also be some support for Gout, which also implies support for the frame of discernment, and indeed any other superset of {Gout}. The next step is to define a belief function which takes account of all the evidences currently available. In his monograph (Shafer, 1976) Shafer first defines such a belief function without reference to a basic probability assignment:

Definition 4.1

Bel: $2^{\Omega} \rightarrow [0,1]$ is a *belief function* over Ω if it satisfies:

i. $Bel(\emptyset) = 0$

ii. $Bel(\Omega) = 1$

iii. for every integer n>0 and collection of subsets $A_1, ..., A_n$ of Ω

$Bel(A_1 \cup ... \cup A_n) \geq$

$$\sum_i Bel(A_i) - \sum_{i<j} Bel(A_i \cap A_j) + ... + (-1)^{n+1} Bel(A_1 \cap ... \cap A_n)$$

The first condition is reiterating the discussion of bpas. The proposition ∅ (false) should not be believed. The second condition restates the fact that Ω, the tautology, should always be believed. The third condition looks a bit daunting at first sight. However, if one considers the case of just two propositions it is much easier to interpret:

$$\text{Bel}(A_1 \cup A_2) \geq \text{Bel}(A_1) + \text{Bel}(A_2) - \text{Bel}(A_1 \cap A_2)$$

That is, the belief in the disjunction of two propositions should be at least as great as the sum of the beliefs in the two individual propositions minus the belief in their conjunction. The need to subtract the belief in the conjunction once has a similar rationale to that of the combination rule of Equation (4.3). Condition (iii) is simply a generalisation of this case. The above definition should give some feel for the properties of a belief function, but it does not tell us how a belief function may be constructed from a basic probability assignment.

As has been mentioned, the bpa gives a measure of the support that is assigned *exactly* to the focal elements of a given frame of discernment. In order to obtain the total belief in a subset A, the extent to which all the available evidence supports A, one needs to sum together the bpas of all the subsets of A (propositions that imply A):

$$\text{Bel}(A) = \sum_{B \subseteq A} m(B) \tag{4.5}$$

This definition is equivalent to the previous definition (Shafer, 1976).

However, the remaining evidence need not necessarily refute A (support its negation $\overline{A}$). Some of it may be assigned to propositions which are not disjoint from A, and hence could be plausibly transferred directly to A in the light of further information. Hence, we may call the extent to which the available evidence fails to refute A, the *plausibility* of A:

$$\text{Pl}(A) = 1 - \text{Bel}(\overline{A})$$

$$= \sum_{B \cap A \neq \emptyset} m(B) \tag{4.6}$$

Since the constraint $B \cap A \neq \emptyset$ is weaker than $B \subseteq A$ for a given set A, it should be clear that:

$$\text{Bel}(A) \leq \text{Pl}(A)$$

Thus the credal status of a proposition A is represented by an interval [Bel(A), Pl(A)]. To reiterate, the lower bound represents the extent to which the proposition is definitely supported, whilst the upper bound represents the extent to which the evidence fails to refute it. Note that the interval [1, 1] represents complete certainty in a proposition, whilst the interval [0, 1] represents a state of ignorance about the truth or falsity of a proposition.

It is easy to show that as a result:

$$Bel(A) + Bel(\overline{A}) \leq 1$$

That is, the law of additivity is not, in general, obeyed for belief functions. This is quite a natural property if belief functions are interpreted as being derived from epistemic probabilities. There are, however, conditions under which the law of additivity is obeyed. If the focal elements of a bpa are all singleton sets (elementary propositions), then it will always be the case that $B \subseteq A$ if and only if $B \cap A \neq \emptyset$ for any focal element B, and any subset A of Ω. Thus, for all such A:

$$Bel(A) = \sum_{B \subseteq A} m(B) = \sum_{B \cap A \neq \emptyset} m(B) = Pl(A)$$

and $Bel(A) = Pl(A) = 1 - Bel(\overline{A})$

i.e. $Bel(A) + Bel(\overline{A}) = 1.$

Such a belief function is referred to as a *Bayesian belief function*, since it corresponds to a point valued and additive belief function. That is, classical probability is a special case of Dempster-Shafer belief.

Before moving on to a discussion of the Dempster rule for combining evidence from different sources, we provide one further definition. We have mentioned that belief may be transferred from a focal element to any of its subsets. This is an important feature which is emphasised in the Transferable Belief Model of Smets (Smets, 1990a). This interpretation of the theory of evidence will be discussed further later, but we will note here that a function can be defined which is a measure of the total belief which could be transferred to any element of a proposition A. This is known as the *commonality function* Q: $2^{\Omega} \rightarrow [0,1]$, where,

$$Q(A) = \sum_{A \subseteq B} m(B) \qquad (4.7)$$

We have defined a basic probability assignment, which is a measure of the belief which a given body of evidence strictly assigns to subsets, focal elements, of a specified frame of discernment. We have shown that this definition allows an expression of ignorance. Belief not specifically allocated to a proposition may be assigned to, for example, the entire frame of discernment. Hence it could plausibly be transferred in this case to *any* proposition on receipt of further information. Belief and plausibility functions may then be constructed from the bpa. This is a very static situation. We will now discuss how further evidence may be pooled as it becomes available.

4.3.3   The Dempster rule of combination.

Recall that Locke viewed probability as an attribute of arguments, and that probability need not necessarily be numerical. We have discussed some rules for combining probabilities from different arguments, and will now discuss the more general rule proposed by Dempster (1968) which is used for combining evidence in the D-S theory of evidence. In so far as Cox's axioms provide a justification for, and statement of, the properties of probabilistic inference, it would be useful to provide a similar axiomatisation for the combination, or "aggregation", of arguments. Such an axiomatisation may be derived from (Ginsberg, 1984):

A1.   It should be commutative and associative. The final result should be independent of the order in which the arguments are identified and in which the probabilities are aggregated.

A2.   Accumulating an argument expressing total ignorance should have no effect on the aggregation.

A3.   If using numerical point value probabilities, the operation should reduce to the usual combination for point probabilities.

A4.   No non-monotonic rule can outweigh a logical certainty.

A5.   The combination of 'certainly believed' and 'certainly disbelieved' is undefined.

A6.   Combination should be invertible. We may wish to be able to 'retract' a probability should an argument become invalidated.

These axioms provide an abstract specification for a combination rule. However, it should be remembered that in no sense are they pre-ordained. What are perceived as desirable properties in one context may turn out to be quite undesirable in another. In particular, we will have more to say about the second axiom concerning the aggregation of arguments expressing ignorance.

The Dempster rule of combination provides a method for combining basic probability assignments which satisfies this specification. Given two bpas m_1 and m_2 which have been obtained from *independent* arguments, we wish to be able to form their *orthogonal sum* $m_1 \oplus m_2$ in such a way that the sum is still a bpa. Consider two propositions A and B with associated probabilities $m_1(A)$ and $m_2(B)$ from the respective bpas. Then the probability of their conjunction $C = A \cap B$ obtained from this assignment will be $m_1(A).m_2(B)$. (Remember the set interpretation of the propositional logic in which conjunction corresponds to set intersection). There may be several pairs of propositions A, B whose conjunction is equal to a given proposition C. The total probability assigned to the proposition C will be the sum of all such contributions: the sum over all probabilities $m_1(A).m_2(B)$ from combined arguments $A \cap B$ which support C. However, it may be that probability is assigned to focal elements in one assignment which are disjoint to focal elements in the other. The combination of such probabilities will assign support to the empty set $\emptyset$. If this occurs, it will violate one of the conditions for a bpa. One way of resolving this potential difficulty is to redistribute the probability assigned to the empty set amongst the non-empty focal elements of the combined bpa by including a normalisation constant in the rule. For a more rigorous justification of the combination rule, see (Shafer, 1976).

We now present Dempster's rule. If m_1 and m_2 are two bpa's obtained from independent evidences, then the combined bpa is given by:

$$(m_1 \oplus m_2)(C) = \frac{\sum\limits_{A \cap B = C} m_1(A) m_2(B)}{1 - \sum\limits_{A \cap B = \emptyset} m_1(A) m_2(B)} \qquad (4.8)$$

The numerator of Equation (4.8) represents the sum over all conjunctions of arguments which support C. The denominator is the normalisation coefficient obtained from the mass assigned to contradictory arguments. Note that the combination will not succeed for the case where the cores of the two bpas are disjoint. That is, where there is total conflict between the two evidences. For in this case, we will have that,

$$\sum\limits_{A \cap B = \emptyset} m_1(A) m_2(B) = 1 \qquad (4.9)$$

and the normalisation coefficient will become zero, leaving the combination of contradictory evidences undefined. We will have more to say about the properties of Dempster's rule, including its behaviour with contradictory or near contradictory evidence, after the following simple demonstration of the rule in use.

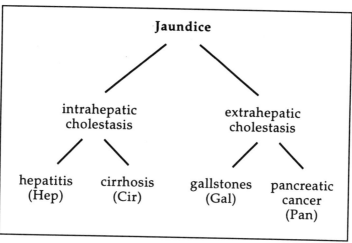

Fig 4.2   *Simplified subclass hierarchy for jaundice.*

4.3.4   A simple case of jaundice.

Gordon and Shortliffe were among the first to consider the use of the Dempster-Shafer formalism for medical diagnosis (Gordon and Shortliffe, 1984). We will use a variant of their simple example of the diagnosis of a case of cholestatic jaundice to illustrate the use of the Dempster rule. Jaundice is a yellowing of the skin which is caused by a pigment produced by the liver being transferred into the blood stream. The excess production of this pigment (bilirubin) may be due to a disease within the liver (intrahepatic cholestasis), or due to a blocking of the bile ducts outside the liver (extrahepatic cholestasis). Types of intrahepatic cholestasis include hepatitis (Hep) and cirrhosis (Cir). Types of extrahepatic cholestasis include gallstones (Gal) and pancreatic cancer (Pan). For the sake of simplicity, we will assume that only these two types of each form of cholestasis are being considered in the hypothesis set. That is, the problem has already been framed with Ω = {Hep, Cir, Gal, Pan} as the set of mutually exclusive and exhaustive hypotheses (the frame of discernment).

Suppose that upon examining the patient, one physician says that she has identified strong evidence that the patient is suffering from intrahepatic cholestasis, and that this evidence makes it very unlikely that the patient is suffering from extrahepatic cholestasis:

$$m_1(\{Hep, Cir\}) = 0.8$$
$$m_1(\{Gal, Pan\}) = 0.2$$

Note that this corresponds to a 'mixed' argument, and that $Bel_1(\{Hep, Cir\}) = Pl_1(\{Hep, Cir\}) = 0.8$ and $Bel_1(\{Gal, Pan\}) = Pl_1(\{Gal, Pan\}) = 0.2$.

A second physician now says that he has quite independent grounds to support the patient not suffering from hepatitis, although he could not rule it out categorically and would not like to commit himself as to whether this evidence affects his belief in any of the other hypotheses:

$$m_2(\{Cir, Gal, Pan\}) = 0.9$$
$$m_2(\Omega) = 0.1$$

Note that this corresponds to a 'pure' argument with evidence supporting the negation of $\{Hep\}$, but no evidence refuting its negation. That is, $Bel_2(\{Cir, Gal, Pan\}) = 0.9$, but $Pl_2(\{Cir, Gal, Pan\}) = 1$.

We now wish to combine the evidence obtained from these two arguments. Applying Dempster's rule (equation 4.8) we obtain:

$$m_1 \oplus m_2 (\{Cir\}) = 0.8 \times 0.9 = 0.72$$
$$m_1 \oplus m_2(\{Hep, Cir\}) = 0.8 \times 0.1 = 0.08$$
$$m_1 \oplus m_2 (\{Gal, Pan\}) = 0.2 \times 0.9 + 0.1 \times 0.2 = 0.2$$

(there is no conflict between the two arguments, so the normalisation coefficient is 1).

$m_1 \oplus m_2$	$m_2(\{Cir, Gal, Pan\})$ $= 0.9$	$m_2(\Omega) = 0.1$
$m_1(\{Hep, Cir\}) = 0.8$	$m_1 \oplus m_2 (\{Cir\})$ $= 0.72$	$m_1 \oplus m_2(\{Hep, Cir\})$ $= 0.08$
$m_1(\{Gal, Pan\}) = 0.2$	0.18	0.02
	$m_1 \oplus m_2 (\{Gal, Pan\}) = 0.2$	

Table 4.1   *Combination of an argument with strong support for "intrahepatic cholestasis" and an argument with strong evidence against "hepatitis".*

The revised belief and plausibility functions can now be evaluated, and we find:

$$Bel_{12}(\{Cir\}) = 0.72$$
$$Pl_{12}(\{Cir\}) = 0.72 + 0.08 = 0.8$$
$$Bel_{12}(\{Hep, Cir\}) = 0.72 + 0.08 = 0.8$$
$$Pl_{12}(\{Hep, Cir\}) = 0.8$$

$$\text{Bel}_{12}(\{\text{Gal, Pan}\}) = 0.2$$
$$\text{Pl}_{12}(\{\text{Gal, Pan}\}) = 0.2$$

The second physician's evidence results in a transfer of belief to the specific hypothesis of cirrhosis. Note that if the second physician had been certain that the cause of jaundice in this case could not be hepatitis, that is $m_2(\{\text{Cir, Gal, Pan}\}) = 1$, the combination would yield a bpa of:

$$m_1 \oplus m_2 \, (\{\text{Cir}\}) = 0.8$$
$$m_1 \oplus m_2 \, (\{\text{Gal, Pan}\}) = 0.2$$

- *all* the belief in intrahepatic cholestasis would be transferred to the one hypothesis of cirrhosis.

4.3.5   Conflicting evidence and Dempster's rule.

There was no conflict between the views of the two physicians, so we did not need to worry about normalisation of the combined bpa. Normalisation in the Dempster-Shafer theory has been a contentious issue, with some arguing that it can lead to counter-intuitive results (Zadeh, 1984; 1986b). We will illustrate this with a fairly extreme case of conflicting evidence. Suppose the same patient as above is being examined by two highly competent, but rather dogmatic physicians. The first says that the patient is definitely *not* suffering from extrahepatic cholestasis, and although there may be some possibility he is suffering from cirrhosis it is almost certainly hepatitis that is the problem:

$$m_1(\{\text{Hep}\}) = 0.9$$
$$m_1(\{\text{Cir}\}) = 0.1$$
$$m_1(\{\text{Gal, Pan}\}) = 0$$

The second physician, however, says that the patient almost certainly *is* suffering from extrahepatic cholestasis, although he does not know at present what type and he would also agree that there was some possibility of the patient suffering from cirrhosis:

$$m_1(\{\text{Hep}\}) = 0$$
$$m_1(\{\text{Cir}\}) = 0.1$$
$$m_1(\{\text{Gal, Pan}\}) = 0.9$$

There is a high degree of conflict between these two evidences, but the cores of the two bpas are not disjoint (they intersect at cirrhosis) and so the combination is defined. But we will need to renormalise:

$$m_1 \oplus m_2 (\{Hep\}) = 0$$
$$m_1 \oplus m_2 (\{Cir\}) = 0.01/K = 1$$
$$m_1 \oplus m_2 (\{Gal, Pan\}) = 0$$

Here $K = 1 - \displaystyle\sum_{A \cap B = \emptyset} m_1(A) m_2(B) = 0.01$.

	m_1	m_2	$m_1 \oplus m_2$
{Hep}	0.9	0	0
{Cir}	0.1	0.1	1.0
{Gal, Pan}	0	0.9	0

Table 4.2 *Combination of two partially conflicting arguments*

The physicians each assign a low degree of belief to the hypothesis of cirrhosis. However, because all the other hypotheses are eliminated by the two arguments, the result after normalisation is to assign certainty to cirrhosis. As we have said, this is believed by some to be counter-intuitive.

The use of normalisation corresponds to applying the closed world assumption: the truth must lie somewhere in the Boolean algebra of propositions derived from the frame of discernment. Unless we have some grounds to disbelieve the evidence (*discount* one or other of the arguments), we must accept that each physician in the above example really has eliminated some of the possible hypotheses. The truth must then lie in those that remain. In this case, there is only one remaining hypothesis and that is cirrhosis. So it must be true. This is doing no more than following the time honoured advice of Sherlock Holmes: "when you have eliminated the impossible, whatever remains, no matter how improbable, must be the truth". From this perspective, the normalisation is justifiable. Harder to justify is the fact that if the physicians assign very small values instead of zero to the appropriate propositions, the combination rule may produce qualitatively different results. The deeper problem is that Dempster's rule is discontinuous in the neighbourhood of total conflict (Clarke, 1988).

An alternative approach is not to renormalise. This may be interpreted as using the *open world assumption* (Smets, 1990a). Belief is assigned to the empty set by the combination of conflicting evidence. That is, we are unable to assign this belief to any of the propositions in the frame of discernment. In this interpretation that belief should, in fact, be assigned to the empty set unioned with all the other hypotheses that have so far *not* been considered in the framing of the problem. Unfortunately, we do not know what those propositions are.

The basic difficulty is that a high degree of conflict, as always, implies that the problem has been incorrectly framed: perhaps one of our sources of evidence is unreliable; perhaps an incorrect assumption has been made; perhaps we are missing information or have not considered all the possibilities. There are many potential sources of contradiction, and we do not have a general method for resolving it. Perhaps we are moving into the domain of meta-level reasoning at this stage. The Dempster rule cannot handle absolutely contradictory evidence, and there is some discomfort at its behaviour near to contradiction. Shafer suggests using *-log(K)* (with K as above) as a measure of the weight of conflict in the combined evidence. This can be used as an indication of when the results need to be treated with some caution. But we still need to develop rational methods for reasoning about the problem to identify the most appropriate way to resolve the conflict. We will discuss issues of meta-level reasoning further in the final chapter of this book.

4.3.6   Dempster's rule compared with Bernoulli and Lambert's rules.

Dempster's rule is a generalisation of Lambert's combination rule for epistemic probabilities which we presented in Section 4.2.2. We will illustrate this with two examples. As the first case, consider the combination of two pure arguments concerning a single proposition A (with Ω being the frame of discernment as usual). We model a pure argument with a bpa which assigns a probability to the proposition. The difference from unity of this probability is then assigned to the frame of discernment. This means that as new evidence is identified this remainder may be assigned at some later stage to the proposition or to its negation. We do not know which at this stage.

For the first argument:

$$m_1(A) = p_1$$
$$m_1(\Omega) = 1 - p_1$$

And for the second argument:

$$m_2(A) = p_2$$
$$m_2(\Omega) = 1 - p_2$$

Then, since the normalisation coefficient K is equal to 1,

$$m_1 \oplus m_2 (A) \quad = \sum_{A_i \cap B_i = A} m_1 (A_i) \, m_2 (B_i)$$

$$= p_1 p_2 + p_1 (1 - p_2) + p_2 (1 - p_1)$$

$$= 1 - (1 - p_1)(1 - p_2)$$

which is the rule which Bernoulli gave, and the appropriate specialisation of Lambert's rule, for pure arguments.

In the more general case, a simple argument will assign some probability to a proposition, and some probability to its negation. However, unlike Bayesian probability, some belief may remain unassigned. So we will have the following bpa's:

$$m_1(A) = p_1$$
$$m_1(\overline{A}) = q_1$$
$$m_1(\Omega) = 1 - (p_1 + q_1)$$

And for the second argument:

$$m_2(A) = p_2$$
$$m_2(\overline{A}) = q_2$$
$$m_2(\Omega) = 1 - (p_2 + q_2)$$

In this case, the normalisation coefficient is no longer zero and we obtain:

$$m_1 \oplus m_2 (A) \quad = \frac{p_1 (1 - (p_2 + q_2)) + p_2 (1 - (p_1 + q_1)) + p_1 p_2}{1 - (p_1 q_2 + p_2 q_1)}$$

$$= \frac{p_1 + p_2 - p_1 p_2 - p_1 q_2 - p_2 q_1}{1 - p_1 q_2 - p_2 q_1}$$

and

$$m_1 \oplus m_2 (\overline{A}) \quad = \frac{q_1 (1 - (p_2 + q_2)) + q_2 (1 - (p_1 + q_1)) + q_1 q_2}{1 - (p_1 q_2 + p_2 q_1)}$$

$$= \frac{q_1 + q_2 - q_1 q_2 - p_1 q_2 - p_2 q_1}{1 - p_1 q_2 - p_2 q_1}$$

These are Lambert's general rules for combining arguments.

4.3.7   Dempster's rule and the voting problem.

In Section 4.3.3 we presented a set of axioms which would seem to be reasonable properties for a combination rule which is used to aggregate epistemic probabilities derived from arguments. There seems to be little to dispute in any of them, bar one. That is the second one: accumulating an argument expressing total ignorance should have no effect on the aggregation.

It is quite straightforward to show that Dempster's rule does indeed satisfy this axiom. What is more difficult is satisfying oneself that this is a reasonable property in all circumstances. We hypothesised a situation in the introductory chapter (Section 1.2.1) in which 100 clinicians were asked which of two drugs they would prescribe a given patient. In the case where 1 clinician said "drug A", but 99 said "don't know", we postulated that there should be some expression of this profound degree of ignorance in the pooled evidences. However, if these evidences are combined using Dempster's rule, the answer will merely reflect the commitment of the one clinician who favoured drug A.

A directly analogous problem has been addressed in social choice theory; one may view the above scenario as experts "voting" for a preferred option. However, the problem of specifying the conditions which an ideal voting procedure should satisfy is not an easy one. There is usually some form of dominance, as we have with the use of Dempster's rule. Nevertheless, Dubois and Koning (1991) have produced a model of the pooling of evidence which satisfies an axiom system from social choice theory, proposed by Arrow (1963).

4.4   How to act on a belief

Having constructed a framework for combining evidence to obtain an overall measure of belief in a hypothesis, the next question to ask is, how should one act upon this belief? Classical decision theory is very much based around Bayesian probability as a measure of belief. Indeed rational betting behaviour as a model for decision making provides much of the justification for Bayesian probability, as we have seen. In classical decision theory, one approach is to assess the (point value) probability for the possible outcomes, multiply each by a measure of the utility of the respective outcome, and 'simply' choose that outcome which maximises the resulting expected utility (Lindley, 1985). This is certainly not the only approach. For example, one may adopt a "risk-averse" (as opposed to a "risk-selective") strategy and take that decision which minimises the possible loss. However, given that Belief and Plausibility functions provide an interval value for the credibility of a given hypothesis and intervals do not admit of a simple ordering, a modified scheme is needed for making decisions in Dempster-Shafer theory (Clarke, 1988).

The most straightforward approach is to accept the doctrine of Lindley and others, and offer a transformation which maps Dempster-Shafer belief into point value probabilities for all propositions. This transformation is then applied whenever one needs to act upon the current state of belief. Early proposals were to do this by using a generalisation of the principle of insufficient reason (Dubois and Prade, 1982; Williams, 1982). The insufficient reason principle states that in the absence of further information, belief in a set of mutually exclusive propositions should be evenly distributed amongst those propositions. Thus, if I believe that a tossed coin will certainly either land heads up or land tails up, I should assign a probability of 1/2 to each of the two possible outcomes. The generalised insufficient reason principle states that the probabilities in a bpa should be evenly distributed amongst the elementary propositions in the focal elements, if a decision needs to be made (Smets, 1990b):

$$p(A) = \sum_{B \subseteq \Omega} m(B) \frac{|A \cap B|}{|B|} \qquad (4.10)$$

For each focal element B in the bpa, m(B) is distributed equally among the elementary propositions in B. The probability p(A) assigned to any proposition A is then the sum of those parts of the bpa that were assigned to A. (Smets, 1990b) provides a full axiomatic justification of this transformation.

From the perspective of decision making, this provides a two level model of belief. There is a *credal level* at which beliefs are maintained and revised (using the D-S model, or perhaps any other model which is thought appropriate in a given situation). Then when an action needs to be performed, or a decision made, beliefs are transformed to the *pignistic level* (from the Latin word *Pignus* for bet) using the above transformation. At first sight the need to transform beliefs into point value probabilities would seem to weaken the justification for an alternative model at the credal level (i.e D-S). However, (Smets and Kennes, 1989) provides a number of examples whereby this two level model provides qualitatively different answers to those obtained through framing the problems entirely within the Bayesian probability model.

Converting beliefs and plausibilities into a point value probability may be disregarding some of the potential of the Dempster-Shafer formalism. For example, if a risk averse-strategy was appropriate for some decision

making task, then one would look at the plausibilities of the least favourable outcomes. Alternatively, in a risk-selective strategy one may compare
the beliefs of the favourable outcomes. Such decisions about which strategy to take would have to be taken at the meta-level, and again we are suggesting that meta-level reasoning should be regarded as an important
aspect of reasoning under uncertainty.

4.5   Evidential reasoning applied to robot navigation

4.5.1   The problem of robot navigation.

The Dempster-Shafer style of evidential reasoning has been used in a
number of applications. We have chosen to illustrate its use in an experimental piece of AI research (Kak et al, 1990). This is partly for the sake of
adding a little variety to the rather heavy slant towards medical examples,
but it is also because this example does very clearly illustrate the flexibility
that may be achieved using the D-S formalism. In this example, the problem is structured 'on the fly' as it were. There are various mechanisms for
proposing propositions as members of the frame of discernment. Then potential sources of evidence are identified and the respective bpas calculated
using simple geometrical reasoning. As evidence accumulates, more complex, and hierarchical, relationships between data elements can be exploited. In turn, this information is used to refine the framing of the problem
further, enabling still more sources of evidence to be brought to bear.

The basic problem is this. Is it possible to build a system to enable a robot to navigate automatically through a complex environment? The robot
has an on-board television camera together with an image processor. The
processor can take an input image from the camera and convert the pixel
data into a collection of piecewise linear segments representing edges that
have been detected. Furthermore, the robot has a 3-D model of the space it
is to navigate through stored in its on-board computer. Using this model
and approximate knowledge of its position and orientation in this space, it
may construct a map of the image it expects the camera to see. The idea is
to use the relationships between the elements in the expected map to constrain the possible interpretations of the line segments derived by the preprocessor from the observed image. Using simple geometry, the robot may
then obtain a more precise estimate of its position from the reconstructed
observed image.

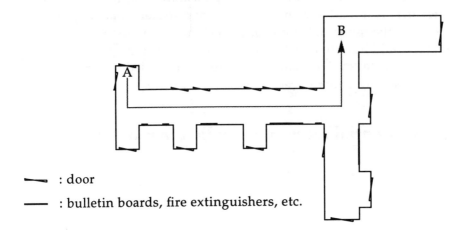

━━▄ : door

━━━ : bulletin boards, fire extinguishers, etc.

Fig 4.3   *Plan of hallways used in the robot navigation experiments (after Kak et al, 1990).*

A group in the Robot Vision Laboratory at Purdue University have been developing a robot navigation system along these lines (Kak et al, 1990). Figure 4.3 shows a plan of the laboratory hallways which they used in the experiments reported in the above paper. Although it was quite a simple environment, they believed that it was not possible for their robot to navigate inertially, 'in the blind', from point A of the figure, to point B. This was because there were many unquantifiable factors which affected the motion of the robot. For example, the uneven weight distribution of the robot and the slipperiness of the floor would cause uncertainties in the direction of travel and the distance travelled. To give an indication of the sort of uncertainties involved, a commanded turn of 45° would introduce an uncertainty of orientation of about 2°, and a commanded straight line motion would result in an associated uncertainty of about 10% in distance travelled, and up to 15° error in the direction travelled. So, as the robot moved along, it needed to update periodically its expected position. The Purdue group chose to use the technique outlined above to do this.

4.5.2   The image interpretation system.

The image interpretation was carried out in a system called PSEIKI (for Production System Environment for Integrating Knowledge with Images). Phrased succinctly, the expected image is presented to PSEIKI as a geometrical hierarchy of abstractions. The program will then attempt to construct

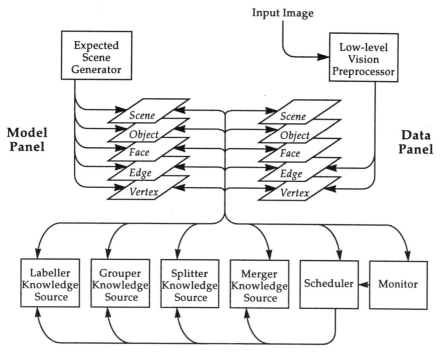

Fig 4.4   *Architecture of PSEIKI (After Kak et al, 1990).*

abstraction hierarchies of the perceived image taking cues from the abstraction hierarchy of the expected image. The Dempster-Shafer model for uncertain reasoning is used to associate belief measures to each possible label for the elements in the construction hierarchy, enabling the most likely interpretation of the perceived image in terms of the expected image to be identified. This all sounds very abstruse, but should become much clearer with some examples.

Figure 4.4 outlines the architecture of PSEIKI. The system is implemented as a 2 panel 5 level blackboard. Using the current estimate for the position for the robot, the expected scene generator will supply an *abstraction hierarchy* for the expected scene to the model panel. So, what is meant by an abstraction hierarchy?

This is really quite simple. Figure 4.5 shows the hierarchy for a simple object. A scene is a set of objects. As in Figure 4.4, an object is in turn a set of faces, each of which is a set of edges, each of which is a set of vertices. A symbolic representation of the perceived image is obtained from the image

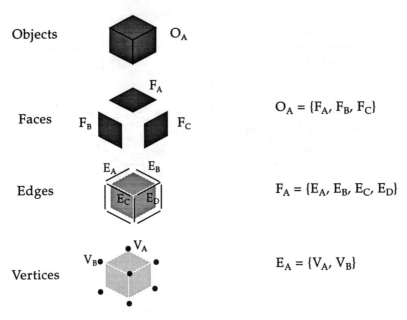

Objects O_A

Faces $O_A = \{F_A, F_B, F_C\}$

Edges $F_A = \{E_A, E_B, E_C, E_D\}$

Vertices $E_A = \{V_A, V_B\}$

Fig 4.5   *Simple abstraction hierarchy for a cube shaped object. Elements of one level are defined in terms of elements of the next lower level.*

preprocessor. This is represented as piecewise linear segments, and is deposited in the lowest two levels of the data panel.

At this stage, edges and vertices in the perceived image may be identified. However, there may be several linear segments which could be grouped to form a single edge in the model panel. For example, in the example of images captured in the model and data panels shown in Figure 4.6, data segments E_8 and E_{10} could possibly be grouped and interpreted as model edge E_E. There may also be missing vertices in the data panel, and/ or possibly spurious lines and vertices resulting from artefacts of the camera image. For example, the vertex of the edges E_{17} and E_7 may be merely due to a misalignment between two segments corresponding to the same model edge (E_D).

It is quite easy for us to see that the object represented in the data panel of Figure 4.6 is "most likely" the same object as that in the image panel. It is also quite easy to postulate which line segments should be grouped to form boundaries of which faces. PSEIKI performs the same function by:

1. Labelling edges in the data panel with the name of the edges in the model panel which they are most likely to correspond to.

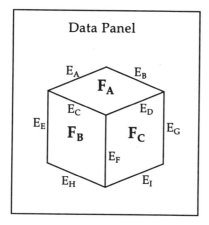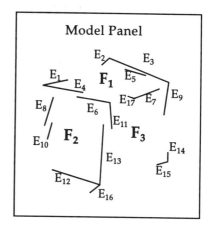

Fig 4.6   *A simple example of image interpretation. The frame on the left depicts the information contained in the data panel; that on the right, the information obtained from the image preprocessor (After Andress and Kak, 1988).*

2. Grouping edges in the data panel on the basis of the corresponding groupings of edge labels according to faces in the model panel.

3. Revising its initial labelling on the basis of evidence obtained from the geometrical relationships which should be satisfied on the basis of these groupings.

4. Progressing in this way up the abstraction hierarchy (grouping faces to form objects, and so on) until all the elements in the data panel are associated with labels in the model panel.

4.5.3   Accumulation of evidence.

The association of edges in the data panel with edges in the model panel is initialised purely on the basis of proximity information. The Labeller Knowledge Source (KS) of Figure 4.4 will pool together all the model edges whose centres of mass are within a specified radius, r_{max}, of the data edge under consideration. This constructs the frame of discernment $\Theta_{initial}$ for that data edge. Notice, though, that this construction procedure requires that the data image be reasonably close to the model image in the first place. Having constructed the frame of discernment, sources of evidence now need to be identified which will provide arguments in favour of the data edge being associated with one or other of the labels in $\Theta_{initial}$. This is achieved using similarity and dissimilarity metrics, as illustrated in the following example.

Consider the data edge E_1 of Figure 4.6, and suppose that using the above technique PSEIKI has constructed $\Theta_{initial} = \{E_A, E_C, E_E\}$. Kak et al (1990) use the analogy that each model edge in $\Theta_{initial}$ "is an expert and tells us, by using similarity and dissimilarity metrics, how much belief it places in its similarity to the data edge E_1". For example, the expert corresponding to edge E_A provides the following evidence as basic probability assignment A:

$$m_A(\{E_A\}) = \text{similarity\_metric}(E_1, E_A) \qquad (4.11)$$
$$m_A(\{\neg E_A\}) = \text{dissimilarity\_metric}(E_1, E_A) \qquad (4.12)$$
$$m_A(\Theta_{initial}) = 1 - m_A(\{E_A\}) - m_A(\{\neg E_A\}) \qquad (4.13)$$

(Recall that $\{\neg E_A\}$ corresponds to the set complement of $\{E_A\}$, which equals $\{E_C, E_E\}$ in this case). Similarly, experts C and E, corresponding to model edges E_C and E_E respectively, give the following bpas:

$$m_C(\{E_C\}) = \text{similarity\_metric}(E_1, E_C) \qquad (4.14)$$
$$m_C(\{\neg E_C\}) = \text{dissimilarity\_metric}(E_1, E_C) \qquad (4.15)$$
$$m_C(\Theta_{initial}) = 1 - m_C(\{E_C\}) - m_C(\{\neg E_C\}) \qquad (4.16)$$

and

$$m_E(\{E_E\}) = \text{similarity\_metric}(E_1, E_E) \qquad (4.17)$$
$$m_E(\{\neg E_E\}) = \text{dissimilarity\_metric}(E_1, E_E) \qquad (4.18)$$
$$m_E(\Theta_{initial}) = 1 - m_E(\{E_E\}) - m_E(\{\neg E_E\}) \qquad (4.19)$$

These three evidences are then combined using Dempster's rule to give an aggregated measure of belief in each of the three possible hypotheses. The model edge with the highest belief (say E_A in this case) is then assigned as a label to data edge E_1.

In each case, the similarity and dissimilarity metrics are based on a simple analysis of the geometrical relationships between the specified line segments. Each metric returns a value in the [0,1] interval. Should the similarity and dissimilarity metrics for a specific bpa sum to greater than 1, then they are normalised so that the resulting values do satisfy the requirements for a bpa. Of course, as can be seen from equations (4.11) - (4.19), if they sum to less than unity, then the unassigned mass is given to the frame of discernment.

Once the Labeller KS has assigned labels to each data edge, it is the turn of the Grouper KS to group the data edges on the basis of the hierarchical structure of the corresponding model edges. For example, according to the abstraction hierarchy of Figure 4.5, model edges $\{E_A, E_B, E_C, E_D\}$ bound face F_A. Those data edges which are attached to these labels are grouped together. Suppose the grouper has identified $\{E_1, E_2, E_5, E_7, E_6, E_4\}$ as a possible grouping. This forms an element, F_1, of the face level in the abstraction hierarchy, and the current label assigned to F_1 would be F_A (as this was the basis of the grouping, although this may be subject to revision on the basis of further evidential reasoning).

The belief values for all the child nodes of F_1 $\{E_1, E_2, E_5,$ etc.) may now be updated on the basis of a comparison between their geometrical relationships and the corresponding relationships between the edges in the model panel. Consider now the contribution that E_5 may make to the belief that edge E_1 has label E_A. If E_5 has current label E_X (perhaps $X = B$), then the update bpa may be generated on the basis of a comparison of the geometrical relationship between E_A and E_X in the model with the relationship between E_1 and E_5 in the data panel. If $E_5{:}E_1$ is the rigid body translation between E_5 and E_1, and $E_X{:}E_A$ is the rigid body translation between E_X and E_A, then a relational similarity metric may be defined on the basis of a comparison of these two transformations; relational_similarity_metric($E_5{:}E_1$, $E_X{:}E_A$). See (Andress and Kak, 1989) for full details of this metric. Then E_5 may be thought of as an "expert" offering a bpa concerning E_1 having label E_A on the basis of these geometrical relationships:

$$m_{Update:5}(\{E_A\}) = m_5(\{E_X\}).relational\_similarity\_metric(E_5{:}E_1, E_X{:}E_A)$$

$$m_{Update:5}(\{\neg E_A\}) = m_5(\{E_X\}).relational\_dissimilarity\_metric(E_5{:}E_1, E_X{:}E_A)$$

$$m_{Update:5}(\Theta) = 1-m_{Update:5}(\{E_A\})-m_{Update:5}(\{\neg E_A\})$$

Similarly, every element in the grouping will provide an update bpa $m_{Update:i}$ ($i \in \{2,5,7,6,4\}$). These will be combined with the current belief for the label of E_A, again using Dempster's rule.

It may happen that as a result of this update operation the largest mass may be assigned to a singleton proposition which is not the current label for E_1. This may, in turn, initiate a comprehensive restructuring of the data interpretation (Kak et al, 1990).

4.5.4   The application of image interpretation to navigation.

This discussion has focused on the identification of the sources of evidence concerning the possible labels for edges. The same technique is used as the

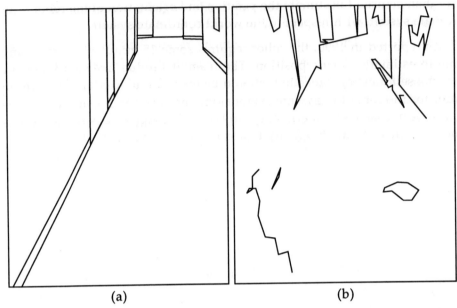

(a)   (b)

Fig 4.7   *(a) shows the expectation map after the robot has travelled some distance
along the corridor. There was significant misregistration between the expectation map and the actual camera image. (b) shows the data edges from the
scene node with the highest probability mass assigned to it (redrawn from
Kak et al, 1990).*

interpretation progresses up the hierarchy to identify possible faces and
objects. Hopefully this brief description will suffice to give a flavour for
the technique used by PSEIKI to interpret a camera image in terms of an expected model. So how is this interpretation used to assist robot self-loca-
tion?

At the end of the processing cycle, PSEIKI will have a selection of possible scenes (where a scene is an assignment of labels), each with a different degree of belief associated with it. The navigation module controlling
the robot then selects the scene with the highest probability mass assigned
to it. Figure 4.7a, shows the expectation map at one stage of the navigation
exercise. Figure 4.7b shows the corresponding scene with the highest probability mass obtained from an analysis of the actual camera image. The
navigation module has worked its way through the abstraction hierarchy
to obtain those edges with the highest probability mass (usually only those
exceeding a high threshold, say 0.9, are retained). The misalignment between these edges and the corresponding edges in the expectation map

may then be used to estimate the position and orientation of the robot's co-ordinate system with respect to the world coordinate system.

As reported in 1990, the robot requires some 15 minutes of processing time to estimate its true position. The team at Purdue University believe that the self location procedure should be carried out after 6m of travel in order for the robot to navigate safely along the corridor. So, at present this is still very much an experiment in robot self navigation. Nevertheless, it does demonstrate the flexibility that can be achieved using the Dempster-Shafer approach and we feel it makes for an exciting demonstration of its potential.

4.6   Discussion

In this chapter, we have introduced the Dempster-Shafer theory of evidence in the context of epistemic probability. Although this is in line with Shafer's own presentation of the theory (Shafer, 1976; 1978), it is, in a sense, a post hoc justification of the model. Dempster's original presentation of the rule, which bears his name, was in the context of a generalisation of statistical inference to probability distributions which induced upper and lower bounds on the probability of an event (Dempster, 1967; 1968). Nevertheless, it is Shafer's development of the theory of evidence from Dempster's foundational work which is of relevance to AI.

Our presentation of the Dempster-Shafer theory has, however, emphasised those aspects of the theory which are concerned with the pooling of arguments, perhaps at the expense of certain other of its attributes. As a consequence, we will be returning to D-S in the next chapter to provide a slightly different interpretation of it as a model for uncertain reasoning with imprecise data.

The Dempster-Shafer theory differs from Bayesian probability in a number of aspects. Perhaps the most important differences between the belief functions of Dempster-Shafer theory, and Bayesian probabilities are that:

a.   beliefs need not be additive,

b.   beliefs can be assigned to sets of propositions rather than of necessity to each individual proposition, and

c.   as a consequence, it is possible to pool evidence with respect to hierarchically nested hypothesis sets.

These are significant departures and we have argued that there are circumstances where these properties are both rational and useful. Because of these differences from Bayesian probability, we would expect that D-S violates some of Cox's axioms (Section 2.2). This is indeed the case. Axiom B2, scalar continuity, is certainly violated; two numbers, Bel and Pl, are used to represent belief. Axiom B6 is also violated; we may simultaneously hold a low belief in both a proposition and its negation. However, the really central issue is the violation of axiom B3; completeness. The important point, and this is the focus of the discussion of D-S in Chapter 5, is that belief in D-S need not be assigned to every well-defined proposition.

4.6.1   Knowledge representation.

Dempster-Shafer theory satisfies, in a natural way, more of Bonissone's desiderata of uncertainty management (Section 1.2) than Bayesian probability. Consequently, we would expect the theory of evidence to allow greater expressiveness in knowledge representation. This is the case, although there are some potential difficulties.

Specifically, the formalism permits the expression of ignorance or partial evidence (desideratum 5), as we have discussed above. In addition, although the decision whether to normalise or not is a contentious issue (see Section 4.3.5), the normalisation coefficient of equation 4.8 does provide a measure of dissonance between the various information sources (desideratum 4). However, in its normalised form, Dempster's rule of combination (eqn. 4.8) does assume the exhaustiveness and exclusiveness of the hypotheses (contra desideratum 8). This is the assumption which Smets' unnormalised model tries to overcome (Smets, 1990a), although this revision is not without its critics (e.g. Wilson, 1992; Paass, 1988). Shafer's original proposal was to *discount* one of the sources of evidence, in the case of extreme conflict (Shafer, 1976); that is, reduce the overall credibility of one or more of the conflicting sources by transferring belief mass to the frame of discernment. Of course, the choice of which source(s), and by how much, still requires some meta-knowledge about the problem (Section 4.3.5).

With respect to our typology of uncertainty (Figure 1.2 of Section 1.1.3), the normalisation coefficient also allows for a representation of inconsistency and anomaly. As we have seen, it may be used to provide a grading of anomaly, although it should be recalled that Dempster's rule is strictly undefined in the case of outright contradiction. The unnormalised model of Smets, in which belief that should be assigned to the empty set is assigned to a proposition representing the "open world", has very strong similarities to the use of "any other hypothesis" nodes in Bayesian networks (Section 2.9.1.1). However, this is slightly more contentious than the use of "any other hypothesis" nodes, as we have seen.

Another of Bonissone's desiderata which is not satisfied is (7). This is because the theory of evidence does make strong assumptions of evidence independence. There are, however, many applications for which these assumptions are valid. For example, Wilson (1992) provides an interpretation of D-S (the "Sources of Evidence" Framework) in which the assumptions appear quite natural. This interpretation is restricted to the combination of "simple support functions" (which correspond to the pure arguments of Section 4.2.1), though. It is really a matter of ensuring that the model fits the application domain.

4.6.2   Knowledge engineering.

Although Dempster-Shafer theory does seem quite natural as a model of subjective belief, a problem does arise with the elicitation of the numerical coefficients. The basic probability assignments correspond to an assessment of the impact of evidence on belief in a hypothesis. However, as was discussed in Chapter 2, in a domain such as medical diagnosis it is often much easier, and more reliable, to assess the impact of the hypothesis on belief in the evidence (for example, the belief that specific symptoms will be observed, given a disease is easier to assess than the belief in a disease given some symptom). As we saw, the use of Bayes' rule allows a certain amount of freedom in the choice of direction of influence that needs to be elicited. This freedom is not available in the D-S model.

However, the claim is that the theory of evidence provides a way of modelling purely subjective belief. Many of the biases which a strict Bayesian probabilistic system claims to avoid are assessed in terms of classical decision theory and betting behaviour. However, Shafer argues that the theory of evidence need not rely on assigning a meaning to its measures of belief, and justifying its rules, by appeal to rational betting behaviour (Shafer, 1981). His view, developed with Tversky, was that subjective probability judgements should be made by comparison of one's evidence to a scale of canonical examples. One of his obligations in developing the theory of evidence was to provide such a scale of canonical examples, together with a method for breaking the task of comparison down to simpler judgements. This task was addressed in (Shafer, 1976; 1981).

In fact, as we have suggested in Section 4.4, the dominance of a decision theory based on point value assignments of additive probabilities is not necessarily clear cut. There may well be situations in which an agent's betting behaviour reflects a degree of caution or ignorance in a specific situation. In these cases, measures of belief or of plausibility may, in fact, be more appropriate to use as a basis for one's actions, rather than using the pignistic transformation of Smets. Further discussion of decision making using imprecise probabilities can be found in (Smith, 1965; Williams, 1974; Walley, 1991).

4.6.3   Computational considerations.

In this chapter we have usually only considered examples in which Dempster's rule is used to combine evidence from two sources. In any large scale application evidence will generally need to be combined from a much larger number of sources. Here, the computational problems become quite intense. Orponen (1990) shows that the problem of computing belief is exponential in the number of evidences to be combined; the general problem quickly becomes computationally intractable as the number of sources of evidence increases. However, as with Bayesian belief networks, there have been a number of developments which allow efficient computation in certain circumstances.

At quite an early stage, Barnett (1981) showed that it was possible to calculate the combined belief in linear time in the case where all the evidence either supported, or opposed, singleton sets. This algorithm was used in the work reported in Section 4.5.

Quite a lot of work has been carried out on the propagation of belief functions in networks. These draw on hypertree and hypergraph representations of the network in a similar way to the L & S algorithm of Chapter 2. Foundational work on this can be found in, for example (Shenoy and Shafer, 1986; Shafer, Shenoy and Mellouli, 1987; Shenoy and Shafer, 1990; Xu, 1991). This work has resulted in a number of efficient implementations. These include DELIEF (Zarley et al, 1988), MacEvidence (Hsia and Shenoy, 1989), and Pulcinella (Saffiotti and Umkehrer, 1991). The last of these, Pulcinella, is particularly interesting as it can be reconfigured to propagate either Bayesian probabilities, Dempster-Shafer belief or Possibilities (Chapter 5) as required by the user.

Two slightly different approaches to the development of graphical algorithms have also been taken. Kennes and Smets (1990) have used the fast Möbius transform to speed up the computation. This is an approach which is analogous to the use of fast fourier transforms for efficient data analysis. Wilson, on the other hand, provides a Monte-Carlo algorithm which allows the combination of evidence to be calculated to any given accuracy in a time which is linear in the number of sources (Wilson, 1991; 1992). The excellent computational properties of this Monte-Carlo algorithm suggest that it should become a standard approach for the calculation of Dempster-Shafer belief.

4.7   Conclusions

Dempster-Shafer theory is a semantically richer formalism than Bayesian probability, primarily because it allows an expression of partial knowledge. It is not without its critics (Cheeseman, 1988; Pearl, 1990), however, and there are still some difficulties which remain in connection with the elicitation and interpretation of belief functions. Nevertheless, D-S has rapidly evolved into a mature discipline with many supporters, and a good understanding of its strengths and limitations has emerged.

In fact it is becoming increasingly clear that there are many domains where D-S is a natural and appropriate model of reasoning to use. In a recent paper, Lohmann (1991) described the use of evidential reasoning for the classification of satellite images. She reported that this approach produced successful results where classical Bayesian approaches to classification had consistently failed in the past. With that, we rest our case!

5
Reasoning with Imprecise and Vague Data

Imprecision that is intrinsic in natural languages is, in the main, possibilistic rather than probabilistic in nature. (Zadeh, 1978).

5.1   Introduction

In this chapter, we will be looking at models of uncertain reasoning which allow for imprecision and vagueness in a natural way. They achieve this by the use of a set theoretic component in the model. We will revisit the Dempster-Shafer theory in order to discuss its handling of imprecision, and introduce fuzzy sets and possibility theory in connection with vagueness.

In Chapter 4, the Dempster-Shafer theory of evidence was presented as a model of epistemic probability. That is, as a model for attributing purely subjective estimates of belief to propositions based on the evidence, or arguments, concerning those propositions. We discussed the Dempster rule of combination as a method of pooling evidence. In that chapter, a justification for the Dempster-Shafer theory was given at a philosophical level by appeal to a line in which probability was seen as an epistemic notion; as an attribute of opinion. The Dempster rule of combination was presented as a generalisation of earlier work of Bernoulli and Lambert in which a variety of rules were put forward for combining measures of evidence for arguments.

At a purely functional level, on the other hand, a justification for the Dempster-Shafer theory which is often given is that it allows for an expression of *ignorance* in a way which Bayesian probability cannot. For example, we may have evidence which suggests that a patient is suffering from arthritis, but be unable to draw any finer distinction about which form of arthritis from this evidence. The Dempster-Shafer theory allows us to assign a belief mass to "arthritis", which is the set of all possible forms of arthritis. Upon identifying further, more specific evidence, some or all of this belief may be transferred to a subset of arthritis. Here we are initially ignorant about the precise distribution of belief to all the forms of arthritis. The Dempster-Shafer theory allows us the choice of not committing to a precise distribution of belief, whereas Bayesian probability does require a precise measure of belief to be assigned to each proposition in the frame of reference. Here ignorance arises in two guises. Firstly, we have insufficient information to establish the truth or falsity of the proposition "arthritis" and so are *uncertain* as to its validity. Secondly, the proposition itself is *imprecise*; it covers a number of possibilities (rheumatoid arthritis, osteoarthritis and gout, say) and we are ignorant as to which one is in fact the case.

We will consider a further refinement of imprecision. If we say someone is suffering from "arthritis", this covers a number of possibilities, but each is equally possible. However, if we say someone is "medium height", this is more than an imprecise statement. There is an element of *vagueness*, a gradedness of the possibilities. That is, there are no sharp boundaries to the set of possible values for their height. The values just become less possible the more they depart from a value of, say, 1.75m. If someone was given the information that "Paul was medium height", then they may think it "quite possible" that Paul was 1.75m tall, "not possible" that he was 2m tall, and be "rather surprised" if he turned out to be 1.65m tall. We will introduce fuzzy sets and possibility theory in order to model reasoning with vague data.

5.1.1   Uncertainty, imprecision and vagueness.

In the preceeding section we informally introduced a taxonomy of ignorance in which we considered imprecision and uncertainty as forms of ignorance, and vagueness as a form of imprecision. We will now present a more rigorous statement of these concepts.

Information is ultimately derived from sensory data. We may be more, or less, confident in the sensors which provide this data, and more or less confident about the conclusions which can, in turn, be drawn from this data. For example, a clinician may have obtained, from some test, a value for the calcium level in a blood sample which has a 0.98 probability of being correct. She then uses this to refine a patient's diagnosis. The uncertainty in the test data will influence her final confidence in the diagnosis. Alternatively, you may seek information from three different friends on the profits a certain company made in the last year. One friend, who is not terribly reliable, says he thought the profits were "greater than £5m". A second friend, whom you trust a bit more, says the profits were "greater than £10m". The third friend has a good head for figures and says quite confidently that the profits were "greater than £15m". You summarise this information with a statement that the profits for the last financial year were "very high".

Uncertainty is ultimately derived from the reliability of the sensors which provide information.

Let Θ be a space of sensors. They may, for example, be a set of consultants providing medical data, or perhaps be a set of radar beams providing information on the locations of ships at sea. Our confidence in the reliability of these sensors leads to a probability distribution p being imposed on the space of sensors:

$$p : 2^{\Theta} \rightarrow [0,1]$$

That is, to each sensor $\{\theta\} \in 2^{\Theta}$ is assigned a number in the [0,1] interval corresponding to the reliability of that sensor. These sensors provide us with our raw information, and the probability distribution on the sensors induces a probability distribution on the information. The precise nature of the induced probability distribution will depend on the nature of the information supplied by the sensors.

Let Ω be the frame of discernment we are interested in. For example, Ω may be a set of all possible ship locations, disease states, murderers, or whatever. It is assumed that Ω is an exhaustive set of mutually exclusive hypotheses for the problem under consideration. What sort of information can the sensors supply?

Suppose the sensors $\{\theta_1, \theta_2, \theta_3\}$ provide information on the pathophysiological state of a person. They might, for example, provide a measure of the body temperature. The sensors may return precise values for the body temperature. For example, we might receive the value 98.6°F from sensor θ_1. In this case, the probability distribution on sensors will induce a probability distribution on temperatures.

On the other hand, the sensors might return imprecise values. For example, from sensor θ_2, we might receive the information that the temperature t lies in the range $98 \leq t \leq 98.8$; that is, t lies within the set $\{98.0, 98.1,$

98.2, 98.3, 98.4, 98.5, 98.6, 98.7, 98.8} (if we allow only a finite set of discrete values). In this case, the probability distribution on sensors induces a mass distribution on *sets* of temperature values. We will see that this corresponds to the Dempster-Shafer model of Chapter 4.

Finally, the sensors might return a vague value for the temperature. For example, they might present the information that "the temperature is high", which gives a set of possibilities without any precisely defined limits. This will lead us to the study of fuzzy sets and possibility theory.

Prior to the introduction of fuzzy sets, we will provide a brief revision of set theory and its use to model imprecise data. This will lead us to some preliminary work on possibility theory, and a revisitation of Dempster-Shafer theory, but from a different perspective to that of Chapter 4.

5.2   Crisp sets and imprecision

In conversation, one will often make very general statements about a certain situation. For example, instead of giving a specific condition, one may say that such and such is "suffering from cancer", or they "have arthritis", or whatever. This may be because this is sufficient information to impart in the context, or it may be because one has insufficient information available upon which to base a more precise statement. So, for very general diagnoses one might want to consider a frame of discernment Ω where, say,

$$\Omega = \{cancer, arthritis, ulcer\}.$$

However, one may wish, or need, to be more specific about the medical condition of the person under discussion. A frame of discernment which contains specific instances of the above is:

$\Omega' = \{$leukaemia, lung cancer, breast cancer, rheumatoid arthritis, osteoarthritis, gout, peptic ulcer, gastric ulcer$\}$

Sadly, there are many more forms of cancer than we have listed. In a sense, Ω' is a *refinement* of Ω. We can be more precise about what we mean by this.

The following mapping, $\hat{\Pi}$, can be defined:

$\hat{\Pi}(\{cancer\}) = \{$leukaemia, breast cancer, lung cancer$\}$

$\hat{\Pi}(\{arthritis\}) = \{$rheumatoid arthritis, osteoarthritis, gout$\}$

$\hat{\Pi}(\{ulcer\}) = \{$peptic ulcer, gastric ulcer$\}$

This is an instance of a *refinement mapping*, $\hat{\Pi}: 2^\Omega \to 2^{\Omega'}$ between two frames of discernment. There are a number of properties which we would expect such a mapping to satisfy, and conditions i) - iv) in Definition 5.1 ensure that these are satisfied for any refinement Ω' of a frame of discernment Ω. Clearly, in a refinement we do not wish to ignore any of the information expressed in terms of the original frame of discernment. Condition (i) of Definition 5.1 ensures this does not happen. Secondly, the terms in the original frame Ω represent distinct concepts. We would not expect a refinement to result in some ambiguity in concepts; some overlap in meaning. Condition (ii) expresses this formally, and our instance of $\hat{\Pi}$ satisfies this. Neither would we expect the refined frame Ω' to contain any additional concepts which were unrelated to those in Ω. Condition (iii) ensures that the refinement is 'minimal' in this sense. Finally, we would expect a conceptual structure to have an identical map to the sum of its components. This is condition (iv).

Definition 5.1   (Shafer, 1976)

A set Ω' is called a refinement of Ω if there is a mapping $\hat{\Pi}: 2^{\Omega} \rightarrow 2^{\Omega'}$ such that:

   i) $\hat{\Pi}(\{\omega\}) \neq \varnothing$ $\forall \omega \in \Omega$
   ii) $\hat{\Pi}(\{\omega\}) \cap \hat{\Pi}(\{\omega'\}) = \varnothing$ if $\omega \neq \omega'$
   iii) $\cup\{\hat{\Pi}(\{\omega\} \mid \omega \in \Omega\} = \Omega'$
   iv) $\hat{\Pi}(A) = \cup\{\hat{\Pi}(\{\omega\}) \mid \omega \in A\}$

Let us just clarify for the moment that we are not at present considering any reliability in our source of information. We merely have the case where we are provided with some information which is an *imprecise concept*, cancer say, which may be expressed as a *set* of concepts in a refined frame of discernment ({leukaemia, breast cancer, lung cancer} in our example); the imprecise information has lead us to consider a set of *possibilities*. At the moment there is no grading on these possibilities. It is conventional to say that a pathology (in this case) has possibility 1 if it is an element of this set, and possibility 0 if it is not. We will see later that it is quite natural to consider a finer grading of possibilities.

Let us make this a bit more precise. Following (Dubois and Prade, 1988a), suppose we have an imprecise measurement M of the value x of an attribute. For example, an attribute of a person might be their height, taking a value x from the range [0, 2] (in metres). In our example, we might call the attribute we are interested in "pathological state", which may take a value x from the frame Ω or Ω', as above. We may then postulate an imprecise proposition of the type "x belongs to the subset I". Two modalities naturally arise as qualifiers for this proposition:

i)   If M∩ I ≠ ∅, then "x ∈ I" is *possibly* true.

ii) If M ⊆ I, then "x ∈ I" is *necessarily* true.

An original "measurement", M, of a person's pathological state as "arthritis" corresponds to the set {rheumatoid arthritis, osteoarthritis, gout} in the refined space Ω'. Suppose this information is now present in a database. We can then model a query "has he got gout?" by the more prosaic "does the value x of this person's pathological state belong to the subset {gout}?". The answer, according to (i) would be "possibly". This seems to capture the intuitive usage of the term (although see Chapters 7 and 8 for more detailed discussions on the roles of verbal uncertainty expressions).

Suppose some additional information became available, which ruled out the possibility of gout. Then we would have a resulting measurement M' = {rheumatoid arthritis, osteoarthritis}. Now we might query the database with "has he got arthritis", or, "does the value of his pathological state belong to the subset {rheumatoid arthritis, osteoarthritis, gout}?" From (ii) the answer would be that this was necessarily so; if we know that a value belongs to a set of hypotheses, then it necessarily belongs to any superset of that set.

Remember that for the present we are not considering any gradation to the degree of membership of a set. In general terms, to any set A we may associate a *characteristic function* μ_A which takes as domain the 'universal set' Ω and returns a value in the set {0,1}, where:

$$\mu_A(\omega) = \begin{cases} 1 \text{ if } \omega \in A \\ 0 \text{ if } \omega \notin A \end{cases}$$

Such a characteristic function defines a *crisp set*; for any ω we may say precisely whether it does or does not belong to that set.

Since we are not at present considering gradations to the characteristic function of a set, we can only define discrete valued measures of possibility and necessity. However, it is still useful to define such measures, and we will see later how allowing a finer grading of the characteristic functions of sets ('fuzzy sets') induces a grading on these possibility and necessity measures.

We are also perfectly trusting our sensors. They admittedly may only give us imprecise information, but we are treating that information as 'sure'. Let the universal set, or frame of discernment be Ω, and E ⊆ Ω a sure event. Then we may define possibility and necessity measures, taking values in {0,1}, for the moment, as follows:

Definition 5.2

The function $\Pi: 2^\Omega \rightarrow \{0,1\}$ defined by

$$\Pi(A) = 1 \quad \text{if } A \cap E \neq \varnothing$$
$$= 0 \quad \text{otherwise}$$

is a *possibility* measure.

Definition 5.3

The function $N: 2^\Omega \rightarrow \{0,1\}$ defined by

$$N(A) = 1 \quad \text{if } E \subseteq A$$
$$= 0 \quad \text{otherwise}$$

is a *necessity* measure.

5.2.1   Some properties of possibility and necessity measures.

We make the closed world assumption that the frame of discernment Ω covers all the possibilities. That is, Ω may be considered as the 'always sure' event. Then:

$$\Pi(\Omega) = N(\Omega) = 1.$$

Since *something* must be true, we associate the empty set $\varnothing$ with the contradiction, or always impossible event:

$$\Pi(\varnothing) = N(\varnothing) = 0.$$

As a reminder (see Section 4.3.1), if A is an event, then its contrary is $\overline{A}$ = Ω-A. The reader should find it fairly easy to convince him or herself that the following hold, and that they are intuitively plausible properties of possibility and necessity measures.

i) $\forall A, B \subseteq \Omega \quad \Pi(A \cup B) = \max(\Pi(A), \Pi(B))$.
   The union of two events is possible if either of the two events is possible.

ii) $\max(\Pi(A), \Pi(\overline{A})) = 1$
   Of two contradictory events, one at least is completely possible. It could be that we consider both as possible.

iii) $\forall A, B \subseteq \Omega \quad N(A \cap B) = \min(N(A), N(B))$
   The necessity of a conjunction of two events is restricted to that of the least necessary event.

iv) Saying that an event is possible commits us very little; in a state of partial ignorance we may consider both an event and its negation as possible. However, when we say an event is necessary we are making the much stronger statement that we consider it as a sure event. We have that

$$\min(N(A), N(\overline{A})) = 0$$

That is, we cannot have two contradictory events being simultaneously necessary.

v) $\forall A \subseteq \Omega,$ $\Pi(A) = 1\text{-}N(\overline{A}).$

Here we have a duality property of possibility and necessity measures. This corresponds to the property of modal logics of possibility and necessity in which a proposition is considered possible if its contrary is not necessary ($\neg\Box\neg P \overset{d}{=} \Diamond P$; read $\overset{d}{=}$ as "is equal to by definition"). This gives us an alternative definition of possibility in terms of necessity: to the extent that we cannot rule out the contrary of an event, that event is possible.

vi) $\forall A \subseteq \Omega$ $\Pi(A) \geq N(A)$

An event becomes possible before it becomes necessary. This is consistent with the above comments that possibility is a weaker notion than necessity. However, because of the duality of possibility and necessity, one can make stronger statements of the relationship between the two than this. Firstly, if an event is (the least bit) necessary then it must be (completely) possible:

$$\forall A \subseteq \Omega \quad N(A) > 0 \Rightarrow \Pi(A) = 1$$

Secondly, if we doubt the possibility of an event (to any extent) then that event cannot be (the least bit) necessary:

$$\forall A \subseteq \Omega \quad \Pi(A) < 1 \Rightarrow N(A) = 0$$

(The bracketed qualifiers look forward to when we allow grades of possibility and necessity).

5.2.2   Imprecise data induces imprecise probabilities.

Earlier we said that at a fundamental level we had a space of sensors Θ which was the source of our information about the world. To this space we assigned a probability distribution p reflecting our confidence in those sensors. However, it is not the elements of the space Θ, but the information which they provide, which is of prime interest. It may be that this information is provided as imprecise concepts. If we wish to query the database with more precise queries, it is appropriate to map the imprecise data to a refined space. As we have discussed, the data is then expressed in terms of sets of precise concepts. In sum, we have an *observation mapping* $\Gamma: \Theta \rightarrow 2^{\Omega}$, in which the sensors return imprecise data expressed as subsets of the frame of discernment Ω.

The probability distribution on Θ then induces, via the mapping Γ, a structure on Ω which represents our partial beliefs about the actual state of the world. The result is that 'belief masses' are assigned to subsets of Ω. The resulting mass assignment, $m:2^{\Omega} \rightarrow [0,1]$ is such that:

i) $m(\emptyset) = 0$

ii) $m(\Omega) = \displaystyle\sum_{A \subseteq \Omega} m(A) = 1$

The subsets $A \subseteq \Omega$ for which $m(A) > 0$ are called 'focal elements'. With that, it should be clear that we have returned to the domain of belief functions (Chapter 4).

As a reminder, $m(A)$ is the total amount of belief committed *exactly* to A. On the basis of further information, this mass may be transferred to any of the possibilities covered by A. For example, we may have evidence for the imprecise datum 'arthritis' to which we assign a confidence of 0.8; $m(\{osteoarthritis, rheumatoid arthritis, gout\}) = 0.8$. We are not committing ourselves to how this belief is distributed amongst the possibilities. It may be transferred to the singletons {osteoarthritis}, {rheumatoid arthritis}, or {gout}, or indeed to any subset of "arthritis". Any one of these possibilities may have all, none, or some of this initial belief assignment transferred to it.

What this means is that given a database of imprecise information with an induced mass distribution, we cannot (in general) be precise about the belief this entails for any query we might present to the database. We can, however, provide meaningful bounds.

Consider a proposition $B \subseteq \Omega$. As a cautious estimate, we may consider all those focal elements which make B necessary (given an imprecise datum A, B is necessary if $A \subseteq B$). That is, we sum all the belief which is bound within B:

$$Bel_m(B) = \sum_{A \subseteq B} m(A) \qquad\qquad (5.1)$$

This gives a lower bound for the belief in B.

Alternatively, we may be more optimistic and consider all those focal elements which make B possible (given an imprecise datum A, B is possible if $A \cap B \neq \emptyset$). That is, we sum all the belief which is potentially transferable to B:

$$Pl_m(B) = \sum_{A \cap B \neq \emptyset} m(A) \qquad (5.2)$$

This gives an upper bound for the belief which may be transferred to B.

From the perspective that there is an underlying probability distribution which induces this belief structure, these belief (Bel) and plausibility (Pl) functions may be regarded as lower and upper bounds, respectively, on the probability of B.

5.2.3   Conditioning and belief revision with belief functions.

In Chapter 4 we saw how information from distinct sources of evidence could be combined using Dempster's rule. However, combination of evidence is not the only operation which is of interest. In probabilistic reasoning we considered the effect of *conditioning* on one or more nodes in a belief network (see Section 2.4). That is, we asked; if some information was known with certainty, how did this affect our belief in the other nodes in the network? In a similar way, we may ask how belief functions should be revised if some information becomes available which is certain.

We will describe two approaches which may be taken to this problem, here. A full discussion of both within the framework of mass distributions induced by observation mappings can be found in (Kruse et al, 1991); we will only outline their justification and present the resulting conditional/revised mass distributions.

Let us first set up a small example. Suppose our information is obtained from four experts: $\Theta = \{\theta_1, \theta_2, \theta_3, \theta_4\}$ (with apologies for the rather unimaginative choice of names!). To reflect our confidence in the experts' judgement, we assign a probability distribution to 2^Θ:

$$p(\{\theta_1\}) = 0.4, \ p(\{\theta_2\}) = p(\{\theta_3\}) = p(\{\theta_4\}) = 0.2$$

These experts have been asked to pass judgement on the state of health of an arthritic patient.

We will consider a restricted frame of discernment:

$$\Omega = \{osteoarthritis, rheumatoid \ arthritis, gout\}.$$

- Expert θ_1 says the patient is suffering from osteoarthritis.

- Expert θ_2 says the patient either has osteoarthritis or rheumatoid arthritis.
- Expert θ_3 says the patient either has rheumatoid arthritis or gout.
- Expert θ_4 does not specialise in arthritis, and has no opinion on the matter.

We thus have the observation mapping $\Gamma:\Theta \to 2^\Omega$ defined by:

$\Gamma(\theta_1) = \{osteoarthritis\};$

$\Gamma(\theta_2) = \{osteoarthritis, rheumatoid\ arthritis\};$

$\Gamma(\theta_3) = \{rheumatoid\ arthritis, gout\};$

$\Gamma(\theta_4) = \varnothing.$

Now, as we have said, the probability distribution on the sensor space Θ will induce a belief mass distribution on the frame of discernment Ω. We will refer to this induced distribution as $\Gamma[p]$, where $\Gamma[p]:2^\Omega \to [0,1]$. As we should expect, the above information is sufficient to determine $\Gamma[p]$ (Kruse et al, 1991):

$$\Gamma[p](A) \stackrel{d}{=} \begin{cases} \dfrac{p(\{\theta \in \Theta \mid \Gamma(\theta) = A\})}{p(\{\theta \in \Theta \mid \Gamma(\theta) \neq \varnothing\})} & \text{if } A \neq \varnothing \\ 0 & \text{otherwise} \end{cases} \qquad (5.3)$$

The denominator provides a normalisation coefficient. In effect, we ignore those sensors which provide no information (for which $\Gamma(\theta) = \varnothing$) and renormalise the mass of those which do provide information. Note that at least one sensor *must* provide some data; the distribution is undefined if $\{\theta \in \Theta \mid \Gamma(\theta) \neq \varnothing\} = \varnothing$. Then we sum the confidences of those sensors which agree on a data item (they reinforce each other) and assign the result as a belief mass to the datum.

In the case of our experts in arthritis we obtain:

$m(\{osteoarthritis\}) = 0.5;$

$m(\{osteoarthritis, rheumatoid\ arthritis\}) = 0.25;$

$m(\{rheumatoid\ arthritis, gout\}) = 0.25.$

5.2.3.1 Conditional mass distributions.

We will consider the impact of the arrival of some absolutely reliable, yet imprecise, information. If ω_0 is the attribute value we are interested in finding out, this information says that for sure $\omega_0 \in E$, where $E \subseteq \Omega$

Given this information, we may take a cautious, or sceptical, approach and accept (from the sensors) only that information which is in agreement with it. Here the decision maker is given very little freedom. She may only accept or reject data, and does this on the basis of whether it is, or is not, in agreement with the sure information E. The first step is to define a conditional observation mapping, $\Gamma_E : \Theta \rightarrow 2^\Omega$:

$$\Gamma_E(\theta) \stackrel{d}{=} \begin{cases} \Gamma(\theta) & \text{if } \Gamma(\theta) \subseteq E \\ \varnothing & \text{otherwise} \end{cases} \tag{5.4}$$

Suppose, in the case of our example, we obtain some information which surely rules out gout. Put another way, we have the sure information E = {osteoarthritis, rheumatoid arthritis}. Then the observation mapping which is strictly in agreement with this is:

$\Gamma_E(\theta_1) = (\{\text{osteoarthritis}\});$

$\Gamma_E(\theta_2) = (\{\text{osteoarthritis, rheumatoid arthritis}\});$

$\Gamma_E(\theta_3) = \varnothing;$

$\Gamma_E(\theta_4) = \varnothing.$

The data from θ_3 was in partial disagreement with the information E, which we trust implicitly, so we reject it.

The result of modifying the observation mapping Γ to the conditional mapping Γ_E is that all belief is transferred to E. Consequently, the original mass distribution must be rescaled to obtain the conditional mass distribution:

$$m(A \mid E) \stackrel{d}{=} \begin{cases} \dfrac{m(A)}{\text{Bel}_m(E)} & \text{if } A \subseteq E \\ 0 & \text{otherwise} \end{cases} \tag{5.5}$$

The result of using this conditional mass distribution in the calculation of the belief, Bel, and plausibility, Pl, functions is that we obtain:

$$\text{Bel}_{m(. \mid E)}(A \mid E) = \frac{\text{Bel}_m(A \cap E)}{\text{Bel}_m(E)} \tag{5.6}$$

$$\text{Pl}_{m(. \mid E)}(A \mid E) = \frac{\text{Pl}_m(A \cup \overline{E}) - \text{Pl}_m(\overline{E})}{1 - \text{Pl}_m(\overline{E})} \tag{5.7}$$

Returning to the example. From the original mass distribution, we had that Bel(E) = (0.5+0.25) = 0.75. So, the conditional mass distribution, given E, is:

$$m(\{osteoarthritis\} \mid E) = 0.5/0.75 = 0.67$$
$$m(\{osteoarthritis, rheumatoid\ arthritis\} \mid E) = 0.25/0.75 = 0.33$$

Prior to conditioning we had:

$$Bel_m(\{osteoarthritis\}) = 0.5$$
$$Pl_m(\{osteoarthritis\}) = 0.75$$

$$Bel_m(\{osteoarthritis, rheumatoid\ arthritis\}) = 0.75$$
$$Pl_m(\{osteoarthritis, rheumatoid\ arthritis\}) = 1$$

$$Bel_m(\{rheumatoid\ arthritis, gout\}) = 0.25$$
$$Pl_m(\{rheumatoid\ arthritis, gout\}) = 0.5$$

After conditioning we have:

$$Bel_{m(.\mid E)}(\{osteoarthritis\} \mid E) = 0.67$$
$$Pl_{m(.\mid E)}(\{osteoarthritis\} \mid E) = 1$$

$$Bel_{m(.\mid E)}(\{osteoarthritis, rheumatoid\ arthritis\} \mid E)$$
$$= Pl_{m(.\mid E)}(\{osteoarthritis, rheumatoid\ arthritis\} \mid E)$$
$$= 1$$

$$Bel_{m(.\mid E)}(\{rheumatoid\ arthritis, gout\} \mid E) = 0$$
$$Pl_{m(.\mid E)}(\{rheumatoid\ arthritis, gout\} \mid E) = 0.33$$

There are, of course, other queries we might make.

5.2.3.2 Belief revision.

With belief revision we will take a more credulous approach. Again, we are given some sure information E. In the case of conditioning, we said we will only consider data (from the sensors) which is *necessarily* in agreement with E. With belief revision, we say we will consider all information which is compatible with E, which is *possibly* in agreement with E. We then revise this information to be consistent with the sure information. In effect, the decision maker is being offered more freedom than in the previous case. Instead of accepting or rejecting data from the sensors, he is allowed to revise the observation mapping Γ to $\Gamma_E : \Theta \to 2^\Omega$, where:

$$\Gamma_E(\theta) \stackrel{d}{=} \Gamma(\theta) \cap E.$$

For our example, this gives:

$$\Gamma_E(\theta_1) = \{osteoarthritis\};$$

$\Gamma_E(\theta_2) = \{\text{osteoarthritis, rheumatoid arthritis}\};$

$\Gamma_E(\theta_3) = \{\text{rheumatoid arthritis}\};$

$\Gamma_E(\theta_4) = \varnothing.$

This leads to a revised mass distribution $m_E : 2^\Omega \to [0,1]$, where:

$$m_E(A) \stackrel{d}{=} \begin{cases} \dfrac{\displaystyle\sum_{E \cap C = A} m(C)}{1 - \displaystyle\sum_{C \cap E = \varnothing} m(C)} & \text{if } A \subseteq E \\[6pt] 0 & \text{otherwise} \end{cases} \qquad (5.8)$$

Note that, as with Dempster's rule of combination (Section 4.3.3), there is a normalisation factor which rescales m_E by a factor which corresponds to the extent to which the original distribution disagrees with E. Note also that the revised distribution is undefined in the case where there is an absolute contradiction between the sure information E, and the original distribution m; that is, if $\text{Bel}_m(\overline{E}) = 1$.

After this rescaling, the net effect of the revision is to transfer mass from the original focal elements to subsets of those focal elements which are in agreement with E.

The revised mass distribution for this example is:

$m_E(\{\text{osteoarthritis}\}) = 0.5$

$m_E(\{\text{osteoarthritis, rheumatoid arthritis}\}) = 0.25$

$m_E(\{\text{rheumatoid arthritis}\}) = 0.25$

In this case, the original mass assigned to {rheumatoid arthritis, gout} has been transferred to its subset {rheumatoid arthritis} ($\subseteq$ E).

As with the case of conditioning, one can produce equations which directly relate the belief and plausibility functions before and after revision. These are:

$$\text{Bel}_{m_E}(A) = \frac{\text{Bel}_m(A \cup \overline{E}) - \text{Bel}_m(\overline{E})}{1 - \text{Bel}_m(\overline{E})} \qquad A \subseteq \Omega \qquad (5.9)$$

$$\text{Pl}_{m_E}(A) = \frac{\text{Pl}_m(A \cap E)}{\text{Pl}_m(E)} \qquad A \subseteq \Omega \qquad (5.10)$$

Note the interesting symmetry between the resulting equations for conditioning and for belief revision. In one, we renormalise by the lower bound of our former belief in E (sceptical), in the other we renormalise by the upper bound of our former belief in E (credulous).

We now calculate the revised belief and plausibility functions to complete our example:

$$\text{Bel}_{m_E}(\{\text{osteoarthritis}\}) = 0.5.$$

$$\text{Pl}_{m_E}(\{\text{osteoarthritis}\}) = 0.5 + 0.25 = 0.75.$$

$$\text{Bel}_{m_E}(\{\text{osteoarthritis, rheumatoid arthritis}\})$$
$$= \text{Pl}_{m_E}(\{\text{osteoarthritis, rheumatoid arthritis}\})$$
$$= 0.5 + 0.25 + 0.25 = 1.$$

$$\text{Bel}_{m_E}(\{\text{rheumatoid arthritis, gout}\}) = 0.25.$$

$$\text{Pl}_{m_E}(\{\text{rheumatoid arthritis, gout}\}) = 0.25 + 0.25 = 0.5.$$

Again, there are other queries we might make. Note we get a significantly different result to the case of conditioning. This is as we might expect owing to the quite different ways in which conditioning and belief revision respectively deal with data which is partially inconsistent with the sure information E.

5.2.4   Review of imprecision.

In Chapter 4 we traced the roots of the Dempster-Shafer theory of evidence back through the work of Bernoulli and Lambert to seventeenth century notions of epistemic probability. In this first part of the Chapter 5 we have reviewed the Dempster-Shafer theory as a vehicle for handling imprecise data. A mass distribution on subsets of the frame of discernment Ω is modelled as being induced by an underlying probability distribution on a set of sensors which provide imprecise information. Note that we are not saying that the sensors will be explicitly represented in a database. Merely that a mass distribution m *can be viewed* as having been induced by a probability distribution on an underlying sensor space.

In Chapter 4 we saw how evidence from independent sources may be combined using Dempster's rule. In this chapter we looked at two further operations which may be carried out on imprecise data. These emphasised the view of belief masses as potentially movable, or transferable, to any subset of their focal elements, given some sure information E. In the first case we generated the conditional mass distribution, given E. We handled this by considering only that data which formerly made E necessary, and

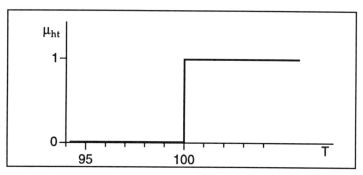

Fig 5.1   *A possible characteristic function for "high temperature".*

discarding the rest. The mass distribution was scaled by a factor Bel(E) to ensure it was normalised.

In the case of belief revision, we considered that data which formerly made E possible, and revised it to be consistent with E. This necessitated mass being transferred to subsets A ∩ E of the focal elements E. This time the revised distribution was renormalised by the factor Pl(E). There are, as yet, few clear guidelines as to which operation, conditioning or belief revision, to use in which circumstances. There is a great need for practical experience with both.

5.3   Vague and approximate concepts

5.3.1   Fuzzy sets.

We have looked at the use of (crisp) sets to represent imprecise concepts. We represented the concept arthritis, for example, as the set of values {rheumatoid arthritis, osteoarthritis, gout} for the attribute "pathological state". Crisp sets have an associated characteristic function which returns a value from {0, 1} depending on whether an element is, or is not, a member of the set (Section 5.2). For example, we might say that someone's temperature was "high" if it had a value ≥ 100°F. The concept "high temperature" would then have an associated characteristic function μ_{ht} as shown in Figure 5.1.

However, this does intuitively seem to be an overconstrained representation of the concept "high temperature". Are we right to give a precise cut off between when a temperature may be regarded as high, and when as not

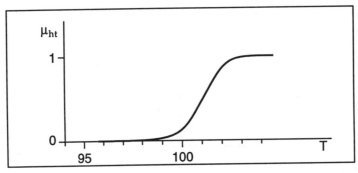

Fig 5.2   *A more realistic characteristic function for "high temperature".*

high? Certainly we would say that a temperature of 110°F was high. Equally certainly, a temperature of 98.6°F would be normal, and not high. But as the temperature rises from 99°F, so we would say it was high with increasing conviction. We might, perhaps, prefer to use a characteristic function such as that shown in Figure 5.2.

That is, we now allow the characteristic function to take values in the [0, 1] interval, so we have a continuous grading of set membership between 0 and 1. Such fuzzy sets were first introduced by Zadeh (1965).

Definition 5.4   after (Zadeh, 1965)

Let Ω be a frame of discernment (set of all possible values x for an attribute). Then a *fuzzy set* A in Ω is characterised by a membership function μ_A: $\Omega \to [0, 1]$. The value $\mu_A(x)$ for $x \in \Omega$ represents the "grade of membership" of x in A. The characteristic function μ_A can be thought of as a measure of the degree of compatibility of x with the concept A.

Note that although Ω may be an infinite domain, such as the set of all real numbers for example, for the sake of simplicity we will only consider finite, discrete domains in most of the formal definitions. We will not generally make such a restriction in the examples, and all the definitions are modifiable to cover the case of infinite domains.

Examples of vague concepts which might be expressed as fuzzy sets abound: the set of *short* people; the set of all real numbers *much greater* than 1; the set of *serious* illnesses; the set of *painful* side effects. Many of these would be represented by a characteristic function which is highly subjective, and which may need to be revised in a different context. For example,

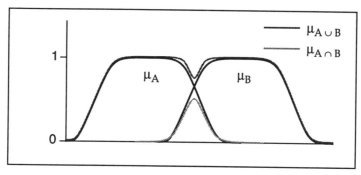

Fig 5.3   *The union and intersection of two fuzzy sets.*

in the 1960's we might have characterised the set of fast saloon cars (in a restricted domain) by the function; μ_{fc}(Mini Minor) = 0, μ_{fc}(Mini Cooper) = 0.3, μ_{fc}(Mini Cooper S) = 0.8, μ_{fc}(Jaguar) = 1. With the changes in technology over the last thirty years, these values are no longer appropriate (although they might still be from the perspective of a cyclist).

There are a number of relations and connectives on ordinary, or crisp, sets which need to be redefined for the case of fuzzy sets. We will give the original definitions presented by Zadeh (1965; 1968). However, these are not the only legitimate definitions; there are a number of alternatives which still produce a coherent formalism (see e.g. Guinan, Streicher and Kerre, 1990).

In the following, A, B and C are fuzzy sets in Ω and x a variable which may take any value in Ω. Figure 5.3 illustrates the union and intersection of two fuzzy sets.

Containment:	$A \subseteq B$	iff $\forall x.\mu_A(x) \leq \mu_B(x)$.
Equality:	$A = B$	iff $\forall x.\mu_A(x) = \mu_B(x)$.
Complementation:	$C = \overline{A}$	iff $\forall x.\mu_C(x) = 1-\mu_A(x)$.
Union:	$C = A \cup B$	iff $\forall x.\mu_C(x) = \max(\mu_A(x), \mu_B(x))$.
Intersection:	$C = A \cap B$	iff $\forall x.\mu_C(x) = \min(\mu_A(x), \mu_B(x))$.

Most of the expected properties of a boolean algebra (see Section 4.3.1) are satisfied by these definitions of the fuzzy connectives union, intersection and complementation. For example, it is easily verified that de Morgan's laws and the distributive laws hold for all fuzzy sets A, B, C in some universe Ω:

i) $\overline{A \cup B} = \overline{A} \cap \overline{B}$;

ii) $\overline{A \cap B} = \overline{A} \cup \overline{B}$;

iii) $C \cap (A \cup B) = (C \cap A) \cup (C \cap B)$;

iv) $C \cup (A \cap B) = (C \cup A) \cap (C \cup B)$.

(e.g. in the case of (i) $1 - \max(\mu_A, \mu_B) = \min(1 - \mu_A, 1 - \mu_B)$).

However, two properties of a boolean algebra do not hold. In general, we will have $A \cup \overline{A} \neq \Omega$, and $A \cap \overline{A} \neq \varnothing$ for A in Ω, since:

$$\forall x.\ 0 < \mu_A(x) < 1 \quad \max(\mu_A, 1 - \mu_A) < 1$$
$$\min(\mu_A, 1 - \mu_A) > 0.$$

As an aside, a succinct statement of this situation is that we have "a complete distributive lattice with pseudocomplementation" (Dubois and Prade, 1988a). The meaning of "distributive" and "pseudocomplementation" should be clear from the preceding discussion. The word "lattice" essentially refers to the partial order placed on subsets of a universe Ω by the set containment relation, $\subseteq$ (for example, {a, b} is "less than" {a, b, c}, because {a, b} $\subseteq$ {a, b, c}).

Three further definitions will complete our survey of the very basics of fuzzy set theory. It is possible to represent a fuzzy set in terms of crisp sets by introducing the idea of an α-cut. An α-cut of a fuzzy set A is the crisp set of values which are compatible with the concept (represented by) A to a level at least α. For example, the set {Mini Cooper, Mini Cooper S, Jaguar} contains the items which are compatible with the concept "Fast Car" to at least level 0.3, the set {Jaguar} contains those items which are compatible to level at least 0.9 (and, in fact, to level 1).

Definition 5.5

If A is a fuzzy set in Ω, then the α-*cut* A_α is defined by:

$$A_\alpha = \{\omega \in \Omega \mid \mu_A(\omega) \geq \alpha\}.$$

(e.g. Fast_Car$_{0.3}$ = {Mini Cooper, Mini Cooper S, Jaguar}).

Zadeh's representation theorem clarifies how a fuzzy set may be represented by a set of crisp sets; the family of its α-cuts. First notice that in the case of Fast_Car, we had:

$$\text{Fast\_Car}_{0.3} \supseteq \text{Fast\_Car}_{0.9} \supseteq \text{Fast\_Car}_1\ (=\{\text{Jaguar}\}).$$

This is a quite general property of α-cuts. That is, the family C(A) of α-cuts, with $0 < \alpha \leq 1$, is monotone:

For all A_β, $A_\gamma \in C(A)$ ($= \{A_\alpha \mid \alpha \in [0,1]\}$)
if $0 < \beta \leq \gamma \leq 1$, then $A_\beta \supseteq A_\gamma$.

We will now state Zadeh's representation theorem (Zadeh, 1971)

Theorem 5.1

Let A be a fuzzy set in Ω. Then:

$$\forall \omega \in \Omega, \mu_A(\omega) = \sup\{\alpha \mid \omega \in A_\alpha\}$$

(sup(A) is the least upper bound of the elements of a set A. For example, sup$\{2, 5, 8, 15\}$ = 15).

What this means is that we can reconstruct the characteristic function of a fuzzy set from its class of α-cuts. Again, we will briefly illustrate this with the example of Fast_Car. It should be easy to see that:

μ_{fc}(Mini Minor) $= \sup\{0\}$ $= 0$

μ_{fc}(Mini Cooper) $= \sup\{0, 0.3\}$ $= 0.3$

μ_{fc}(Mini Cooper S) $= \sup\{0, 0.3, 0.8\}$ $= 0.8$

μ_{fc}(Jaguar) $= \sup\{0, 0.3, 0.8, 1\} = 1$

We have recovered the original characteristic function.

Any monotone family of sets $\{A_\alpha \mid \alpha \in [0,1]\}$ such that $\alpha_i < \alpha_j \Rightarrow A_{\alpha i} \supseteq A_{\alpha j}$ will form the set of α-cuts of a fuzzy set A defined by the characteristic function of theorem 5.1.

Two specific α-cuts are of interest.

Definition 5.6

The α-cut at level 1 is the *core*, $\mathring{A}$, of a fuzzy set A in Ω:

$$\mathring{A} = \{\omega \in \Omega \mid \mu_A(\omega) = 1\}.$$

A *strong α-cut*, $A_{\bar\alpha}$, is defined using a strict inequality:

$$\forall \alpha \in [0, 1), A_{\bar\alpha} = \{\omega \in \Omega \mid \mu_A(\omega) > \alpha\}.$$

Definition 5.7

The strong cut at level 0 is the *support*, S(A), of a fuzzy set A in Ω:

$$S(A) = \{\omega \in \Omega \mid \mu_A(\omega) > 0\}$$

5.3.2   Graded possibility distributions.

In Section 5.2 we introduced possibility and necessity measures which returned values from $\{0, 1\}$. We will now see how these definitions can be refined to provide gradings of possibility and necessity.

In Section 5.2 we considered a variable x representing the unknown
value of some attribute of interest. If Ω was the range of the variable x, then
we could say that "x = ω", for some $\omega \in \Omega$, was "possibly true" if ω was a
member of a crisp subset of Ω obtained from some (imprecise) measure-
ment. More formally, if $M \subseteq \Omega$ was a measurement, then $x \in I$ was possibly
true if $M \cap I \neq \varnothing$ (where in this example we are considering the case where
$I = \{\omega\}$ for some $\omega \in \Omega$). In effect, the imprecise datum M has induced a
"possibility distribution" on the singletons $\{\omega\}$, for all $\omega \in \Omega$, where

$$\Pi(\{\omega\}) = 1 \qquad \text{if } \{\omega\} \subseteq M$$
$$= 0 \qquad \text{otherwise.}$$

In the first case, we say "x = ω" is (perfectly) possible. In the second
case, "x = ω" is impossible.

Note, first, the important distinction between the semantics of probable
and possible. Suppose we have a large set of possible values for x, and we
have equal confidence in any one of them being the true value. Then we
should assign a uniform probability distribution to those values, which
sums to unity; the probability of any individual value being the true case
will be low. To quote Shackle (1961): "Thus a hypothesis can be rated 'improbable' not because anything in its own nature disqualifies it but because
it is crowded out from attention". In distinction, we may say all of these
values are equally *possible*, and assign each one a possibility equal to unity.

However, that is not to say that we need necessarily only speak of a
value being either "possible" or "impossible". In natural language one often grades possibility: something is *perfectly* possible; something is *just*
possible (although we would not be all that surprised if it turned out not to
be the case). The idea of grading possibility and necessity can be captured
quite naturally by considering vague data, represented by fuzzy sets, as
opposed to imprecise data. We will follow (Dubois and Prade, 1991a) quite
closely in introducing graded possibility distributions.

The possibility measure Π was defined over subsets of Ω. We will take
as primitive a *possibility distribution* π_x which is defined over the elements
of Ω themselves. (Effectively $\pi_x(\omega) = \Pi(\{\omega\})$). The function $\pi_x: \Omega \rightarrow [0, 1]$
represents a "flexible restriction" (Dubois and Prade, 1991a) on the values
of x, subject to the following constraints. For $\omega \in \Omega$,

$\pi_x(\omega) = 0$ means "$x = \omega$" is impossible,

$\pi_x(\omega) = 1$ means "$x = \omega$" is perfectly possible.

The flexibility arises because we may take π_x to range between 0 and 1, subject to the above interpretations at the extreme values.

If our sources of information are consistent, we would always expect some value(s) in Ω to be perfectly possible; Ω is taken to cover all possibilities. So we will usually expect the following normalisation condition to hold for any possibility distribution:

$$\exists \omega \in \Omega \; \pi_x(\omega) = 1. \qquad (5.11)$$

Now, how do we make the connection with fuzzy set theory? If the only information we have is that "x lies in A" for some set $A \subseteq \Omega$, then the possibility distribution is defined by the characteristic function μ_A of that set. That is,

$$\pi_x(\omega) = \mu_A(\omega) \quad \forall \omega \in \Omega \qquad (5.12)$$

So, if A is a crisp set, $\pi_x(w) = 1$ if $\omega \in A$ and $\pi_x(w) = 0$ otherwise. If the set A is a fuzzy set, then π_x will range over [0,1]. In either case, we can say "x is A". For example, Ronald's *pathological state* is *arthritis* represents a possibility distribution where $\pi_{ps}(\omega) = 1$ if $\omega \in \{$osteoarthritis, rheumatoid arthritis, gout$\}$. Alternatively, Julia's *height* is *tall* represents a possibility distribution π_{height} taking gradings of possibility increasing between 0 and 1 as the value of height increases (up to a certain limit).

It should be emphasised that possibility distributions are *not* just membership functions. Given that it is the only information that we have, then a fuzzy set membership function may be used as a tool to *represent* a possibility distribution.

Note the two extreme cases for a possibility distribution:

- complete knowledge; we know the value of x to be precisely ω_0. That is, $\pi_x(\omega_0) = 1$, and $\pi_x(\omega) = 0$, $\forall \omega \neq \omega_0$.

- complete ignorance; anything is possible. That is, $\pi_x(\omega) = 1$, $\forall \omega \in \Omega$

5.3.3   Graded measures of possibility and necessity.

Definitions 5.2 and 5.3 in Section 5.2 introduced possibility and necessity measures on sets of propositions which returned values from $\{0, 1\}$, given some information which is sure, although imprecise. We now have a way of representing vague data using possibility distributions. Can we provide revised definitions of the possibility and necessity measures such that they

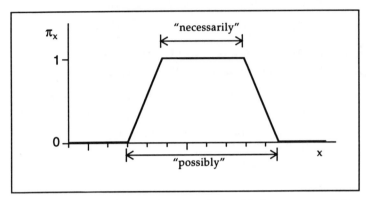

Fig 5.4   *Simple example of the qualitative relationship between possibility and necessity.*

return graded values in the [0,1] interval? This is indeed the case, and we will present the revised definitions in this section.

Let π be a normalised possibility distribution defined over the frame of discernment Ω. Then:

Definition 5.8

The function $\Pi: 2^{\Omega} \to [0,1]$ defined by:

$$\Pi(A) = \sup\{\pi(\omega) \mid \omega \in A\}$$

is a possibility measure.

Definition 5.9

The function $N: 2^{\Omega} \to [0,1]$ defined by

$$N(A) = \inf\{1 - \pi(\omega) \mid \omega \notin A\}$$

is a necessity measure[1].

It should be straightforward for the reader to satisfy him or herself that these definitions coincide with 5.2 and 5.3 in the case where the possibility distribution π is represented by a membership function of a crisp set A. Please take the trouble to do so!

All the properties of Section 5.2.1 hold, of course, for these definitions of possibility and necessity. Note that the final property (vi) is more meaningful now we allow grades of possibility and necessity ($N(A) > 0 \Rightarrow \Pi(A)$

---

1. "inf(A)" is the greatest lower bound of a set A.

= 1, and $\Pi(A) < 1 \Rightarrow N(A) = 0$). Figure 5.4 is a simple illustration of this property.

5.3.4   Modelling possibility and necessity in the information sources framework.

The information sources, or context model, introduced by (Kruse et al, 1991; Gebhart and Kruse, 1993) can be used to provide further insight into the origin of possibility distributions. The following is a simplified discussion, but should provide a reasonably accurate illustrative account.

In Section 5.1.1 we had a space of sensors which provided some information. A probability distribution over the space of sensors induced a mass distribution over subsets of the frame of discernment Ω. Now again we have a space of sensors, Θ, providing imprecise information. But this time we say that there is a high degree of coherence between the information which is supplied. If $\Gamma: \Theta \to 2^{\Omega}$ is the information mapping, then some ordering may be imposed on the sensors such that if $\Gamma(\theta_i) = A_i$, $\forall i$. $1 \le i \le n$, then $A_1 \subseteq A_2 \subseteq \dots \subseteq A_n$. (Assuming there are n sensors in Θ). Again, the probability distribution on the sensor space induces a mass distribution on subsets of the frame of discernment Ω, but this time we have a *consonant mass distribution*; the focal elements are not necessarily in agreement, but they *are* consistent with one another.

Note first that this sequence is monotone. Recall from the opening of Section 5.3 that a fuzzy set may be represented by a monotone sequence of crisp sets; the α-cuts. An α-cut of a fuzzy set A contains all those possible values which are compatible with the concept represented by A to level at least α. Now, with the case of the consonant mass distribution we may interpret $m(A_i)$, $1 \le i \le n$, as the belief mass assigned to the statement "possibly $\omega \in A_i$". For each of the focal elements we obtain from equation 5.2:

$$Pl(A_i) = \sum_{A_i \cap A_j \ne \varnothing} m(A_j) = \sum_{i \le j \le n} m(A_j)$$

If we take $Pl(A_i) = \alpha_i$, $1 \le i \le n$, then A_i may be said to contain those elements of Ω which are possible values to level at least α_i. It looks like Pl is a possibility measure in this case.

In fact, it is straightforward to show that for a consonant mass distribution, for any $B,C \subseteq \Omega$:

i) $Pl(\Omega) = 1$

ii) $Pl(\emptyset) = 0$

iii) $Pl(B \cup C) = \max(Pl(B), Pl(C))$.

These properties are sufficient to characterise Pl as a possibility function (Dubois and Prade, 1988a); $\Pi(A) = Pl(A)\ \forall A \subseteq \Omega.$

(To provide a little more conviction that the above properties hold, note that:

$$Pl(B \cup C) \;=\; \sum_{A_i \cap (B \cup C) \neq \emptyset} m(A_i) \;=\; \sum_{(A_i \cap B) \cup (A_i \cap C) \neq \emptyset} m(A_i)$$

$$=\; \max\left(\sum_{A_i \cap B \neq \emptyset} m(A_i),\ \sum_{A_i \cap C \neq \emptyset} m(A_i) \right)$$

$$=\; \max(Pl(B), Pl(C))$$

provided $A_1 \subseteq A_2 \subseteq \dots \subseteq A_n$)

Finally, since $\Pi(A) \overset{d}{=} Pl(A)\ \forall A \subseteq \Omega$, is a possibility function, we may define a possibility distribution (induced by the consonant mass distribution) by:

$$\pi(\omega) \overset{d}{=} Pl(\{\omega\})\quad \forall \omega \in \Omega \qquad\qquad (5.13)$$

To summarise, each sensor in a space of sensors provides some imprecise datum. A probability distribution on the sensors reflects our confidence in those sensors. This induces a mass distribution on the imprecise data. Although the sensors vary in the precision with which they may constrain the value of a variable, they do display a high degree of coherence. The focal elements A_i of the resulting mass distribution may be viewed as α-cuts. That is, they provide a representation in terms of crisp sets of some underlying vague datum. In sum, the sensors provide a vague datum with an associated possibility distribution.

An example may help to clarify this.

We have a set of sensors $\{\theta_1, \theta_2, \theta_3\}$, and a probability distribution over those sensors:

$$p(\{\theta_1\}) = 0.3,\ p(\{\theta_2\}) = 0.5,\ p(\{\theta_3\}) = 0.2.$$

We wish to know; "what type is Simon's car?".

- θ_1 provides the information that Simon's car is some kind of sporty saloon; either a Mini Cooper, a Mini Cooper S, or a Jaguar. That is:

  $\Gamma(\theta_1) = \{$Mini Cooper, Mini Cooper S, Jaguar$\}$

- θ_2 can be a bit more precise; Simon drives one of the faster saloons, a Mini Cooper S or a Jaguar. That is:

  $\Gamma(\theta_2) = \{$Mini Cooper S, Jaguar$\}$.

- θ_3 says Simon drives a Jaguar:

  $\Gamma(\theta_3) = \{$Jaguar$\}$.

From the probability distribution on the sensor space, we have that:

$$m(\{\text{Mini Cooper, Mini Cooper S, Jaguar}\}) = 0.3;$$

$$m(\{\text{Mini Cooper S, Jaguar}\}) = 0.5;$$

$$m(\{\text{Jaguar}\}) = 0.2$$

Information is being derived from a variety of different perspectives, or contexts. Each source is providing a different set of possibilities, although the sets of possibilities do have a high degree of coherence. Hence, the sources together provide a possibility distribution:

$$\pi(\text{Mini}) \quad = \Pi(\{\text{Mini}\})$$

$$= \sum_{A \cap \{\text{Mini}\} \neq \varnothing} m(A) = 0$$

$$\pi(\text{Mini Cooper}) \quad = \Pi(\{\text{Mini Cooper}\})$$

$$= \sum_{A \cap \{\text{MiniCooper}\} \neq \varnothing} m(A) = 0.3$$

$$\pi(\text{Mini Cooper S}) \quad = \Pi(\{\text{Mini Cooper S}\})$$

$$= \sum_{A \cap \{\text{MiniCooperS}\} \neq \varnothing} m(A) = 0.3 + 0.5 = 0.8$$

$$\pi(\text{Jaguar}) \quad = \Pi(\{\text{Jaguar}\})$$

$$= \sum_{A \cap \{\text{Jaguar}\} \neq \varnothing} m(A) = 0.3 + 0.5 + 0.2 = 1$$

The information from the sensors has together provided us with a possibility distribution which may be represented by the fuzzy set Fast_Car of Section 5.3.1.

Again, this is not to say that the underlying information sources need ever be explicitly represented. The aim is to provide a unifying formal framework, which enables the precise relationships of the various calculi to be represented.

5.3.5   Conditioning and belief revision in possibility theory.

As with belief functions, in its rigorous form the sources of evidence model enables a full analysis of belief revision and conditioning to be carried out. We will only present the resulting formulae here. See (Kruse et al, 1991) for their justification. In the following, Π is a possibility measure on Ω, with associated possibility distribution π. N is the corresponding necessity measure.

5.3.5.1 Conditioning.

Let $B \subseteq \Omega$ be such that $N(B) \neq 0$. Note that this implies $\Pi(B) = 1$. That is, $\sup\{\pi(\omega) \mid \omega \in B\} = 1$; we know ω_0 (the precise value we are seeking) lies in B. It does not make sense to condition on a set which does not have this property as there would be an element of contradiction involved.

Essentially, with conditioning we renormalise the possibility distribution to ensure that $N(B \mid B) = 1$:

$$N(A \mid B) \stackrel{d}{=} \begin{cases} \dfrac{N(A)}{N(B)} & \text{if } A \subseteq B \\ 0 & \text{otherwise} \end{cases} \qquad (5.14)$$

$$\Pi(A \mid B) \stackrel{d}{=} \begin{cases} \dfrac{\Pi(A \cup \overline{B}) - \Pi(\overline{B})}{1 - \Pi(\overline{B})} & \text{if } A \subseteq B \\ 0 & \text{otherwise} \end{cases} \qquad (5.15)$$

5.3.5.2 Belief revision.

In this case, as with belief functions, we are looking to revise data which is consistent with the truth lying in B. That is, instead of the truth necessarily lying in B, we assume it to possibly lie in B before revision. That is $\Pi(B) > 0$ and we revise the data to ensure that $\Pi_B(B) = 1$:

$$N_B(A) \stackrel{d}{=} \begin{cases} \dfrac{N(A \cup \overline{B}) - N(\overline{B})}{1 - N(\overline{B})} & \text{if } A \subseteq B \\ 0 & \text{otherwise} \end{cases} \qquad (5.16)$$

$$\Pi_B(A) \stackrel{d}{=} \begin{cases} \dfrac{\Pi(A)}{\Pi(B)} & \text{if } A \subseteq B \\ 0 & \text{otherwise} \end{cases} \qquad (5.17)$$

5.3.6   Review of vagueness.

We have shown how possibility distributions induced by vague data may be:

  a.   represented by fuzzy sets, and

  b.   interpreted in terms of consonant belief functions.

This covers the very basics of possibility theory. We have looked at two patterns of inference in possibility theory, conditioning and belief revision, but clearly there are many more aspects which could be covered. Further information can be found in (Dubois and Prade, 1988a; 1988b) and in (de Mántaras, 1990).

5.4   Possibilistic logic

A number of applications have been built and reported in the literature which are capable of handling imprecise or vague data. (Dubois and Prade, 1988b) includes a short overview of a variety of applications which use imprecise and uncertain rules and facts. An extended presentation on one specific inference engine, TOULMED, and its application to diabetology can be found in (Buisson et al, 1987). However, in slight contrast to the applications described in Chapters 2, 3 and 4, we will look at the application of possibility and necessity measures to logic programming under uncertainty in this chapter.

In a sense, this discussion is a little premature as we will be focusing on logical approaches to reasoning in the next chapter. However, we will not be going into a great deal of technical detail and "possibilistic logic" does provide an interesting view on possibility theory.

5.4.1   Automated theorem proving.

Let us state the problem. There is now a widespread interest in using formal logic as a vehicle for knowledge representation. Recent developments in automated theorem proving mean that logical deductions can be performed over sets of logical axioms stored in a database by a computer. Many readers will be familiar with Prolog, which is currently the most widely available computer programming language based on automatic theorem proving techniques. At the heart of Prolog is a procedure called *resolution*. This is a simple rule of inference which states that if $p \lor q$ is known to be true (perhaps from some other deductions) and $\neg p \lor r$ is true, then one can conclude that q ∨ r must be true (where p, q, and r are propositions). We will write this as:

$$\frac{p \lor q \qquad \lnot p \lor r}{q \lor r} \qquad (5.18)$$

A little thought is usually needed to convince oneself that this is a perfectly correct rule of inference. However, it can be made to look a little more intuitive by considering an instance of a special case of the rule. We might translate the saying "there's no smoke without fire" as; ¬smoke ∨ fire ("no smoke, or fire"). If we see smoke, then we can conclude there is a fire:

$$\frac{smoke \qquad \lnot smoke \lor fire}{fire} \qquad (5.19)$$

Rule (5.18) is just the general case of this style of inference.

One would not always wish to just "forward chain" through applications of this rule to see what inferences one could make from a database. In the case of logic programming, it is usual to take a more goal directed approach to theorem proving. That is, try and prove on demand that a specified proposition is in fact a consequence of a database. A proof strategy learnt at school is to assume the contrary of what one wants to prove, and see if this leads to a contradiction. Exactly the same technique is employed in automated theorem proving using resolution.

Suppose we specifically want to see if fire is a consequence of {smoke, ¬smoke ∨ fire}. First we add ¬fire to the database to get {smoke, ¬smoke ∨ fire, ¬fire}. After two applications of resolution we obtain the empty proposition □, which corresponds to a contradiction[2]. That is, assuming ¬fire leads to a contradiction, so fire must be true. Figure 5.5 shows the proof tree, where the clause at each vertex is the result of the resolution of the two parent clauses.

Clearly, that is not all there is to automated theorem proving, but it will suffice for this discussion. Further depth may be found in almost any Prolog text book (e.g. Sterling and Shapiro, 1986), and at a more theoretical level in (Chang and Lee, 1973).

---

2. Since the final two propositions to be resolved must be precise contraries for this to occur.

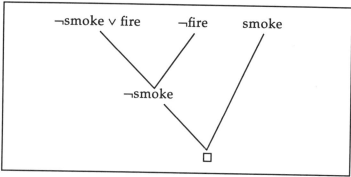

Fig 5.5   *A refutation proof of "fire".*

5.4.2   Truth functionality and uncertainty.

Now, classical logic is "two valued"; a proposition is either true or it is false. However, in reasoning under uncertainty we wish to be able to grade the certainty, or confidence, in the truth of a conclusion. The question is, given a database of uncertain facts, can we develop theorem proving techniques which will return a measure of certainty for the consequences of that database? Here we have a fundamental difficulty.

In Chapters 2 and 3 we mentioned the problem of modularity in connection with the assignment of certainty coefficients to propositions in rule-based systems. In general it is not possible to assign coherently a certainty coefficient to a proposition independently of how it was proven and what else is in the database. We will express this slightly differently here:

- Logics of uncertainty (with precise propositions) are not truth-functional.

We cannot stress this too highly.

What do we mean by truth functionality? Basically, the truth of a complex proposition is a simple function of its constituent propositions. For example: $p \wedge q$ is *true* if p is true *and* q is true; $p \vee q$ is *false* if p is false *and* q is false. We cannot, however, allow grades of truth from the interval [0,1] *and* have truth functionality. See (Dubois and Prade, 1988b) for a proof of this, or refer back to Section 2.2.2 for an informal justification.

This makes things difficult when it comes to trying to develop automatic theorem proving techniques for the case when the propositions in a database are uncertain. The certainty of a conclusion will not in general be a simple function of the certainty of the intermediate steps in its proof.

From the point of view of truth functionality, possibility and necessity measures do seem to have some appeal as qualifiers for logics of uncertainty. For example, although the necessity of a conjunction *is* a function of the necessities of each of its conjuncts ($N(A \cap B) = \min(N(A), N(B))$), the necessities of two disjuncts only provide a constraint on the necessity of a disjunction; in general, $N(A \cup B) \geq \min(N(A), N(B))$.

5.4.3   Possibilistic resolution.

In 1983 Henri Prade proposed using possibility theory as a basis for a logic of uncertainty (Prade, 1983). In the following, we will be considering precise propositions, and not vague or imprecise data. The basic axioms p_i in a database will be assigned subjective measures of possibility $\Pi(p_i)$ or necessity $N(p_i)$. These will satisfy the properties of possibility and necessity measures of the preceding sections.

Some properties are worth emphasising in the context of possibilistic logic. For example, although we have $\forall p. \forall q. \Pi(p \vee q) = \max(\Pi(p), \Pi(q))$, we only have $\forall p. \forall q. \Pi(p \wedge q) \leq \min(\Pi(p), \Pi(q))$. Consider, for example, a state of partial ignorance in which both a proposition and its negation are considered somewhat possible; $\Pi(p) > 0$ and $\Pi(\neg p) > 0$. Despite the fact that $\min(\Pi(p), \Pi(\neg p)) > 0$, we must have $\Pi(p \vee \neg p) = 0$; the possibility of the contradiction must be zero. Similarly, we require that the necessity of the always true proposition, T, be unity. That is $N(p \vee \neg p) = 1$, even though we may have $N(p) < 1$ and $N(\neg p) < 1$. So, in general, $\forall p. \forall q. N(p \vee q) \geq \max(N(p), N(q))$, although we do have $\forall p. \forall q. N(p \wedge q) = \min(N(p), N(q))$.

Here, we will only consider the case where axioms in the database are labelled with necessity measures. These labels represent lower bounds of the certainty of their associated proposition. That is, $(p, (N\ \alpha))$ should be read as "p is certain at least to degree α; $N(p) \geq \alpha$. The resolution rule, equation (5.18), may then be extended for uncertain clauses to (Dubois and Prade, 1987);

$$\frac{\begin{array}{ll} p \vee q & (N\ \alpha) \\ \neg p \vee r & (N\ \beta) \end{array}}{\begin{array}{ll} q \vee r & (N \min(\alpha, \beta)) \end{array}} \qquad (5.20)$$

In words; if α is a lower bound of the necessity of $p \vee q$, and β is a lower bound of the necessity of $\neg p \vee r$, then $\min(\alpha, \beta)$ is a lower bound of the necessity of the resolvent $q \vee r$.

In any proof, the *parent clauses* are the basic axioms used as foundation of the proof (the axioms smoke, ¬smoke ∨ fire, ¬fire in the example of Figure 5.5). We have the following theorem (Dubois, Lang and Prade, 1987):

Theorem 5.2

The degree of certainty (as necessity) in any consequence obtained by repeated applications of the resolution rule (5.20) will be at least equal to that of the least certain parent clause.

Note what is happening here. We are not so much interested in establishing absolute quantitative values of certainty. We are establishing a more qualitative *ordinal* relationship; a consequence is no less certain than the least certain of its parent clauses.

5.4.4   Refutation proofs.

In goal directed theorem proving, we added the negation of the proposition we wanted to prove to the database, and then tried to prove a contradiction. In a similar way, with uncertain reasoning we may add the negation of the proposition to be proven to the database, with necessity equal to 1; assume the proposition is certainly false and try and prove the contradiction. In this case, the following theorem holds (Dubois, Lang and Prade, 1987):

Theorem 5.3

The necessity measure obtained for the empty clause (contradiction), using the above refutation procedure, corresponds to *a* lower bound of the necessity of the proposition to be proven.

We have emphasised that this is *a* lower bound. It may not be the most informative lower bound since it may be possible to generate a proof which is based on different, more certain, axioms. What is now required is a search strategy which ensures that each step in a refutation proof is chosen so that the necessity measure obtained for the empty clause is the greatest possible lower bound for the proposition to be proven. A search strategy which is optimal in this sense is presented in (Dubois, Lang and Prade, 1987). This search strategy has essentially the same computational complexity as the search strategy used in Prolog, so it is efficient.

As a result of the use of possibilistic resolution together with the optimal search strategy we have the following basic properties of possibilistic logic:

i)   the degree of certainty associated with a proof of a proposition is the least degree attached to a proposition in the proof tree;

ii) the degree of certainty associated with a consequence of a possibilistic knowledge base is the greatest degree associated with the proofs yielding the consequence.

This degree of certainty is still a lower bound, but it is the most informative lower bound. However, it is the case that no matter how many different ways a proposition can be proven, the certainty associated with that proposition will not increase above that of the "strongest" proof. That is, in possibilistic logic there is not the notion of reinforcement of arguments that is present in probabilistic reasoning and in the use of Dempster's rule of combination (see also Chapter 7).

5.4.5   Some final notes on possibilistic logic.

Possibilistic logic has been developed into a very sophisticated tool for deductive uncertain reasoning. Only the very basics have been covered here. A more complete description of its current state of development can be found in (Dubois, Lang and Prade, 1993). A current concern with the development of large knowledge bases, which we will return to in Chapter 7, is the difficulty of ensuring consistency over the entire database. One interesting aspect of possibilistic logic is its ability to cope with partial inconsistency (Dubois, Lang and Prade, 1992).

One or two further points are worth making. In Chapter 6 we will emphasise that a formal logic should have an associated semantics; a formal framework for defining possible interpretations of that logic. We have discussed possibility and necessity measures mainly in connection with vague data and fuzzy sets. Then we said possibilistic logic involved *precise* propositions. There is still an underlying connection with fuzzy set theory, however, as possibilistic logic can be given a semantics in terms of fuzzy sets of interpretations (Lang, 1991; Dubois, Lang and Prade, 1993).

It has been claimed that certainty values as necessity measures may be easier to elicit than probabilities, as they express a simple ordinal preference, or priority relationship, rather than an assessment of chance. Dubois and Prade (1988b) contains some discussion of the elicitation of necessity values, as well as their interpretation. Somewhat deeper studies of the relationship between possibilistic logic and more philosophical interpretations of epistemic states can be found in (Dubois and Prade, 1991b; Dubois and Prade, 1992).

5.5   Discussion

We have focused on representing and reasoning with imprecise or vague data in this chapter. This has given us some further insight into the Dempster-Shafer theory of evidence and provided a vehicle for introducing fuzzy sets and possibility theory. The discussion section of Chapter 4 focused on the Dempster-Shafer theory, so we will largely confine this section to fuzzy sets and possibility theory.

Fuzzy sets have not received a great breadth of coverage here. What we have aimed to do is to provide a simplified account of the foundational issues, rather than reiterate material on fuzzy logic and approximate reasoning which already has received wide coverage. A short account of the more technical aspects of fuzzy reasoning can be found in (de Mántaras, 1990). We have often referred to (Dubois and Prade, 1988a); this provides a very good coverage of many aspects of possibility theory and fuzzy reasoning. Our presentation has been particularly influenced by (Kruse et al, 1991), to which the reader is referred for a rigorous account dealing with continuous distributions of variables. The last book covers a great deal of ground which we have not had space to introduce. In particular, their treatment of information and refinement mappings is extended to cover product spaces, which allows a much richer formalism for knowledge representation.

A comprehensive selection of Zadeh's papers can be found in (Yager et al, 1987), which actually provides as good an introduction to fuzzy set theory as any. More recent developments are surveyed in (Zadeh and Kacprzyk, 1992).

Fuzzy techniques have been employed in a number of application domains (Bezdek, 1976; Ishizuka et al, 1981; Mamdani and Gaines, 1981; Mamdani, 1983), but the number of applications is not widespread in the West. There still seems to be a widespread suspicion that fuzzy approaches do not improve upon probability theory (Bonissone, 1987). However, Japanese industry seems to have taken fuzzy logic to its heart; fuzzy controllers are frequently found in electronic consumer goods which have been made in Japan.

The differences between probability theory and possibility theory have been extensively discussed by Zadeh (1986a). He argues that probability theory lacks expressiveness as a language of uncertainty for propositions such as "it is *very likely* that Mary is *young*." where *likely* is a fuzzy probability and *young* is a fuzzy predicate. Zadeh argues that there is no satisfactory manner in which to represent this proposition in probability theory so as to be able to determine the likelihood that Mary is *not very young*.

The view we have presented here is that there *is* an underlying probabilistic semantics for the Dempster-Shafer, and possibility theories. This is, however, augmented by a set theoretic structure which allows for a natural representation of imprecision and vagueness.

5.5.1   Knowledge representation.

Possibility theory and fuzzy logic provide the principal formal systems explicitly devoted to the representation and manipulation of incomplete knowledge manifested as vagueness. With respect to the uncertainty classification of Figure 1.2, this chapter has shown how a numerical calculus may be augmented to deal with both unary aspects of ignorance. There is an underlying numerical calculus which represents partial knowledge (confidence, propensity), upon which is superimposed a set theoretic component to represent indeterminate knowledge (vagueness). Information expressed in terms of fuzzy sets also allows some representation of ambiguity; there may be some overlap between the membership functions of different concepts.

As noted in Chapter 2, it has been argued that fuzziness can be represented as normalised probability density functions (Cheeseman, 1986; Lindley, 1987). However, since this requires a much greater amount of information, it will not always be practical. Furthermore it is not clear that a probability density function is always the most natural way in which to express a term denoting extent on a continuous variable.

We mentioned in the discussion section of Chapter 4 that the Dempster-Shafer theory allows some accommodation of partial degrees of inconsistency. The same remarks apply here. It should also be mentioned that this is an important distinction between the conditioning and belief revision operations discussed in Sections 5.2.3 and 5.3.5. In the case of conditioning, data is only considered which is in agreement with the sure information. In the case of belief revision, all the data which is consistent with the sure information is considered. In the latter, there may be a partial degree of inconsistency between the sure information and the data which is revised.

Slightly different considerations apply to possibilistic logic. Here the motivation was to build an efficiently implementable logic programming language in which propositions were augmented with meaningful and informative subjective confidence bounds. These bounds can be interpreted in terms of a notion of epistemic entrenchment (Gärdenfors, 1988), which is essentially an ordinal relationship reflecting commitment to propositions. Possibilistic logic does not really handle vagueness or imprecision, but it does allow the representation of degrees of partial inconsistency (Benferhat et al, 1993a; 1993b).

5.5.2   Knowledge engineering.

Just as there are difficulties in determining the relevant prior and conditional probabilities for a Bayesian analysis, so the production of membership functions is no simple matter. Empirical derivation of correct membership functions is clearly more difficult than elicitation of single probabilities since more information is required. On the other hand since the coherence constraints on membership functions are weaker than those on probability values, more imprecision can be accommodated.

Elicitation of membership functions have been based on two empirical techniques. The first approach, epitomized by Wallsten et al (1986a), employs direct psychological scaling techniques which build up the membership function over a number of trials. The second is an indirect scaling technique which is easier to administer but which makes the strong assumptions that the resulting membership functions are trapezoidal (as in Figures 5.4 and 5.6).

As an example of a direct scaling technique, Wallsten et al (1986a) displayed two radially divided spinners with segments of opposing colours, denoting different probabilities, on a computer monitor. On each trial one of ten verbal uncertainty expressions was printed above the spinners. The subjects' task was to indicate which spinner probability was best represented by the expression by moving an arrow along a calibrated line, such that the degree of displacement represented the relative appropriateness of the two spinners. Probabilities on the two spinners were varied factorially for each expression and subject, within a previously elicited individual range. This range was intended to represent the maximum and minimum probability points of applicability for each expression. Responses (arrow positions) were analysed using conjoint-measurement theory, and values obtained for each term according to various scaling models. These values were normalized to be non-negative with an arbitrary maximum of 1 and plotted against probability values to produce membership functions for the verbal uncertainty expressions.

Interestingly, their results showed that 33% of the membership functions obtained were multi-peaked. The remaining 67% were either point (4%), flat (2%), monotonic (30%), or single peaked (31%). There was no expression for which all subjects' membership functions had the same shape. Expressions nearer the extremes of the probability scale tended to be monotonic rather than single peaked. Fuzzy membership functions are generally not characterised as having multi-peaked distributions. Such distributions imply either ambiguity in the meaning of an expression, measurement error, or inappropriateness of the variable over which the function is measured. Wallsten et al attributed the multiple peaked nature of some of these functions to measurement error, and it is arguable that the number of multi-peaked distributions would decrease if the sample size of responses from which membership functions are derived were to increase.

As an example of an indirect scaling technique, Zimmer (1986) had subjects first generate a scale of verbal uncertainty expressions in an unspecified task. Next, idealised, noiseless, trapezoidal possibility functions were determined using a modified Robbins-Monro procedure with a matrix of

Index	Verbal Uncertainty Expression	Meaning			
		B	C	B-A	D-C
1	impossible	0	0	0	0
2	extremely unlikely	0.01	0.02	0.01	0.05
3	very low chance	0.1	0.18	0.06	0.05
4	small chance	0.22	0.36	0.05	0.06
5	it may	0.41	0.58	0.09	0.07
6	meaningful chance	0.63	0.80	0.05	0.06
7	most likely	0.78	0.92	0.06	0.05
8	extremely likely	0.98	0.99	0.05	0.01
9	certain	1	1	0	0

Table 5.1   *The Nine Element Term Set L-nine (Bonissone et al, 1987). The first two parameters indicate the lower and upper bounds of necessity in which the membership function is 1, the third and fourth parameters indicate the left and right width of the distribution in which membership is greater than 0 (see Figure 5.6).*

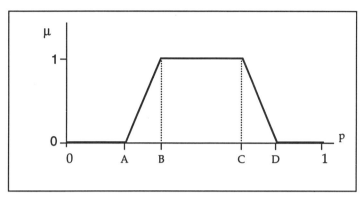

Fig 5.6   *An instance of the parameters A, B, C, D used in Table 5.1.*

two colours of dots, whose proportions varied between 5% and 95% (Zimmer, 1986, p252). The mean number of expressions produced was 5.44.

Using the same model assumption, the RUM system (Bonissone et al, 1987) communicates uncertainty to the user using sets of linguistic uncertainty terms defined as trapezoidal (highly regular) fuzzy membership functions on the unit probability interval. One such set (based on the results of Beyth-Marom, 1982), with the associated parameters, is shown in Table 5.1 (see Figure 5.6 for an illustration of the parameters A, B, C and D).

The bottom line with respect to elicitation, therefore, is that it is either highly laborious, as with the direct technique requiring many trials, or it is assumption ridden. A hybrid technique, in which the fuzzy variables are first piloted using direct scaling, can be used to remove variables with multi-peaked distributions, before using the administratively simpler indirect scaling technique to determine the final functions. It should be emphasised, however, that there will be an error associated with each of the four individual points. This cannot be easily eliminated using the formal coherence properties of the calculus, as is the case for the Bayesian model. For example, we may find that the membership functions for "X is Tall" and "X is Short" overlap.

5.5.3   Computational considerations.

See Section 4.6.3 for a discussion of the computational issues involved with belief functions.

With respect to fuzzy sets and possibility theory, since many of the combination functions involve either min or max operations they are computationally less demanding than Bayesian propagation. Rule based systems which use fuzzy sets for approximate reasoning can be implemented with an order of complexity no higher than the conventional case (Dubois and Prade, 1988b). The processing time for each rule is higher than for the classical case, of course, but this merely provides a constant scaling factor.

Indeed, computation is not a serious problem with possibilistic/fuzzy approaches. In the inference engine SPII-2 (Martin-Clouaire and Prade, 1986), possibility distributions are used to represent imprecision, and uncertainty is represented with a pair of possibility and necessity measures. This system has been tested using a number of realistic sized appraisal problems in petroleum geology (Lebailly et al, 1987).

As a final remark, we would just refer the reader back to Section 5.4 for a demonstration of the computational advantages of possibilistic logic as a logic for uncertain reasoning.

5.6   Conclusions

Fuzzy sets and possibility theory provide a basis for a form of approximate/semi-qualitative reasoning. This makes for a fairly weak form of reasoning, in the sense that the use of max and min operators does not allow any reinforcement of evidences. However, it does also have a side effect of a limited computational overhead, and this is perhaps a significant reason for the interest in this approach from application builders.

Fuzzy logic is currently employed in many technological applications, including, perhaps paradoxically, imaging systems (though note the resulting images are not necessarily fuzzy!). Furthermore there are many Expert System type applications (see Leung et al, 1989) which use fuzzy sets and possibility theory. The theoretical developments of the last two decades have provided these approaches with a well defined and understood semantics, and have helped to ensure that these techniques do now have an established place in the domain of reasoning under uncertainty.

6
Non-monotonic Logic

Life is the art of drawing sufficient conclusions from insufficient premises.
(Samuel Butler).

6.1 Introduction

Since the time of Aristotle, logic has developed as a formalism for modelling the correct construction of arguments which demonstrate that a conclusion *necessarily* follows from a set of premises. It was perhaps in keeping with the Greek obsession with absolutes that there was to be no uncertainty or doubt associated with these arguments. The arguments were used to establish facts; they were deductive proofs. Indeed Aristotle held that deductive proof was the sole basis for establishing facts in mathematics.

In these beginnings, logic was derived from mathematics. The original motivation was to abstract correct forms of mathematical reasoning. However, as time went by, logic came to be considered to be independent of and prior to mathematics and applicable to all reasoning. In this century in particular, many of the developments of modern mathematical logic have been driven by the need to provide a formal foundation for mathematics and for computer science. But in addition, endeavours to model reasoning under uncertainty or reasoning in the absence of complete information have led to a number of extensions of classical logic. These are the subject of this chapter.

By way of introduction, we ought to explain what is meant by the words in the title. We can take the standard Oxford Dictionary definition of logic as "the science of reasoning, proof, thinking or inference". The deductions of non-monotonic logics, however, are not of the nature of categoric proofs. They are *contingent* proofs whose conclusions may become invalidated in the light of further information or in a different context. Non-monotonic logics are, nevertheless, attempts at providing well defined models of reasoning or inference. It is in this sense that they are "logics".

Non-monotonic logics can be viewed as ways of augmenting the conclusions which can be drawn from classical logic in a given context. For example, Aristotle is often attributed the statement that all men are mortal. We may express this fact as a sentence in first order logic: $\forall x.\ man(x) \supset mortal(x)$[1]. If we know that Aristotle is a man, then we are entitled to conclude that Aristotle is mortal. Nothing can make us retract this conclusion. If we are given more information about Aristotle, we may be enabled to conclude more facts about him. But nothing we subsequently learn will change our opinion about his mortality if we reason solely using classical logic. However, there are many occasions when we may "jump" to a conclusion which may not be valid in a different context. For example, it is normally the case that cells in an organism are growth limited in some way. It will usually be quite safe to assume that some cell under study will be growth limited. However, if it is discovered that the cell is a tumour cell, then this conclusion must be retracted in favour of the conclusion that the cell is *not* growth limited. Although we cannot assert that the sentence "$\forall x.cell(x) \supset growth\_limited(x)$" is valid, there are circumstances under which, given cell(obj), we would wish to conclude (provisionally) growth_-limited(obj).

The tumour cell case is an example of non-monotonic reasoning. Classical logic is *monotonic*. As information is added to a given context, the number of theorems which are provable from that context will always increase. All the theorems which were provable before the information was added will still remain provable afterwards. Some additional theorems may be provable too. However, in non-monotonic logics the addition of information to a context may result in some theorems which were derivable before the update no longer being derivable after the context is updated. The number of theorems "provable" from a given context may decrease as information is added to that context.

This chapter will focus primarily on the development of default logic as a form of non-monotonic reasoning. Many other formalisms have been proposed. Each has their merits, and the relationship of many of them with default logic will be discussed. However, this discussion will presuppose a reasonable familiarity with some of the basic concepts of formal logic and so we will start with a brief overview of traditional logic.

---

1. The symbol '$\supset$' may be read as 'implies'.

6.2   A brief overview of formal logic

Some of the statements we wish to make about non-monotonic logics will only make sense if the reader has a reasonable familiarity with the basics of formal logic. In addition, we would like to use a number of words which have a precise technical meaning. Consequently, to make this book as self contained as possible, this section will provide an overview of formal logic. It should be viewed as an extended glossary. Those with little experience of formal logic should read it carefully a couple of times, and will find it helpful to refer back to it frequently whilst reading the remainder of this chapter[2]. We would recommend that even those with some familiarity with logic should read this section quickly as it summarises the context for the subsequent discussion.

Formal logic involves the manipulation of symbols. So we would expect a logic to have a *syntax*; a *language* and a method for constructing *sentences* from the primitives of that language. We would also expect the sentences of a logic to have meaningful interpretations. For example, we may interpret the sentence 'p ∨ ¬p' in classical logic as 'it is raining or it is not raining', or 'she has measles or she does not have measles'. We would agree that each of these last two statements is true. Indeed, we may intuitively feel that 'p ∨ ¬p' would be true whatever 'p' represents; that is, 'p ∨ ¬p' is a *tautology*, it is true in all possible interpretations, in all possible worlds.

Similarly, consider the set of premises S ={p, p ⊃ q}. We may interpret these as I_1={'it is raining', 'if it is raining then the grass will be wet'}, or perhaps I_2={'she has a positive ultra-sound scan', 'if she has a positive ultra-sound scan then she must be pregnant'}. In the first case, we would feel that if each premise in I_1 were true, then 'the grass would be wet' would also be true; in the second case that 'she must be pregnant' would be true whenever the statements in I_2 were true. That is, S *entails* q in all possible interpretations; q *necessarily* follows from S. We may write in this case, S ⊨ q (or, {p, p ⊃ q} ⊨ q) as shorthand for S *semantically entails* q.

The *sequent* S ⊨ q is *valid* if in all interpretations in which S is true, q is also true.

Note that tautologihood and validity are a matter of *semantics*; a matter of the interpretation we give to the sentences of the logic. It should also be

2. As further reading, clear introductions to formal logic can be found in (Johnstone, 1987) and (Mendelson, 1964).

noted that we may wish to construct alternative semantics to that discussed above. For example, we may wish to reject the law of the excluded middle (p ∨ ¬p) and construct a logic (intuitionistic logic) in which this was not a tautology. There are a variety of ways in which a logic may be given a semantics. The approach which is most familiar is to define the meaning of logical propositions in terms of truth tables. This is acceptable for the propositional calculus, but a more powerful approach is required for logics which allow variables and quantifiers of those variables in the language. One such is *model theory*. We will refer to this from time to time, but not in any technical detail. The point is that it is a method of defining in a precise way what is meant by an interpretation of a set of sentences in a logic. Model theory is used to specify the meaning, the semantics, of a logic.

However, the main interest from a computational perspective is that a formal logic can be viewed as a purely syntactic entity. If we can define legal methods of reasoning by performing purely syntactic manipulations on sentences in the logical language, then there is some hope of being able to automate the process; to build machines which can reason. So the question is; is there a purely syntactic method of characterising those sentences which turn out to be tautologies, those sequents which turn out to be valid? The answer turns out not to be that straightforward. However, since we will be focusing on syntactic treatments of logics in this chapter, we will enlarge on the syntactic treatment of logic before discussing the answer to this question in Section 6.2.4. We will use propositional logic by way of example.

6.2.1   The syntax of logics.

As we have seen already, there are a variety of symbols associated with a logic. Some, such as ∨, ∧, ¬, ⊃ are elements *within* the language of the formal logic. Some are used for making statements *about* the logic. We have come across one of the latter, ⊨, already. We will meet another shortly. However, we will continue discussion at the object level for the present.

Connectives such as ∨ (and), ∧ (or), ¬ (not) and ⊃ (material implication) are elements of the *alphabet* of the logic. Specific logics may contain additional, or perhaps fewer, connectives. The alphabet will contain further sets of symbols. For example, in propositional logic there will be a (countable) set of proposition symbols (P_0, P_1, P_2, ...). Predicate logic has a more extensive alphabet which includes a set of quantifiers (∀, ∃) and a set of variable names. Some formal constraints on the way in which elements of the alphabet may be combined to form *well-formed formulae* (wff) of the logic should then be stated. The set of all such formulae constitutes the *language* of the logic.

The logic will also have an inference rule (possibly more than one). In the case of propositional logic this is 'modus ponens': from p and p ⊃ q deduce q.

The final component of the logic is a set of axioms (a designated subset of the well-formed formulae). In the case of propositional logic, for example, we may have:

1) $p \supset (q \supset p)$
2) $(p \supset (q \supset r)) \supset ((p \supset q) \supset (p \supset r))$
3) $(\neg\neg p) \supset p$

together with all substitution instances of these axioms. For example, substitute r ⊃ s for p and t for q in 1) to give:

$$(r \supset s) \supset (t \supset (r \supset s))$$

This is also (implicitly) an axiom.

Strictly, the alphabet, language, set of axioms and the inference rules form a *(meta-level) theory*. However, we will usually use the term *theory* at the object level to denote a set of contingent formulae.

6.2.2   Syntactic entailment.

We will continue with the example of propositional logic. From a given set of propositions, we may use the axioms and the rules of inference to construct proofs of certain other propositions. For example, from the set {p, p ⊃ q, q ⊃ r} we have the following proof of r:

1) p   (given)
2) p ⊃ q   (given)
3) q ⊃ r   (given)
4) q   (1 & 2 modus ponens)
5) r   (3 & 4 modus ponens)

These are purely *syntactic* manipulations of wff in the language of the logic.

Having deduced a formula by a sequence of syntactic manipulations, we may want to step back a level from a logic L and express succinctly that a proposition (r) is deducible from a set of propositions S (S = {p, p ⊃ q, q ⊃ r} in the example) in the logic L. This introduces the notion of *syntactic entailment* and may be expressed thus:

$$S \vdash_L r$$

This can be read as; 'r follows from S in the logic L'. Since it will usually be unambiguous which logic we will be talking about, we will drop the subscript L. The turnstile, ⊢, is not an element of the alphabet of the logic itself. It is a *meta-symbol*. In the case of a tautology t, requiring only the axioms and inference rules to generate its proof, we write:

$$\vdash t$$

These are both statements *about* the logic.

The notion of syntactic entailment may be defined rigorously. The following recursive definition is often used:

A set S of propositions syntactically entails t, written S ⊢ t, if:

1) t is an axiom.
2) t ∈ S.
3) if S ⊢ s for some s, and S ⊢ (s ⊃ t), then S ⊢ t.

For example, consider once more the set S = {p, p ⊃ q, q ⊃ r}. We may write S ⊢ r. It is easy to show that this follows from our definition of syntactic entailment:

From 2), p ∈ S and (p ⊃ q) ∈ S so S ⊢ p and S ⊢ (p ⊃ q).

Consequently from 3) S ⊢ q.

Using 2) again, S ⊢ (q ⊃ r) since (q ⊃ r) ∈ S.

Thus we have S ⊢ q and S ⊢ (q ⊃ r), so using 3) again, we have S ⊢ r.

6.2.3   Axiomatisation of formal logics.

We can use the meta-symbol ⊢ to make general statements about the logic under consideration. For example, the monotonicity property of propositional logic may be expressed thus:

$$\text{if } S \vdash q$$
$$\text{then } S \cup \{p\} \vdash q \text{ for any p.}$$

This simply says that if q follows from a set of formulae S in a logic, then we can add any other well-formed formula p to the set S, and q will *still* follow. This is a known property of classical logics. But we may use statements of this kind as *axioms* for a new kind of logic. That is, we may say what sort of *properties* the consequence relation should have, without necessarily exhibiting a logic which satisfies those properties. Indeed there may be several logics which satisfy a given set of axioms.

An exactly analogous situation arose in geometry in the nineteenth century. There is a well-known axiomatisation of geometry due to Euclid. One of these axioms was always thought to follow obviously from the others; yet no one could produce a proof that this was so. This was the "parallel postulate"; given a straight line and a point not on that line, there is a unique line passing through that point parallel to the given line. All attempts at showing this axiom followed from the others failed. An alternative approach which was then taken was to assume the axiom was false and then attempt to draw a contradiction. If this assumption was contradictory, then the axiom must in fact be true. Rather surprisingly, the parallel postulate could be replaced by either of two alternatives and still generate geometries which satisfied the axioms and were internally consistent. As well as being of interest in themselves, these geometries turned out to be of vital importance in the development of general relativity.

The different axiomatisations were a clear and succinct way of characterising different geometries. In a similar way, different axiomatisations provide a succinct way of characterising different logics. We present first a minimal and, what seems to be, a natural set of axioms which the consequence relation of a logic should 'classically satisfy' (S and S' are sets of formulae, a and p are formulae):

Reflexivity: $S \vdash p$ if $p \in S$

Monotonicity: $$\frac{S \vdash p}{S \cup S' \vdash p}$$

Transitivity: $$\frac{S \vdash a \qquad S' \cup \{a\} \vdash p}{S \cup S' \vdash p}$$

The second and third axioms should be read: "given the entailment relation(s) above the line hold, then the entailment relation below the line must also hold".

The last rule is sometimes known as 'cut'. It can be thought of as an example of lemma generation; 'a' is a result which is proven as a preliminary to proving 'p'. These axioms seem to be natural for a logic whose main application is mathematics (Gabbay, 1990). They are certainly satisfied by propositional and by predicate logics. However, as we have discussed, the second axiom is not satisfied by default logics. Indeed, it is quite obviously not satisfied by any of the non-monotonic logics; this is what gives them their name.

It is, in fact, quite difficult to suggest a set of axioms which a non-monotonic logic should satisfy. We would certainly expect them to agree on reflexivity. Gabbay (1985) proposed a notion of *restricted monotonicity* to replace the second axiom. It is not, however, the case that all the interesting non-monotonic logics satisfy this axiom. Nevertheless it does provide a useful reference point by which different logics may be characterised. In addition, those which do satisfy it have useful computational properties.

Restricted Monotonicity: $$\dfrac{S \vdash p \qquad S \vdash q}{S \cup \{p\} \vdash q}$$

This may be read: "if p follows from a set S and q follows from S, then if we add the formula p to S, q will still follow".

6.2.4   On the relationship between syntax and semantics.

At the beginning of this section we asked the question "is there a purely syntactic method of characterising those sentences which turn out to be tautologies, those sequents which turn out to be valid?" We now return to this question.

A logic is defined by its semantics. Statements made about the syntactic presentation of the logic must be referable back to the semantics of the logic. In particular, any inference which is carried out by purely syntactic manipulations of formulae in the logic must be correct with respect to the semantics; *soundness*. In addition, we would expect to be able to generate proofs by syntactic manipulations of *all* formulae which are valid according to the semantics; *completeness*.

Thus we ideally require of any logical system the following two properties:

Soundness: If $S \vdash p$ then $S \models p$.

Completeness: If $S \models p$ then $S \vdash p$.

That is, the two entailment relations should coincide.

An important result due to Gödel (1931) showed that for propositional and predicate calculus there were proof procedures which could prove (syntax) every true (semantics) formula. That is, these logics were complete. Both logics are also sound.

Unfortunately, our interest in being able to check *automatically* whether a given formula is valid, or true, imposes a more stringent requirement. We would like a *decision procedure*, which is a method for identifying in a *finite* number of steps whether or not a given formula was valid. Herein lies a difficulty. In first order logic we can define a procedure which will terminate in a finite number of steps if a given formula is valid. However, a result due to Church (1936) showed that there can be no such procedure which can be guaranteed to terminate if the formula is *not* valid. That is, if presented with a false formula, such a procedure may run indefinitely. This property of first order logic is referred to by saying that it is *semi-decidable*. This is an important point as it has very serious repercussions for automatic theorem proving in non-monotonic logics.

6.2.5   Locality and non-monotonic logics.

We can now gradually return to the main topic of this chapter. However, before looking at more concrete examples of non-monotonic logics, we will mention one more general property. This is in one sense a strength, whilst in another a weakness of non-monotonic logics.

Let us revisit the monotonic property, but from a slightly different perspective. Suppose all that is currently known about Aristotle and men in general can be expressed by the set S of formulae, where S is the set:

{man(Aristotle), thirsty(Aristotle), $\forall$x.thirsty(x) $\wedge$ man(x) $\supset$ drinks(x),
$\forall$x. man(x) $\supset$ mortal (x), $\forall$x.man(x) $\wedge$ $\neg$rich(x) $\supset$ needs_to_work(x)}

Certainly S $\vdash$ mortal(Aristotle). In fact, we need only consider a small subset S' = {man(Aristotle), $\forall$x. man(x) $\supset$ mortal (x)} of S to generate a proof of mortal(Aristotle). This is a consequence of the *compactness* of classical logic. That is, S $\vdash$ p because for some finite subset $S_p \subseteq S$, $S_p \vdash p$. We do not need to worry about all the formulae in S which are not relevant to the derivation of p (and, as we have said, we can add formulae to S without affecting the derivability of p). We may refer to this as a *locality* property of classical logic (contrast the discussions on modularity in the context of uncertain reasoning in Chapters 2 and 3).

Non-monotonic logics, however, enable us to draw additional *contingent* conclusions over and above those of classical logic, *when it is consistent to do so*. Thus we may assert that a biomolecular cell is growth limited if that conclusion is consistent with all we currently know. If we can somehow contradict this tentative conclusion using any other information that is available to us, then we must retract this conclusion. That is, in the non-monotonic case *all* the information that is present, the entire set S of formulae, must be taken into account somehow to establish the relation S $\vdash$ p for *any* formula p.

The disadvantage of this is that the need to consider all the information in assessing whether a conclusion non-monotonically follows from a set of formulae means that there can be *no* general decision procedure for non-monotonic logics. They are not even semi-decidable. In general non-monotonic logics are undecidable! We will need to explain a little more about the technicalities of the logics to demonstrate why this is so.

6.3   Non-monotonic logics

6.3.1   Proofs as arguments?

We will now start to tie down the general discussions to a specific instance of a non-monotonic logic. We have chosen default logic (Reiter, 1980) as our primary example. Default logic is but one of a number of alternatives. However, most of the alternatives have a well-defined relationship to default logic. That is, it is not clear that they are ultimately any more expressive. Since default logic is perhaps the easiest to understand we will focus on that formalism, although there will be pointers to some of the other approaches.

Broadly speaking, there are two alternative approaches to extending the expressiveness of traditional logic. The first is to extend the language of the logic itself. The second way is not to augment the language, but to provide additional inference rules.

The first approach is that taken in modal logics (e.g. Hughes and Cresswell, 1984), for example, where the language is extended to include the operators $\Diamond$ ("it is possible that") and $\Box$ ("it is necessary that"). Several attempts have been made to develop non-monotonic logics along these lines. The non-monotonic logics of McDermott and Doyle (McDermott and Doyle, 1980; McDermott, 1982) used an operator 'M' which could be read as "it is consistent that". One could then write in the language of their logic (NML) a rule such as:

$\forall$x. Goblet_shaped_spring_flower(x) $\wedge$ M Crocus(x) $\supset$ Crocus(x)   *(r1)*

That is, if we see a small goblet shaped spring flower and it is consistent to assume that it is a crocus (we have no information otherwise) then infer that it is a crocus. Some difficulties arose with the way in which formulae of the form Mq could be derived in NML (e.g. Brewka, 1991a) and it has rather fallen from grace in favour of Autoepistemic Logic (AEL) as a modal non-monotonic logic.

Autoepistemic Logic (Moore, 1985) extends classical logic with the operator L, which should be read as "is believed that". The motivation behind the development of this logic is that it is intended to model the reasoning of an agent with perfect introspection. The intention is to formalise inferences of the following form:

"If I had a sister I would know I had a sister."

"I do not believe that I have a sister."

"Therefore I do not have a sister."

We can rewrite the rule (r1) as a statement in AEL:

Goblet_shaped_spring_flower(x) $\land$ $\neg$L$\neg$Crocus(x) $\supset$ Crocus(x)   *(r2)*

"If I have no reason to believe it is not a crocus, then I will infer that the spring flower is a crocus". We note in passing that there is a restriction on the use of quantification in AEL which prohibits the use of universal quantification in this rule. The rule (r2) should be read as a schema representing all possible ground instances of this rule.

At first glance there looks to be a fairly superficial difference between the two formalisms (the underlying philosophy is obviously quite different). However, the way in which statements of the form 'Lq' are inferred in AEL is quite different from the way in which formulae 'Mq' are derived in NML. We will not go into the details here, but just state without further justification that the formalisation of AEL is widely agreed to be far more satisfactory than that of NML. That is, it seems to capture many of the intuitions about the way in which non-monotonic logics should behave.

We will now look at an example of the second way of extending the inferences which may be drawn from a logic; the provision of additional inference rules. This is the approach taken in default logic. Default logic is an extension of classical logic in that it embodies full first order predicate calculus, but also allows additional rules of the form:

$[\alpha{:}\beta 1, ..., \beta_n/\gamma]$

α, β_1, ..., β_n and γ are well-formed formulae in predicate calculus. α is known as the *prerequisite* of the rule, β_1, ..., β_n its *justifications* and γ the *conclusion*. Such a rule should be read as "if α is true, and it is *consistent* to assume β_1, ...,β_n, then infer γ". Of course, a precise meaning must be given to consistency. This was originally done by showing how the conclusions of a theory in first order logic could be *extended* by the use of such default rules, (Reiter, 1980). It was not until the mid 1980's that some success was achieved in giving default logic a model theoretic semantics (Lukaszewicz, 1985; Etherington, 1987a). A complete statement of a semantics for default logic was not available until 1993 (Besnard and Schaub, 1993).

Returning to our earlier example, the appropriate default rule may be expressed:

[Goblet_shaped_spring_flower(x): Crocus(x)/ Crocus(x)]   (r3)

The reading is: "if x is a goblet shaped spring flower and it is consistent, given all that is currently known, to assume x is a crocus, then infer x is a crocus".

Suppose we also have a rule which states that if a goblet shaped spring flower has six stamens, then it is definitely a Colchicum[3]:

$$\forall x. \text{Goblet\_shaped\_spring\_flower}(x) \land \text{Six-stamens}(x) \supset \text{Colchicum}(x)$$

If we subsequently look more closely at the flower and see that it does indeed have six stamens, then this rule can be used to *rebut* the previously drawn conclusion. Assuming we know that a plant cannot be both a crocus and a colchicum at the same time, then the earlier conclusion that it was a crocus must be retracted; it is no longer consistent to assume it is a crocus and the default rule is no longer applicable. The important point is to define a coherent method for building extensions to a theory in a way which allows such non-monotonic behaviour.

Default rules enable one to jump to conclusions. One does not necessarily wish to seek confirmatory evidence before acting on the cues one is given. On a walk in a local park it is quite safe to say 'oh look at those crocuses' before examining each one closely; the chances are they will all be crocuses. But on visiting the garden of a friend who is an enthusiastic gardener, the following train of thoughts may occur:

"That's an interesting crocus, I've not seen one quite that shade before."

---

3. For those of you who are interested in such things, the often seen crocus is a member of the Iris family and has 3 stamens. Colchicums are often grown as autumn flowering bulbs. They are somewhat misleadingly referred to by some as Autumn Crocuses. They are in fact members of the Lily family (the significance of the 6 stamens), and there are also several spring flowering species in the genus Colchicum.

"It's a bit strange; I'll look a bit closer."

"Oh no, it's a colchicum! That explains it."

This is a very simple example. But it demonstrates a familiar model of commonsense reasoning. Some trigger (prerequisite) leads one to jump to a conclusion. The conclusion may be based on previous experience; in situations in the past where the prerequisite was known to be true, it was typically the case that the conclusion was also true. One may then base an action on this conclusion (in this case, merely express an utterance). This conclusion has, however, been drawn on incomplete information. (That is the useful thing - it enables one to act without the overhead of necessarily accumulating all the information which may have a bearing on the problem.) Perhaps the conclusion leads to the registering of a possible inconsistency ("I've not seen a crocus quite that colour before"). This may lead to further, more specific, information being sought. That information may itself trigger inferences which cause the original conclusion to be retracted.

The important point is that default inferences are not categoric inferences. Default rules may be used to construct *contingent* proofs; proofs whose conclusions may need to be retracted in the light of further information. For this reason it may be more helpful to view a default proof as an *argument* supporting the validity of a proposition, rather than a strict proof of the proposition:

> *a default represents an argument and the way to use that argument* (Besnard, 1989).

Arguments can be thought of as "proofs which can fail"; perhaps through the identification of further information which rebuts the claim (the conclusion of the argument), or through the identification of information which defeats the argument itself. So, we had an argument that a plant was a crocus. This was then rebutted by the claim that it was not a crocus, based on the more specific information that it had six stamens. As an example of defeat of an argument, suppose that on the assumption that he is not feeling tired, it is argued that because it is Sunday Mike will have gone fishing. The discovery that Mike was marking examination papers all night will *defeat* this argument; he was after all very tired and the assumption was not valid. That is, we may produce a further argument which contradicts a claim (which we call rebuttal here), or we may undermine the argument itself (which we refer to as defeating that argument). The interesting thing is that "the way to use arguments" defined in default logics can handle both defeat and rebuttal of arguments (Besnard, pers. comm.). We will discuss this further in Section 6.3.10 once we have given more technical detail to the use of arguments in default logic.

6.3.2   Examples of reasoning styles.

Before leading up to a formal presentation of how the conclusions of a logical theory may be extended by the use of default rules, we will give some further examples which demonstrate some of the reasoning styles which may be captured by default logic.

There has been much discussion as to the exact interpretation one should give to default rules. The archetypal default rule [Bird(x): Flies(x)/ Flies(x)], for example, is often paraphrased as "most birds fly". Besnard (1989) argues strongly against this interpretation. Essentially this is because 'most' has a well defined, if fuzzy, meaning. However, it may be that in a specific context all the birds an agent knows about may be unable to fly (he/she may be at the South Pole, for example). This would not be in contradiction with the default rule; it would simply mean that the default rule would not be applied. Rather than use a word "most" where its precise meaning may depend on context (all, some, or even none), it is more reasonable to view this rule as an example of prototypical reasoning; "birds typically fly, and in so far as it is possible to hold this belief of a bird, we will continue to do so".

The following examples were collected together in (Lukaszewicz, 1990). They each demonstrate how different forms of non-monotonic, commonsense reasoning may be expressed by defaults. However, we would suggest that for each example the default rule [α:β/γ] may be read as "if α is true, in so far as it is possible to hold the belief β, the conclusion γ is true".

Let us look at the examples:

1)   Typically children have two parents.
This is another example of prototypical reasoning. This can be represented by the default:

$$\frac{Child(x): Has\_two\_parents(x)}{Has\_two\_parents(x).}$$

To emphasise once more, this may be read as "for a particular child, so long as it is reasonable to hold the belief that she has two parents, then we will do so".

2)   An example of no-risk reasoning.
Assume that the accused is innocent unless it can be proved otherwise:

$$\frac{\text{Accused(x): Innocent(x)}}{\text{Innocent(x)}}$$

3) Best-guess reasoning.

Assume that the best solution found so far is the best one. This is very characteristic of the motivation behind default logic. We may not have sufficient information to prove a possible solution is the best. But if it is "the best" given our current understanding, then we may act on the assumption that it is the best possible solution (so long as it is consistent to do so):

$$\frac{\text{Best\_so\_far(x): Best\_solution(x)}}{\text{Best\_solution(x)}}$$

We might also add a rule Sherlock Holmes would approve of:

$$\frac{\text{Only\_remaining\_solution(x): Possible\_solution(x)}}{\text{The\_solution(x)}}$$

4) Explicit autoepistemic reasoning.

"We will try and hold progress meetings every Wednesday", (Doyle, 1979):

$$\frac{\text{:Meeting\_on\_Wednesday}}{\text{Meeting\_on\_Wednesday}}$$

5) Subjective autoepistemic reasoning.

We have mentioned this one before: in the absence of evidence to the contrary, assume you have no sister (Moore, 1985). If you had a sister, you would know it, so this rule would not apply:

$$\frac{\text{:}\neg\text{Have\_sister}}{\neg\text{Have\_sister.}}$$

Note that the last two of these rules are 'prerequisite free defaults'. Strictly speaking, they are shorthand for rules in which the prerequisite is 'True'; for example [True: ¬Have_sister/¬Have_sister]. Note also the way negation is being implemented by using this rule. This is not classical negation. However, it is a very often used alternative: if I do not know that something is true, then I will assume that it is false. This is particularly used as a communication convention.

6) Communication convention.

If a train is not timetabled to leave London for Exeter at 10.30am, then it is safe to assume that there will be no train at 10.30:

$$\frac{\neg\text{Timetabled\_at(x): }\neg\text{Departs\_at(x)}}{\neg\text{Departs\_at(x).}}$$

This form of negation may be familiar to many readers if they have used Prolog as a computer programming language. Prolog does not use classical negation. Rather, it uses negation as failure (to prove). That is, if the Prolog interpreter is unable to prove a proposition is a consequence of a program, then it will assume it is false. This has strong similarities to the use of negation in the previous two examples. However, we would emphasise that there are significant differences between the use of negation as failure (naf) in Prolog, and negation by default as expressed using default logic. We will discuss these differences further as we start to progress towards a formalisation of default logic in the next section.

6.3.3   Prolog's negation as failure and non-monotonicity.

Logic programming is a steadily emerging computational paradigm. Many readers will be familiar with Prolog; currently the most successful logic programming language. This language differs from programming in pure logic most notably in two ways. Firstly, Prolog's search strategy can, in certain circumstances, fail to find a solution to a query when there is in fact one. Secondly, Prolog does not use classical negation. The first difference is not of interest here (see, for example, (Deville, 1990) for further discussion of this problem). However, the second is, as Prolog's negation can lead to non-monotonic behaviour. We will use this to illustrate some properties, desirable and otherwise, of non-monotonicity. This discussion will then be used to identify the requirements which underlie the choice of formalisations of default logic.

Just in case the reader is unfamiliar with Prolog, we will give a very quick potted guide. This is mainly to explain the notation we shall use. A good rigorous introduction to Prolog can be found in (Sterling and Shapiro, 1986).

Warning: The notation of Prolog differs from the notation used in the rest of this chapter in that constants have an initial lower case letter, whilst variables have an initial upper case letter.

Loosely speaking, a Prolog program contains a set of facts and a set of rules. Facts are written as, for example:

```
parent(tony,paul).                    (c1)
parent(katherine,paul).               (c2)
```

This should be read "tony is a parent of paul", "katherine is a parent of paul"; 'parent' is the name of the relationship between the two arguments (tony and paul, or katherine and paul). Implications are expressed as clauses in Prolog:

```
father(X,Y):- parent(X,Y), male(X).     (c3)
```

"If X is male, and X is a parent of Y, then X is the father of Y".

Given the additional fact `male(tony)`, a Prolog interpreter would be able to conclude that `father(tony, paul)` was a logical consequence of the above program.

A further point is that if the Prolog interpreter is presented with a query containing uninstantiated variables, then it will return an instance of each of the variables for which the goal is satisfied. For example, we may just ask "who is the father of whom": `|?- father(X,Y).`

With the above program, the interpreter will respond with; X=tony, Y=paul.

We now come on to the treatment of negation in Prolog. Herein lies a difficulty. In general terms, a Prolog program consists of clauses of the form:

$$A:- B_1, ..., B_n.$$

The head of the clause, A, must consist of only one positive literal. The body of the clause (B_1, ..., B_n) may have zero or more positive or negative literals. Clause (c3) is an example of a clause with two literals in its body. Clauses (c1) and (c2) are examples with zero (sometimes referred to as facts as we have done). Now the question is, if we are not allowed to have negated literals at the head of a clause, how can we derive negative information from a Prolog program?

Given the above program, if a Prolog interpreter is presented with the query `|?- father(tony, david).` it will return the answer no. This does not mean that "not `father(tony, david)`" is a logical consequence of the above program. Merely that it has failed to prove that it is. The important distinction is this. If the fact `parent(tony, david)` is now added to the above program, `father(tony, david)` will be provable. The provisional answer not `father(tony, david)` will have to be retracted. That is, Prolog's use of negation as failure to prove, rather than provably false, is non-monotonic.

From the pure logician's point of view, this non-monotonicity of Prolog's negation is a peculiarity. It means that Prolog's negation should be used with extreme caution. However, many practising programmers find Prolog's negation very useful, and very expressive. Indeed "ironically, non-monotonic reasoning has now become fashionable, and one even reads papers suggesting that Prolog is not a proper implementation of it", (Dodd, 1990). Just so!

We will now look at a few simple examples. Suppose we wish to build a simple medical advisor. Aspirin is an effective pain killer for simple aches and sprains. Of course, some people are allergic to the active ingredient, and it should not be used in those cases:

```
prescribe(Person, Drug):-                      (c4)
    suffers_from(Person, Condition),
    relieves(Condition, Drug),
    not allergic_to(Person, Drug).

relieves(muscle_sprain, aspirin).              (c5)
```

Suppose Paul is suffering from muscle sprain:

```
suffers_from(paul, muscle_sprain).             (c6)
```

Now the above program, clauses (c4) to (c6), contains no information about Paul's allergies, so if we ask it what to prescribe,

```
|?- prescribe(paul, Drug).
```

it will respond with `Drug = aspirin`. It has failed to prove `allergic_to(paul, aspirin)`, and so the negated goal succeeds for this instantiation. If we now add the information

```
allergic_to(paul, aspirin).                    (c7)
```

`prescribe(paul, aspirin)` will no longer be a consequence of this program. (But hopefully there will be some other treatment which is suitable!)

In a sense this program is making the default assumption that people are not allergic to treatments unless it has specific information otherwise. Whether this is a safe assumption to make is open to debate. Nevertheless, this is one way of implementing default assumptions (although only for justifications which are negated goals). But is it a 'proper' implementation?

A hypothetical medical Expert System contains rules which enable some default assumptions to be made about parents and their children. it includes the following two Prolog clauses:

```
fertile(A):- has_child(A, C), not adopted(C).  (c8)
adopted(C):- has_child(A, C), not fertile(A).  (c9)
```

That is, if a child is not adopted then his or her parents must be fertile. Conversely, if an adult is infertile then it is safe to assume that their child must have been adopted.

Given no knowledge as to whether a child Carla has been adopted, or whether her parent Alexandra is fertile, what should be concluded? has_ `child(alexandra, carla)` is a fact. Suppose we query whether Alexandra is fertile. The first clause will be called. The first literal in the body of that clause will succeed. In trying to prove the second literal, `not adopted(carla)`, the Prolog interpreter will first try and prove `adopted(carla)`. If it fails to do so, the goal `not adopted(carla)` will succeed and the whole query will succeed. If it fails to succeed, the negative goal will fail and so will the query.

What happens? To try and prove `adopted(carla)` the second clause is called with the variable C instantiated to Carla. `has_child(alexandra, carla)` again succeeds and now `not fertile(alexandra)` is called. To establish whether `not fertile(alexandra)` is true or false, the Prolog intepreter first tries to prove `fertile(alexandra)`. But that is where we came in, and we have not succeeded in establishing the truth or falsity of `fertile(alexandra)` yet. The proof will continue in this circular fashion. Not all Prolog interpreters will behave identically in this situation, but most will just fail to return an answer.

Exactly the same problem arises with the query

    `|?- adopted(carla).`

Is this reasonable? Is there a better solution? If we wish to view negation as failure to prove, as negation by default (assume a proposition is false, so long as it is consistent to do so), then we may postulate that there are two possible solutions to this program. In the first, we assume Carla is not adopted. Then the fertility of Alexandra may be concluded from clause (c8) and the application of clause (c9) is blocked (it would not be consistent to assume simultaneously that Alexandra was not fertile). In the second solution, we do assume that Alexandra is not fertile, and hence conclude that Carla is adopted. These are two alternative scenarios, and there is no way of preferring one to the other given the available knowledge.

A second example (Van Gelder, 1989). A graph (see Figure 6.1) has vertices {a, b, c, d} and edges {(a,b), (c,d), (d,c)}. We may indicate that two vertices, a and b for example, are connected by an edge by writing `edge(a,b)`. A vertex is reachable from a given vertex if there is an unbroken sequence of edges between it and the given vertex. Suppose the given vertex is a. Then we may express this as the following logic program:

`edge(a,b).`	(c10)
`edge(c,d).`	(c11)
`edge(d,c).`	(c12)
`reachable(a).`	(c13)
`reachable(X):- edge(X,Y), reachable(Y).`	(c14)

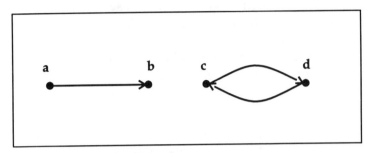

Fig 6.1   *Simple graphical problem.*

In this particular graph, there is an edge between vertices a and b, and also edges between c and d and between d and c. (View this as a directed graph so that an edge between X and Y does not necessarily imply an edge between Y and X). A vertex is reachable if there is an edge between it and another reachable vertex. A moment's thought and it should be clear that this recursive definition is equivalent to the earlier one. Vertex a is reachable.

A vertex is unreachable if there is no continuous path linking it to vertex a:

          unreachable(X):- not reachable(X).   (c15)

Certainly, just by inspecting this program, it is clear that vertex b is reachable. But what about vertex c? There is certainly no edge linking it to either edge a or edge b. Intuitively, one may think that vertex c would be 'unreachable'. So what happens if we run this as a Prolog query?

          |?- unreachable(c)?

From clause (c15), c is unreachable if Prolog fails to prove that it is reachable. Now from clause (c14), c is reachable if there is an edge linking c to another vertex, and that vertex is reachable. Well, there is an edge linking c to d; edge(c,d). But is vertex d reachable? Vertex d is reachable if there is an edge linking it to another vertex which is itself reachable. There is an edge linking vertex d to vertex c; edge(d,c). So, is vertex c reachable? We have been here already! So it goes on, round and round, never succeeding to establish whether or not vertex c is unreachable.

Again, holding the belief 'not reachable(c)' is certainly consistent with the logic program represented by the clauses (c10)-(c15). So, if we augmented this program with a default rule [vertex(X): not reachable(X)/ unreachable(X)], we *would* expect unreachable(c) to be a valid inference.

6.3.4   Logic programming and non-monotonic logics.

Let us just review our current understanding. We have not gone into the details, but just stated that a consequence of the theorem proving technique used in Prolog is that it is not possible to prove negated goals; negated goals at the head of a clause are not allowed (see, for example, (Lloyd, 1984), Chapter 3). An additional rule is needed to allow negative information to be derived. The assumption is made that if something is not known to be true, then it is false (known as the Closed World Assumption, cwa). In order to implement this as a working system, it is only possible to assume false those goals which have failed to be proven in a finite number of steps ('negation as finite failure'). We have given two examples where it seems 'intuitively safe' to assume a negated goal, yet Prolog's proof procedure is unable to decide in a finite number of steps whether or not the goal itself is a consequence of the program.

The importance of all this is that Prolog is an existing implementation of a non-monotonic logic capable of making inferences under incomplete information. Those inferences which include, or depend on, negated goals are in a sense uncertain; belief in them may need to be revised as further information becomes available. But, as we have tried to demonstrate with the above examples, it does not seem appropriate to use Prolog's non-monotonic negation as the basis for a default mechanism. In the absence of a specific proof of a negated goal, we may wish to employ as a contingency "assume that goal is false just so long as it is consistent to do so". Prolog's negation as finite failure fails to do this in certain circumstances.

The semantics of negation as finite failure has been widely discussed in the logic programming/deductive database community. Several alternative semantics for negation have been proposed (e.g. Przymusinska and Przymusinski, 1990), which give a more 'convincing' treatment of some of the examples for which Prolog gives a more contentious solution. In the next section we will develop a formal definition of the 'extension' of a logic program which has a more reasonable interpretation of "negation by default". This will subsequently be expanded into Reiter's presentation of default logic in which justifications, or assumptions, may contain positive as well as negative formulae, and negated formulae may also be derived in the classical sense.

We have made a brief and fairly superficial digression into logic programming. The remainder of this chapter will be increasingly focused on default logic. However, from the preceeding, it should be clear that there are very strong connections between this work and developments in the logic programming/deductive database world. We will refer to the links where appropriate, although without going into any of the technical details.

6.3.5   Specification of a database extension.

Default rules are used to *extend* the inferences which may be drawn from a theory expressed in classical logic. For this reason, the set of consequences of a default theory is referred to as its *extension*. The original paper on default logic by Reiter (Reiter, 1980) included two alternative (but equivalent) formal definitions of the precise contents of such an extension. Neither of them are particularly easy to read on first meeting them. So, in order to give some understanding of the intuitions which lie behind Reiter's definition, we will first discuss some of the properties which such a specification should satisfy. To simplify matters still further, we will initially think in terms of a database in which only negated formulae can be present as justifications in an inference rule, and in which this is the *only* place where negated formulae can appear. As this is not classical negation, we will use the symbol '~' rather than '¬' to prefix a negated term.

Many of the terms used in this section are taken from the abstract framework for default logics presented in (Froidevaux and Mengin, 1992).

Let us first look at some simple examples to see what sort of properties we want. Consider first the following rule:

$$P \wedge \sim Q \wedge \sim R \supset S$$

Suppose we have the proposition P asserted into a database, together with this rule. What extra information should be included in the extension of this database? The following sets of propositions are consistent with this database: $\{P, Q\}, \{P, R\}, \{P, S\}$[4].

In constructing the extension we wish, as will be discussed later, to make the minimum change which is consistent with the database. Adding any one of these three sets of propositions will be a minimal change. But, given P, concluding S from this rule seems to be the most appropriate change to make. That is, in a sense which will be made more specific later, this rule is *applicable* and should be applied.

Consider now the following pair of rules:

---

4. They are in fact models of the database. So in an informal sense, we are looking at defining the semantics of our form of negation by selecting which are the appropriate models.

$P \wedge \sim Q \supset R$

$R \wedge \sim S \supset Q$

Suppose P is asserted, and that is all, bar these two rules. $\sim$Q is consistent with the current state of the database, so we might add R to the extension. $\sim$S is consistent with this extended database (containing R). So the second rule may be applied and Q added to the extension. But this undermines the consistency of assuming $\sim$Q in applying the first rule to deduce R.

We would like to construct the extension in such a way that the extension is still consistent after all the conclusions have been added to it *and* the justification of each conclusion remains consistent with the resulting database. (As a reminder, by justification we mean the negated literals which are assumed false in applying the rules.)

We shall refer to an extension which has this property as being *regular*.

The final example which we will introduce in this section does not need explicit reference to the negative antecedents in the rules, so they will not be included. It may be possible for some form of self-supporting reasoning to be triggered. For example, suppose we have the rule set:

1) $P \supset Q$

2) $Q \supset R$

3) $R \supset Q$

In the case where P is asserted into the database, we would expect Q (from rule 1) and R (from rule 2) to both be included in the extension. What if P is now retracted from the database for some reason? Well, now R supports the derivation of Q, and Q supports the derivation of R. Both propositions are supported in a sense, but in the absence of P we would not expect them to be included in the extension.

We require that any proposition which is included in the extension must be derivable (in an ordered sequence of inference steps) from asserted facts. (Froidevaux and Mengin, 1992) refer to this property as *groundedness*; the set of inference rules used to construct the extension must be *grounded* in the set of asserted facts.

There are two further properties to consider before we present a formal specification of the extension of a database which satisfies these requirements. We have mentioned that a rule is applicable if its positive antecedents can be derived, and if the assumption of its negated antecedents is consistent. We require that the extension be *saturated*; all rules which are applicable should be applied.

These definitions of applicability and saturation are a bit vague at the moment. They will be tightened up later on, but one reason for not doing so now is that there are several possibilities for their precise definitions. The distinctions between these alternatives will become clearer once we have an initial model to play with.

So, the extension should be saturated. What is the second further property? This has already been mentioned in the discussion of Prolog as a non-monotonic logic. We gave an example in which there were two alternative scenarios: one in which a parent, Alexandra, was not fertile and her daughter was adopted; the second in which the daughter, Carla, was not adopted and her parent was fertile. We should consider the possibility that there may be several extensions to a given theory.

To recap:

- The set of rules used to construct an extension should be *grounded* in the set of asserted facts.

- Rules which are *applicable* should be applied. Indeed, all applicable rules should be applied so that the extension is *saturated*.

- The extension should be constructed in such a way that it remains *regular*. That is, it is consistent and the justification of each of the rules used to construct the extension remains consistent with the resulting extension.

This last requirement actually makes things quite difficult. Not so much from a purely theoretical point of view. But if one wishes to implement such a system for constructing extensions there is a problem. As each rule is applied, in order to maintain regularity it will have to be checked for consistency with the *completed extension*. That is, we need some oracle to tell us what the end result is going to be *before* we start to construct it! Automatic theorem proving in default logic is going to be difficult!

6.3.6   Formal definition of an extension.

We are now in a position to give the first of several alternative definitions of the extension of a theory. This first one is intended to be primarily illustrative, although it does make a connection between the use of negation in logic programming and default logic in a simple way.

A *default-negation theory* N is defined as consisting of a set of atomic propositions (or facts), W, and a set of rules R. Each rule in R is specified as a triple: (positive antecedents, negative antecedents, consequent). A rule is satisfiable (or active) with respect to a set of propositions E, if all the positive antecedents and none of the negative antecedents, are present in E. Note again for emphasis that this is not the same as classical negation in which the negated antecedents would have to be a *consequence* of a database for the rule to be satisfiable. Note also that there is only one consequent (which is a positive atomic proposition). With the use of ground rules, there is no loss of generality with this, as rules with multiple consequents can always be rewritten as multiple rules with single consequents.

The rule used in the medical advisor of Section 6.3.3 may be expressed in propositional form as a rule for a default-negation theory as:

({suffers_pain, aspirin_relieves_pain}, {allergic_to_aspirin}, prescribe_aspirin)

If it were not for the different interpretation of negation, this would be equivalent to the following rule in the syntax of classical logic:

suffers_pain $\wedge$ aspirin_relieves_pain $\wedge$ $\neg$allergic_to_aspirin $\supset$ prescribe_aspirin

We now define the extension of a default-negation theory which contains all and only the conclusions of a set of facts and a set of rules which can be consistently drawn.

Definition 6.1

E is an extension of a default-negation theory (W, R) if

i) $E = \bigcup\limits_{i=0}^{n} E_i$ for some $n \in \mathbf{N}$ (the natural numbers)

ii) $E_0 = W$

iii) $\forall\, i \geq 1$

    $E_{i+1} = E_i \cup \{C \mid \exists\ (P,N,C) \in R \bullet P \subseteq E_i, N \cap E = \varnothing\}$

iv) $\forall\ (P,N,C) \in R, P \subseteq E \wedge N \cap E = \varnothing \supset C \in E.$

It is very difficult to get one's mind around a definition like this on first meeting it. That is one of the main reasons why we have initially presented a simpler form than Reiter's general definition. Simplified it may be, but it is still worth explaining in words what this signifies.

The extension is constructed from a sequence of sets E_i $(1 \leq i \leq n)$; condition (i). The first set in this sequence is just the set of contingent facts W; condition (ii). Each set in the sequence is derived from the previous set in the sequence; condition (iii). This is done by adding to the previous set, E_i, the consequents C of all those rules (P, N, C) whose positive antecedents are present in E_i ($P \subseteq E_i$) and for which the assumption of the negated antecedents will not contradict any fact in the resulting extension E, *when it is complete* ($N \cap E = \emptyset$). For the resulting extension to be complete, we must have applied all those rules which can consistently be applied; condition (iv).

Conditions (i), (ii), and (iii) ensure that the rules used to construct the extension are grounded in the set of facts W. A consequent is only added to the conclusion set if it could be derived from the fact set in a finite sequence of inferences, and if the derivation will not be invalidated by the later addition of further consequences to the extension. We gave above the condition for a rule to be *active*. But we also want the assumption of negated antecedents to remain consistent as further rules are applied. So, for an active rule to be *applicable*, we require the extra condition that the negated antecedents will *remain* absent as further rules are applied to complete the construction of the extension. This requires the set of negated antecedents of an applicable rule to be disjoint from the complete extension E in order for the extension to remain regular. Consequently, this is a non-constructive definition of an extension; as discussed at the end of the last section, it requires the presence of an oracle.

Condition (iv) ensures that every rule which is applicable is indeed applied; that is, the extension is *saturated*.

Example 1

In our requirements analysis we used an example concerning the fertility or otherwise of Alexandra to demonstrate an aspect of the behaviour of Prolog's negation which we wished to improve on. Unfortunately, we do not use first order rules in this definition of an extension, so explicit reference to Carla and Alexandra will have to be dropped for the moment. Consider the following two rules:

parent_has_child ∧ ~adopted_child ⊃ fertile_parent

parent_has_child ∧ ~fertile_parent ⊃ adopted_child

If we also have the fact, parent_has_child, this knowledge may be represented as a default negation theory (W, R), where:

W = {parent_has_child}

R = { ({parent_has_child}, {adopted_child}, fertile_parent),
       ({parent_has_child}, {fertile_parent}, adopted_child)}.

With the interpretation of negation used in the above definition of an extension, this theory has two possible extensions. These are {parent_has_-child, fertile_parent} in which adopted_child cannot be concluded, and {parent_has_child, adopted_child} in which fertile_parent cannot be concluded.

Example 2

In eliciting our requirements for the definition of an extension, we considered a theory containing the fact P, together with the two rules:

$$P \wedge \sim Q \supset R$$

$$R \wedge \sim S \supset Q$$

This may be represented by the default-negation theory (W, R) where:

$W = \{P\}$
$R = \{(\{P\}, \{Q\}, R), (\{R\}, \{S\}, Q)\}$

The problem was that application of the second rule would undermine the justification (the assumption of not Q) for the application of the first rule. Consider what happens with the above definition of an extension. P is known, and so $E_0 = W = \{P\}$. Now, suppose E is an extension of this theory. Suppose Q, S ∉ E. Then $E_1 = E_0 \cup \{R\}$, since $\{P\} \subset E_0$, $E \cap \{Q\} = \varnothing$. Now, $\{R\} \subset E_1$ and $E \cap \{S\} = \varnothing$, so the second rule could and should be used to construct E_2. But this means $E_2 = E_1 \cup \{Q\}$ and we said Q ∉ E (= $\cup E_i$).

We have a problem. We must apply all the applicable rules, yet we cannot apply these two rules in a way which is consistent with the definition of an extension. That is, this theory has no extension. (If we knew either of the additional facts Q or S, however, the theory would have an extension; {P} or {P, R, S} respectively).

These two examples illustrate a general property of this choice of definition of an extension. Depending on the nature of the facts and rules, a theory may have none, one, or several extensions associated with it.

So, the effort was worthwhile. We have produced what seems to be a more satisfactory treatment of negation. Like Prolog, it makes a sort of Closed World Assumption in that the things we do not know to be true are assumed false. But unlike Prolog, it allows the possibility of alternative scenarios if there are two or more rules with conclusions which are in conflict. It also satisfies a set of requirements which we have identified as needing to be satisfied by a coherent definition of an extension.

6.3.7   Problems with default-negation extensions.

The definition of the previous section is rigorous and satisfies the requirements which were outlined in Section 6.3.5. However, there are a number of difficulties which we need to address.

- Perhaps the most obvious is that it is a non-constructive definition. That is, it enables us to check if a given set of propositions is indeed an extension of a theory. But it does not specify a procedure for constructing the extensions of a theory if they are not already known. It is easy enough to guess candidate extensions for the simple examples used so far. But for a database containing thousands, if not millions, of data items, a more effective procedure is clearly required.

We will move a little way towards addressing this problem, but the development of a proof theory for default logic gets highly technical, so we cannot go into this in much detail.

- This has been a purely syntactic treatment of 'negation by default'. We need to assign a meaning to negated formulae; we need a semantics.

We will outline the development of a semantics for default logic in Section 6.3.16.

- The above definition of an extension allows propositions to be assumed false if it is consistent to do so (the proposition itself cannot be proven). This is the only way a negated proposition can be derived. In addition, the justifications or assumptions in a rule can only be negated propositions.

That is, in terms of default logic, it is as if we only allowed default rules of the form:

$$\frac{\alpha_1 \wedge \ldots \wedge \alpha_m : \sim\beta_1, \ldots, \sim\beta_n}{\gamma}$$

where α_i, β_i, γ are atomic propositions ($\equiv (\{\alpha_1, \ldots, \alpha_m\},\{\beta_1, \ldots, \beta_n\}, \gamma)$ in our notation). In addition, the set of facts W can only contain atomic propositions.

With the above restrictions, a default-negation extension is equivalent to an extension characterised by the more general definition which will be introduced in Section 6.3.9 (Krause et al, 1993b). However, that more general definition will allow the prerequisites, justifications and consequents of default rules to be arbitrary formulae in first-order predicate calculus. It will also allow W to contain arbitrary formulae, and enable all classical consequents, in addition to default conclusions, to be included in the extension.

- The definition of an extension satisfies the requirements of Section 6.3.5. However, we have also mentioned some properties which the consequence relation of a non-monotonic logic should satisfy (Section 6.2.3). Clearly, negation by default is non-monotonic, but does it satisfy the property of restricted monotonicity of Section 6.2.3? It does not!

What is the consequence relation, though? A cautious, or sceptical, approach would be to say that a proposition was a consequence of a theory if it was a member of all extensions of that theory. This is really a bit too strict as we are interested in all the alternative scenarios, so we will take a 'credulous approach'; that is, a proposition is a consequence of a theory if it is a member of at least one extension.

Since the consequence relation is different to that of classical logic, we will represent it by $\mathrel{|\!\sim}$ rather than $\vdash$. In addition, we are interested in the consequences of a set of facts W given a set of rules R. So we will parameterise the relation by R and write $W \mathrel{|\!\sim}_R P$ if P is a consequence of W given the rule set R.

We have the following definition.

Definition 6.2

For a negation by default theory P = (W, R), and a proposition p, $W \mathrel{|\!\sim}_R p$ if $p \in E$ for some extension E of P.

Restricted monotonicity can be expressed by the following meta-rule:

$$\frac{W \mathrel{|\!\sim}_R p; \quad W \mathrel{|\!\sim}_R q}{W \cup \{p\} \mathrel{|\!\sim}_R q}$$

But default negation does not satisfy this rule. To see this, consider again the theory

W = {parent_has_child}

R = { ({parent_has_child}, {adopted_child}, fertile_parent),
        ({parent_has_child}, {fertile_parent}, adopted_child)}.

Then $W \mathrel{|\!\sim}_R$ fertile_parent. Also, $W \mathrel{|\!\sim}_R$ adopted_child. But $W \cup$ {fertile_parent} $\mathrel{|\!\not\sim}_R$ adopted_child; the propositions fertile_parent and adopted_child belong to different extensions.

Restricted monotonicity is not a property of the more general definition of a default extension either (to be discussed in Section 6.3.9). If, and this is not uncontroversial, we wish default logic to satisfy restricted monotonicity, then we will either have to revise the definition of an extension, or restrict the type of rule which may be used. Both approaches will be discussed.

6.3.8   An 'almost constructive' definition of an extension.

The definition of default-negation extensions, as with the definition of Reiter's default logic, is a non-constructive definition. That is, it enables us to check if a set of propositions is indeed an extension of a given theory. But it does not give us a procedure for constructing that set in the first place. We have intimated in Section 6.2 that automatic deduction for non-monotonic logics is a hard problem, and indeed this is so. Proof procedures do exist for restricted fragments of default logic (e.g. Etherington, 1987b; Dressler, 1988; Junker, 1989; Bonté and Lévy, 1989), and Lévy has presented a method for constructing extensions of general propositional default theories (Lévy, 1991). However, in this section we will present an 'almost constructive' definition of default-negation extensions, which can be thought of as a first step towards developing an automated procedure for constructing extensions.

The term 'non-constructive' was applied to Definition 6.1 because the defining sequence E_i required the presence of an 'oracle', in that reference was made to the resulting extension E at each step in the sequence. The defining sequence of the equivalent definition below does not require the presence of an oracle. The construction of each successive member of the defining sequence only refers to the results of the previous constructions. However, it is not a proper constructive definition because once the sequence is complete a check must be made to see if the resulting set of propositions is indeed an extension of the theory. Some constructions may fail this test. Consequently, this definition is an 'almost constructive' definition (Besnard, pers. comm.) because we do not know whether or not the result of the construction is indeed an extension until *after* it has been constructed.

The almost constructive definition differs from Definition 6.1 in that it includes an additional sequence F_i which accumulates the negated antecedents (or justifications) of rules as they are applied. When a rule is used to construct a successor set in the sequence E_i, we now say that its negative antecedents should not already be known ($N \cap E_i = \emptyset$) and should not become known ($C \notin F_{i+1}$). The negative antecedents are accumulated in the sequence F_i so that a check can be made to ensure that no rule will subsequently be applied which will alter the status of the negative antecedents of a previously applied rule (or even the rule itself; hence the reference to F_{i+1}). Here it is:

Definition 6.3

E is an extension of a default-negation theory (W,R) with respect to F if and only if (iff):

i) $E = \bigcup\limits_{i=0}^{n} E_i, F = \bigcup\limits_{i=0}^{n} F_i$ for some $n \in \mathbf{N}$

ii) $E_0 = W, F_0 = \varnothing$

iii) $\forall\, i \geq 1$

$E_{i+1} = E_i \cup \{C \mid \exists\, (P,N,C) \in R \bullet P \subseteq E_i, C \notin E_i, N \cap E_i = \varnothing, C \notin F_{i+1}\}$

$F_{i+1} = F_i \cup \{N \mid \exists\, (P,N,C) \in R \bullet P \subseteq E_i, C \notin E_i, N \cap E_i = \varnothing, C \notin F_{i+1}\}$

iv) $\neg\exists\, (P,N,C) \in R \bullet P \subseteq E, C \notin E, N \cap E = \varnothing$.

Do not overlook one feature of this definition. Before any rule is applied, a check is made that its consequent is not already known ($C \notin E_i$). This is to prevent justifications being unnecessarily added to R and blocking future rule applications. This is a form of argument subsumption (see also Rychlik, 1991) in which if there are two or more possible ways of concluding a proposition, we choose only one and ignore the others[5].

Once the putative extension has been constructed, a check must still be made to ensure that all the conclusions which could consistently be included in the extension have indeed been included. The defining sequence alone does allow sets of propositions to be constructed which are not true extensions in the sense of Definition 6.1. These would fail to satisfy condition (iv) and so would be rejected, and construction would have to be re-attempted with the rules being applied in a different order.

Definition 6.3 is equivalent to Definition 6.1 (Krause et al, 1993b). It can be easily translated into a Prolog program which enables extensions of propositional default-negation extensions to be constructed (although not particularly efficiently). This differs in behaviour from Prolog's negation as failure in the examples of Section 6.3.2. With the case of Alexandra and Carla, it allows two possible extensions. One contains *fertile(Alexandra)* but not *adopted(Carla)*. The other contains *adopted(Carla)* but not *fertile(Alexandra)*. In the graphical problem illustrated in figure 6.1, the extension in-

---

5. In our case the choice is non-deterministic. In the case of Rychlik, the choice is made on well defined grounds.

cludes the proposition *unreachable(c)*. This is in contrast to the Prolog interpreter which was unable to draw any of these conclusions.

This almost constructive definition can be generalised to give an almost constructive definition of Reiter's default logic (which will be presented in the next section). In the sense that the constructive step generates the fewest 'spurious' extensions of any of the extant definitions, it is the 'best that can be done' (at the time of writing) towards the production of a constructive definition (Moinard, 1992).

6.3.9   Reiter's default logic.

So far, for simplicity, we have been exploring a restricted case of default logic in which the justifications of default rules are negated terms and these are the only form of rule allowed in the database. However, the original motivation for default logic was to provide rules which would *extend* the conclusions which may be drawn from a classical theory. We will now discuss Reiter's original formulation of default logic (Reiter, 1980). In this formulation, a set of first-order well-formed formulae (wffs) W is augmented by a set of default rules D to give a *default theory* $\Delta = (D,W)$. Default rules were introduced on page 153. In all that follows, it will be assumed that the default rules and the formulae in W are *closed*. That is, they do not contain free variables (for example, $\forall x.\exists y.p(x,y) \supset q(x,y)$ is closed, whereas $\forall x.p(x,y) \supset q(y)$ is not – y is not bound to any quantifier in the latter sentence).

Reiter originally presented two equivalent definitions of a default extension. These will be discussed here in the reverse order to that taken by Reiter in order to make the connection with the earlier discussions.

In the following definition, $\mathit{Th}_L(E)$ denotes the set of all consequences of the well-formed formulae E according to the logic L (in this case L is classical first-order logic, but other logics may be used). It can be seen that at each step in the defining sequence E_i, all classical consequences, as well as all the consequences of the applicable default rules, are added.

It will also be seen that this definition does not explicitly include the saturation condition (iv) (or an equivalent thereof) of Definition 6.1. However, the same effect is achieved by requiring that at each stage, E_{i+1} includes the set of consequences for *all* defaults which are applicable. We made the saturation condition explicit in Definition 6.1 as we needed a similar condition in Definition 6.3.

Definition 6.4

Let $\Delta=(D,W)$ be a closed default theory. Then a set of closed wffs E is a Reiter's extension (of Δ) iff:

i) $E = \displaystyle\bigcup_{i=0}^{\infty} E_i$

where

ii) $E_0 = W$ and

$\forall\, i \geq 1,$

$E_{i+1} = \mathit{Th}_L(E_i) \cup \{\gamma \,|\, [\alpha{:}\beta_1, ..., \beta_n/\gamma] \in D \wedge \alpha \subseteq E_i \wedge \neg\beta_1, ..., \neg\beta_n \notin E\}$

In Definition 6.4, the extension is defined by adding to the classical consequences of a set of formulae, $\mathit{Th}_L(E_i)$, all those default conclusions which may be consistently believed. It should be clear that this definition satisfies the requirements of Section 6.3.5. That is, the set of defaults used to construct the extension is grounded in W. The extension is saturated, as we have discussed, and it is regular. That is, the default conclusions are only added to the extension if their justifications will be consistent with the resulting extension ($\neg\beta_1, ..., \neg\beta_n \notin E$). As with the default-negation extensions, this consistency check makes this a non-constructive definition (each subset is defined with respect to the resulting extension).

Reiter started with a slightly different form of definition of an extension of a default theory. Of the two, Definition 6.4 is probably the more intuitive, which is why we have chosen to focus attention on it. However, the alternative definition is of interest. It is equivalent to Definition 6.4 (Reiter, 1980), and we give it here:

Definition 6.5

Let $\Delta=(D,W)$ be a closed default theory. Let L be the set of closed wffs formed using the language of first order predicate logic. For any set $S \subseteq L$, let $\Gamma(S)$ be the *smallest* set such that:

i) $W \subseteq \Gamma(S)$

ii) $\mathit{Th}_L(\Gamma(S)) = \Gamma(S)$

iii)   If $[\alpha{:}\beta_1, ..., \beta_n/\gamma] \in D$, $\alpha \in \Gamma(S)$ and $\neg\beta_1, ..., \neg\beta_n \notin S$, then $\gamma \in \Gamma(S)$

Then a set of closed wffs $E \subseteq L$ is an extension for Δ iff $\Gamma(E)=E$. That is, iff E is a *fixed point* for the operator Γ.

The condition that Γ(S) be the smallest set satisfying the above properties ensures the groundedness of the set of default rules used to construct the extension. Property (ii) ensures all classical consequences are included in the extension, whilst property (iii) ensures the regularity of the extension. That E is a fixed point of the operator Γ means that all the applicable rules must be applied. In other words, it is an alternative way of expressing the saturatedness property of the extension.

6.3.10   Default proofs as arguments.

We suggested in Section 6.3.1 that a default may be viewed as "an argument and the way to use that argument". In that section we considered the notions of argument *rebuttal*, in which the claim of an argument is contradicted, and argument *defeat*, in which the argument itself is undermined. Default logic handles these two properties quite neatly.

Consider again the case of Professor Lethian and Dr. Fortunatus. Dr. Fortunatus' secretary hears that the London rail termini are closed. He argues that as Professor Lethian usually comes to his appointment by train, he will be delayed. So we should assume he will be delayed. Dr. Fortunatus says, however, that if the Professor had caught an earlier train then he would not have been delayed, and that would rebut the secretary's argument. Alternatively, the Professor may be coming by bus, in which case that undermines the assumption of his coming by train and so defeats the argument.

Let us have a look at this in more detail. We have one default rule:

δ: closed_stations: travelling_by_train(x)/delayed(x).

We have two rules:

r_1: $\forall$x.caught_early_train(x) $\supset$ ¬delayed(x)

r_2: $\forall$x.caught_bus(x) $\supset$ ¬travelling_by_train(x)

Note that we have so far been talking about closed default theories in which the formulae contain no free variables. The default rule δ, on the other hand, does apparently contain free variables. This should strictly be read as a 'schema' representing all possible instantiations of this rule.

Now consider the default theory $\Delta = (\{\delta\}, \{closed\_stations, r_1, r_2\})$. The prerequisite of δ is contained in W = {closed_stations, r_1, r_2}. Since there is no way of concluding ¬*travelling_by_train(Lethian)*, the extension will contain *delayed(Lethian)* from application of the default rule δ with x instantiated to *Lethian*:

$$delayed(Lethian) \in E$$

Now, suppose Professor Lethian did catch an early train. We have the default theory Δ'=({δ}, W'), where W' = W∪ {caught_early_train(Lethian)}. Now, suppose we try to apply the argument δ in favour of Professor Lethian being delayed. This then means that *delayed(Lethian)* would be in the extension. But the extension must also contain all classical theorems of W' and the default conclusions. In particular, from rule r_1 we may now conclude ¬*delayed(Lethian)*. If *delayed(Lethian)* is in the extension then we must conclude ⊥, *falsity*. classical logic does not support contradictory theories. If we know both a proposition p and its negation ¬p, we have a proof of ⊥. In addition ⊥ ⊃ q for any proposition q. That is, once we have support for falsity, we can conclude anything. In particular, we can conclude ¬*travelling_by_train(Lethian)*, and the default rule cannot be consistently applied. That is, the logical conclusion of ¬*delayed(Lethian) rebuts* the argument for him being delayed:

$$delayed(Lethian) \notin E'$$

Finally, suppose Professor Lethian caught the bus. Now Δ"=(D, W") where W" = W ∪ {caught_bus(Lethian)}. What can we say about the extension E" of this theory? Again, suppose we try to use the default δ as an argument in favour of the Professor being delayed. This time we use rule r_2 to conclude ¬*travelling_by_train(Lethian)*. That is, it is not consistent to assume *travelling_by_train(Lethian)* and so the argument is defeated. Its justification is undermined:

$$delayed(Lethian) \notin E''.$$

6.3.11   Some other properties of Reiter extensions.

Since there are close similarities between default-negation extensions and Reiter's extensions, it should be no surprise that they have very similar general properties. We will mention some with little further discussion.

- Both of Reiter's definitions are non-constructive. The almost constructive Definition 6.3 can be modified to be equivalent to Reiter's definition (Moinard, 1992) and an automated proof procedure does exist for the propositional case (Lévy, 1991). However, for the general first order case there is a serious problem.

- Reiter's default logic can have no decision procedure. In the general case it is not decidable. We mentioned in Section 6.2.5 that classical logic was semi-decidable. That is, whilst it is possible to obtain a terminating procedure for deciding if a theorem is a consequence of a theory, there is no procedure which is guaranteed to terminate if a formula is *not* a consequence of a theory. Reiter's definition relies on being able to establish when the negation of the justification of a default rule is not a consequence of a theory before it can be applied. That is, deciding if a formula *is* a consequence of a theory depends upon being able to establish that another formula *is not* a consequence of a theory. The latter has no decision procedure. Consequently, the former has no decision procedure. That is, the most general formulation of Reiter's default logic is *not decidable*.

- We still have to outline a semantics for Reiter's default logic.

- In its general form, Reiter's default logic does not satisfy restricted monotonicity.

- A general default theory may have none, one or several extensions. As we will see later, there are some theories which have no Reiter extensions, but for which it can be argued that extensions should exist.

6.3.12   Normal defaults.

All of the examples in Section 6.3.2, bar one, conform to a simple pattern of the justification and the consequent being identical: $\alpha:\beta/\beta$. In a case where α is true and it is consistent to assume β, then do assume β. Such defaults arise frequently, as we have seen, and as a class they do have some useful properties. they are referred to as *normal defaults* and we will briefly discuss some of their properties in this section.

Definition 6.6

A default theory $\Delta=(D,W)$ is *normal* iff all the defaults in D are normal.

Perhaps the most significant property of normal defaults is one which enabled Reiter to develop a proof theory for normal defaults at an early stage (Reiter, 1980; Besnard, 1989). We mentioned in Section 6.2.3 that one advantage of logics which satisfy restricted monotonicity is that they have useful computational properties. The ability to add formulae (subject to certain constraints) to a context without affecting what has already been proven gives a degree of *locality* to the generation of proofs. Normal default theories do have a kind of locality property which is often referred to as *semi-monotonicity*. That is, they are local over the domain of defaults in that no extension of a normal default theory $\Delta=(D,W)$ is decreased if additional defaults are added to D. Put succinctly, a default theory is semi-monotonic if it is monotonic with respect to defaults. However, it *is* still necessary to consider all axioms, W, and theorems in establishing a proof.

Non-monotonic logics must have some sort of global computational requirement in order for them to be non-monotonic. That is, additional information must sometimes result in a *retraction* of beliefs. But the following theorem, stated without proof, means that it may be sufficient to consider only a proper subset of all the normal defaults in order to generate a default proof.

Let gd(E, Δ) denote the set of *generating defaults* of the extension E from the theory Δ. Loosely, the generating defaults of an extension are all the defaults that can be consistently applied to construct the extension. Then we have:

Theorem 6.1   (Reiter, 1980).

Suppose D and D' are sets of closed normal defaults with $D \subseteq D'$. Let E be an extension for the closed normal default theory Δ=(D,W). Then the theory Δ'=(D', W) has an extension E' such that (s.t.)

(i) $E \subseteq E'$

(ii) $gd(E, \Delta) \subseteq gd(E', \Delta')$.

The significance of this theorem is that we may construct the extension of a default theory Δ=(D,W) by stepping incrementally through the defaults in D. A second result immediately follows from Theorem 6.1.

Theorem 6.2

Any normal default theory has at least one extension.

Consider the theory Δ=(D,W). (∅, W) is also a normal default theory, whose extension E contains just the theorems of W. Since $\emptyset \subseteq D$, from Theorem 6.1 Δ must have an extension E' s.t. $E \subseteq E'$.

Further discussion of the properties and proof theory of normal defaults can be found in (Besnard, 1989) and (Reiter, 1980). Many have argued that normal defaults are the only ones that are required, but we will see in the next two sections that there are serious limitations to their expressiveness. We will first look at an alternative formulation of default logic.

6.3.13   Lukaszewicz' extensions.

In Reiter's original paper of 1980 he argued that *all* naturally occurring defaults could be expressed as normal defaults. In the case of non-normal defaults $[\alpha:\beta/\gamma]$, Lukaszewicz (1985) proposed that they be translated into normal defaults by following the simple translation scheme:

$$\frac{\alpha:\ \beta}{\gamma} \ \Rightarrow \ \frac{\alpha:\ \beta\wedge\gamma}{\beta\wedge\gamma}$$

But this does not always work. For example, the argument for someone being a suspect if they have a motive and it is consistent to assume they are guilty may be expressed as the following non-normal default:

$$\frac{\text{has\_motive}(x):\ \text{guilty}(x)}{\text{suspect}(x)}$$

It would not be reasonable to translate this into the following normal default. The conclusion would be too strong.

$$\frac{\text{has\_motive}(x):\ \text{guilty}(x) \wedge \text{suspect}(x)}{\text{guilty}(x) \wedge \text{suspect}(x)}$$

If it is not possible to restrict the form of the default rules, then might it not be possible to modify the definition of default logic in order to regain the desirable properties of normal default theories? That is, is it possible to provide a definition of an extension such that an extension is guaranteed to exist, and the resulting logic is semi-monotonic? Lukaszewicz provided just such a definition (Lukaszewicz, 1988).

In the almost constructive definition of default-negation extensions (Definition 6.3), arguments are defended against subsequent contradiction by recording their justifications, and checking for possible contradiction of previously recorded justifications as each new rule is applied. In view of the fact that Reiter's logic is not semi-monotonic, we would not necessarily expect such a procedure to result in an extension. This is the reason for a final check needing to be made to see if the resulting set of formulae is indeed an extension.

In Lukaszewicz' definition, arguments are defended against subsequent contradiction by recording their justification. This means that the notion of applicability of a default rule is more cautious for a Lukaszewicz extension than for a Reiter extension. In Lukaszewicz' definition a rule may not be applied if it contradicts a justification of another rule which has been applied. In contrast, in a Reiter extension a rule may not be applied only if its own justification is not consistent with the extension. It is this cautious applicability which results in the semi-monotonicity of Lukaszewicz' version of default logic (Froidevaux and Mengin, 1992).

Perhaps it would be useful to give one example to illustrate the motivation behind this alternative definition. Suppose on Sundays, if I am not tired I go fishing. On the other hand, if I have worked hard the day before and I have to get up early I usually find I am tired. When the holidays start and I am not going fishing, I can, of course, wake up late. Suppose that it is the start of the holidays, I worked very hard to get things finished at work before the holidays started, and it is now Sunday. Will I go fishing, will I wake up late, or will I do neither and spend the day walking about like a zombie? We can represent this problem as a default theory (D, W) where:

D = $\{\delta_1, \delta_2, \delta_3\}$ with

δ_1 = [Sunday: I_go_fishing $\wedge \neg$ I_am_tired / I_go_fishing]

δ_2 = [I_worked_hard: I_am_tired $\wedge \neg$ I_wake_up_late / I_am_tired]

δ_3 = [Holidays: I_wake_up_late $\wedge \neg$ I_go_fishing / I_wake_up_late]

W = {Sunday, I_worked_hard, Holidays}

This default theory has no Reiter extensions, but Lukaszewicz thinks that the following three alternatives should be valid extensions:

W $\cup$ {I_go_fishing}; W $\cup$ {I_am_tired}; W $\cup$ {I_wake_up_late}.

As with Reiter, Lukaszewicz first gives a fixed point definition of the modified extensions. For ease of comparison with our definition of a Reiter extension, we quote here the equivalent definition in terms of a sequence of sets. For succinctness, here and in some of the following we make the following identities for a default rule $\delta = [\alpha:\beta_1, ..., \beta_n/\gamma]$:

$$pre(\delta) = \{\alpha\}$$
$$jus(\delta) = \{\beta_1, ..., \beta_n\}$$
$$cons(\delta) = \{\gamma\}$$

Definition 6.7

Let E and F be sets of closed wffs. E is a modified extension (m-extension) w.r.t. F of the closed default theory $\Delta = (D,W)$ iff:

$$E = \bigcup_{i=0}^{\infty} E_i, \quad F = \bigcup_{i=0}^{\infty} F_i$$

where:

E_0 = W; $F_0 = \varnothing$

and $\forall i \geq 0$

- $E_{i+1} = \mathcal{T}h_L(E_i)$

$\cup \{\gamma \mid [\alpha:\beta_1, ..., \beta_n/\gamma] \in D, \alpha \in E_i, \forall \varphi \in F \cup \{\beta_1, ..., \beta_n\}, E \cup \{\gamma\} \nvdash \neg\varphi\}$

- $F_{i+1} = F_i$

$\cup \{\beta \mid \beta \in jus(\delta),$

$\delta = [\alpha:\beta_1, ..., \beta_n/\gamma] \in D, \alpha \in E_i, \forall \varphi \in F \cup \{\beta_1, ..., \beta_n\}, E \cup \{\gamma\} \nvdash \neg\varphi\}$

As with Reiter, Lukaszewicz also gave an equivalent fixed point definition of m-extensions:

Theorem 6.3

Let $\Delta = (D, W)$ be a default theory. Then for any pair of sets of formulae
(S,U), $\Gamma_1(S,U)$ and $\Gamma_2(S,U)$ are the smallest sets satisfying:

  i) $W \subseteq \Gamma_1(S,U)$

  ii) $\mathit{Th}_L(\Gamma_1(S,U)) = \Gamma_1(S,U)$

  iii) If $[\alpha{:}\beta 1, ..., \beta_n/\gamma] \in D$,

         $\alpha \in \Gamma_1(S,U)$, and $\forall \varphi \in U \cup \{\beta 1, ..., \beta_n\}$, $S \cup \{\gamma\} \not\vdash \neg\varphi$ then

              $\gamma \in \Gamma_1(S,U)$ and

              $\beta 1, ..., \beta_n \in \Gamma_2(S,U)$.

Then a set of formulae E is a *modified extension (m-extension)* for Δ with respect to (w.r.t.) a set of formulae F iff $E = \Gamma_1(E, F)$ and $F = \Gamma_2(E,F)$.

E is an m-extension for Δ iff $\exists F$ s.t. E is an m-extension for Δ w.r.t. F (F is the
set of justifications supporting E).

In view of the earlier discussion it should be no surprise that we have
the following properties of m-extensions (proofs can be found in Lukaszewicz, 1988).

Theorem 6.4

Every default theory has at least one m-extension.

Theorem 6.5   Semi-monotonicity.

Let D and D' be sets of defaults such that $D \subseteq D'$. Let E be an m-extension
of the default theory $\Delta = (D,W)$ w.r.t. F. Then the default theory $\Delta' = (D',W)$
has an m-extension E' with respect to a set F' such that $E \subseteq E'$ and $F \subseteq F'$.

Let us look at the fishing example again. With Reiter's definition there
is no extension to this theory. For suppose the extension contains *I_go_fish-
ing* from applying rule δ_1. Then the justification of δ_2 is consistent and so
this rule is applicable. But it cannot be applied without undermining the
justification of δ_1; this would violate the regularity of the extension. Similarly, if δ_2 is applied, δ_3 is still applicable but cannot be applied without undermining the justification of δ_2. If δ_3 is applied, δ_1 is applicable but cannot
be applied without undermining the justification of δ_3 with the conclusion

I_go_fishing. It is not possible to construct a regular, saturated extension to this theory with Reiter's notion of applicability.

However, with Lukaszewicz' definition, there are three possible extensions, as we have said. Suppose δ_1 is applied and *I_go_fishing* is included in an m-extension w.r.t. F. We must have $\neg I\_am\_tired \in$ F. Then δ_2 is not applicable because $E \cup cons(\delta_2) \vdash \neg(\neg I\_am\_tired)$ and $\neg I\_am\_tired \in$ F. δ_3 is clearly not applicable (we need to be more cautious about applying rules). So E=W$\cup${*I_go_fishing*} is saturated using Lukaszewicz' notion of applicability. Similarly, it can easily be shown that W$\cup${*I_am_tired*} and W$\cup${*I_wake_up_late*} are possible m-extensions for this theory.

This is one example, there are others, where Lukaszewicz definition seems to give more intuitive results than Reiter's. However, there are others where Reiter's definition seems preferable. The following example needs a little background information.

Zoologists have divided the animal kingdom into many orders, each order grouping animals with some common characteristics and a common ancestor. The order *Carnivora* includes the Cat, Dog, Bear, Raccoon, Weasel, Civet and Hyena families. As the name suggests, the carnivores are usually meat eaters. The rather attractive little Red Panda is a member of the Raccoon family (it and the Giant Panda have been separated into a family of their own by some authorities, although still within the order *Carnivora*). A native of the Himalayas and western China, it is a relatively recent discovery to western science, having been first recorded in the early nineteenth century (some fifty years before the first recorded sightings of the Giant Panda). The first Red Panda to be brought into captivity rather confused its keeper at the London Zoo. Although known to be a member of the carnivores, it ate little of the meat it was offered as food. It became weaker and weaker. Fortunately, by a happy accident its keeper let it wander into one of the ornamental flower beds where it started to eat the plants! The Red Panda, as with the Giant Panda, had evolved away from the meat eating diet of its immediate ancestors to become predominantly a vegetarian.

Based on this information, we can start to implement an advisor for Zoologists in default logic.

Red Pandas are certainly carnivores:

r_1: $\forall x.red\_panda(x) \supset carnivora(x)$

But unless they are placed in unusual circumstances, Red Pandas have a diet of assorted herbs and fruit:

$$\delta_1: \frac{\text{red\_panda}(x): \text{eats\_herbs}(x) \land \neg\text{unusual}(x)}{\text{eats\_herbs}(x)}$$

Of course, carnivores do usually eat meat, but given the above example, we ought to check they are not known to be herbivores before we assume this:

$$\delta_2: \frac{\text{carnivora}(x): \text{eats\_meat}(x) \land \neg\text{eats\_herbs}(x)}{\text{eats\_meat}(x)}$$

Suppose Herby is a Red Panda and consider the default theory

$$\Delta = (\{\delta_1, \delta_2\}, \{\text{red\_panda(Herby)}, r_1\}).$$

Now, with Lukaszewicz' definition, E_1={*red_panda(Herby), eats_herbs(Herby), carnivora(Herby)*} is an m-extension of Δ. With δ_1 applied, although we can conclude *carnivora(Herby)*, application of δ_2 is blocked. This is an answer we would expect. However, if δ_2 is applied first the application of δ_1 is blocked, as its conclusion would contradict the justification of δ_2 (we must have *eats_meat(Herby)* $\land$ *¬eats_herbs(Herby)* $\in F_2$. Hence, E_2= {*red_panda(Herby), carnivora(Herby), eats_meat(Herby)*} is also an m-extension of Δ (with respect to F_2). This seems contrary to what was intended.

In contrast, E_1 is the only Reiter extension of Δ (we hope that by now the reader will find it easy to convince him or her self of this). In this particular case, this result seems to be the preferable one. The rules have been written with the intent that the more specific rule δ_1 should override the more general rule δ_2.

The simple fact is, if we do wish to enable default logic to express a preference between competing extensions (E_1 and E_2 in this case), then we cannot also have semi-monotonicity. In this last example, we have demonstrated a way in which some preference on the basis of specificity can be encoded into the default rules for Reiter's default logic. The notions of interacting defaults and prioritising extensions are important research topics and warrant further discussion.

6.3.14   Interacting defaults and specificity.

As has been mentioned several times now, depending on its precise nature, a default theory may have none, one or several Reiter extensions. We have discussed two approaches to ensuring that a default theory has at least one extension; the use of normal defaults, and Lukaszewicz' m-extensions. But as well as trying to eliminate the possibility of a theory having no extensions, there has been much work aimed at trying to restrict the occasions when a default theory may have multiple extensions (see, for example, Reiter and Criscuolo, 1981; Moinard, 1990). This can get to be quite an involved topic, so we will just aim to illustrate some of the issues with the Red Panda example.

The rules δ_1 and δ_2 in Section 6.3.13 were presented with little explanation as to why their precise form was chosen. We will stick with "Red Pandas are carnivores" as a categorical rule:

r_1: $\forall x.$ red_panda(x) $\supset$ carnivora(x)

However, the simple way of expressing the dietary requirements of Red Pandas and of carnivores is to say:

Assume a carnivore eats meat if it is consistent to do so:

$$\delta_3: \frac{\text{carnivora(x): eats\_meat(x)}}{\text{eats\_meat(x)}}$$

But, assume a Red Panda does not eat meat:

$$\delta_4: \frac{\text{red\_panda(x): } \neg\text{eats\_meat(x)}}{\neg\text{eats\_meat(x)}}$$

Now, the default theory $(\{\delta_3, \delta_4\}, \{r_1, \text{red\_panda(Herby)}\})$ has two Reiter extensions. In one, Herby does not eat meat. But in the other Herby does; there is nothing to stop δ_3 being applied (and if it is applied, it will block δ_4).

The two defaults δ_3 and δ_4 interact in such a way that they cannot simultaneously be applied. Which is what we want. But we do intuitively feel that there should be some priority of the application of δ_4 over δ_3. δ_4 does express more specific information after all.

The approach we took to encoding this prioritisation was to reference a specific property of the Red Panda in the justification to the carnivora rule δ_2. Red Pandas do not eat meat, they usually eat herbs. Carnivores do usually eat meat unless they are known to eat herbs. Both these rules are still default rules because there may be grounds for believing a carnivore eats neither meat nor herbs (when it is a suckling, for example).

We needed non-normal defaults to express this prioritisation. Furthermore any attempt at defending justifications of default rules once applied would also destroy the intended prioritisation. Hence the comment at the end of the last section that semi-monotonicity is not compatible with expressing priorities amongst defaults (see also Brewka, 1991a). But there is a weakness in this scheme. We are beginning to lose the modularity of the default rules. One of the motivations behind default logic was the absence of explicit reference to the exceptions to a default rule in favour of a more general consistency property. We did not need to know in advance all the goblet shaped spring flowers which are not crocuses; we just need an ability to recognise when one is not a crocus. However, with the prioritisation expressed in rules δ_1 and δ_2, we are beginning to make explicit reference to the exceptions within the rules themselves. If we discover a subspecies of Red Panda which usually just eats berries, we cannot just add this rule to the database. We have to be able to conclude that it is unusual in order to block the application of δ_1. But we also need to add "$\land \neg eats\_berries(x)$" to the justification of δ_2 in order to block the generation of a possible extension in which a member of this hypothetical subspecies is believed to eat meat.

There are a number of alternative approaches to this problem. Different solutions are presented in each of (Froidevaux, 1986), (Touretzky, 1984) and (Poole, 1985). There is unfortunately insufficient space to discuss these here, but (Moinard, 1990) may be referred to for a critique of the various approaches, together with some more general thoughts on preference by specificity.

6.3.15   Other definitions of default extensions.

It is almost getting to the state where the production of alternative formulations of default logic is becoming a major growth industry. As we have tried to indicate with the comparisons between Reiter's original definition, and Lukaszewicz' revised formulation, there are no absolute criteria for preferring one over another. It is essentially a matter of choosing the one whose behaviour best suits the application in hand. A framework for providing a careful analysis of the precise distinctions between all the major formalisms is provided in (Froidevaux and Mengin, 1992), and this should be consulted for more detail on the following remarks. We will merely refer to the different versions, without detailed definitions.

We have mentioned restricted monotonicity as possibly being a desirable property of non-monotonic logics. The nearest we have got to that has been the semi-monotonicity of normal defaults and m-extensions. However, work by Makinson and others on providing a formal basis for more philosophical work on belief revision, suggests that non-monotonic logics should satisfy a slightly revised form of restricted monotonicity (Makinson, 1989). This is often referred to as cumulativity (Brewka, 1991b).

In restricted monotonicity, adding a theorem of a set of premises to that set of premises does not change the derivable formulae (Section 6.2.3). We gave a 'credulous' version of restricted monotonicity in Section 6.3.7 and pointed out that neither default-negation, nor Reiter's default logic satisfy this[6]. Versions of default logic have been defined which do satisfy a form of restricted monotonicity using a credulous notion of entailment.

Definition 6.8

A default logic is cumulative iff it satisfies the following property. If there exists at least one extension of $\Delta=(D,W)$ containing a formula φ, then E is an extension of Δ iff E is an extension of $\Delta'=(D, W \cup \{\varphi\})$.

The versions of default logic which we have discussed so far are not cumulative (Brewka, 1991a). However, Brewka has defined a version of default logic which is cumulative in this sense (Brewka, 1991b). His original definition would not allow any expression of prioritisation, but he was able to modify his original definition to be priority preserving.

The almost constructive definition of default-negation extensions involves a simple notion of argument subsumption. There was a non-deterministic choice about which arguments to subsume; merely that any argument once applied was assumed to subsume all arguments with the same conclusion. Rychlik provided specific criteria to decide whether one argument should subsume another (Rychlik, 1991). Rychlik's c-extensions are semi-monotonic and enjoy a property which he calls rational maximisation of beliefs; essentially believe as much as possible by applying as few defaults as possible. However, the semi-monotonicity does mean c-extensions have the same weaknesses with respect to priority preservation as m-extensions.

Further attempts to make default logic semi-monotonic or cumulative have been provided by (Guerreiro et al, 1990) and (Schaub, 1991) respectively. Work towards producing constructive definitions of extensions is being pursued, and is exemplified by (Delgrande and Jackson, 1991) and (Tan and Treur, 1991).

---

6. Credulous, because a set of premises was said to entail a proposition if it was a member of at least one extension. This is in distinction to a sceptical notion of entailment where a set of premises entails a proposition if it is a member of all extensions.

6.3.16   The semantics of default logics.

So far, this chapter has looked at default logic at a purely syntactic level. That is, we have described how sets of well-formed formulae may be subject to purely syntactic manipulations to establish whether or not a set is an extension of a default theory. However, in order to gain a deeper understanding of any logical system it is necessary to provide a semantics for that system; a meaning is given to the logic by saying what the constraints are on the possible interpretations of the formulae in that logic. This is a distinctive and almost indispensable feature of logics as a mathematical formalism. In Section 6.2 we gave a very loose description of an interpretation of a logic. It is not really possible to do much better here, as the precise definition of the formal semantics of a logic is usually quite technical. Further details on the semantics of propositional and first order logic can be found in (Johnstone, 1987), (Mendelson, 1964) or (Gallier, 1987).

The usual approach is to give a model theoretic semantics to a logic. We will not give a precise characterisation of a model of a theory, merely present some examples to demonstrate the intuitions behind the concept.

Consider the finite set of propositional symbols L={P,Q,R,S}. Let W={P, ¬Q} be a set of axioms. Then the models of W (with respect to L) would be:

$\varphi_1 = \{P, \neg Q, R, S\}$

$\varphi_2 = \{P, \neg Q, \neg R, S\}$

$\varphi_3 = \{P, \neg Q, R, \neg S\}$

$\varphi_4 = \{P, \neg Q, \neg R, \neg S\}$

Here, read P as proposition P is true, and ¬P as proposition P is false. Loosely, the models represent all possible truth assignments for the set of propositions in L which are compatible with the axioms W.

A set of axioms Γ semantically entails a formula P (Γ ⊨ P) if P is true in all possible models of Γ. In the above example, W ⊨ P and W ⊨ ¬Q (not surprisingly). More interestingly, if we had W'={P, P ⊃ ¬Q}, φ_1, ..., φ_4 would also be the only models of W' (we could not have Q without ¬P, but we cannot have ¬P as P ∈ W'). So, again we have W' ⊨ ¬Q.

Now consider the case where W"={P}. There are far more possible models, but the only valuation common to them all is P. We can conclude very little. φ_1 to φ_4 are models of W", but so are φ_5 to φ_8:

$\varphi_5 = \{P, Q, R, S\}$

$\varphi_6 = \{P, Q, \neg R, S\}$

$\varphi_7 = \{P, Q, R, \neg S\}$

$\varphi_8 = \{P, Q, \neg R, \neg S\}$

Suppose we now extend the theory W" with some default rules to give the default theory $\Delta = \{W", \{P:Q/Q, Q:R/R\}\}$. These default rules can be used to restrict the class of models of W", and this idea provides the basis for the development of a model theoretic semantics of default logic (Lukaszewicz, 1985; Besnard, 1989).

Let $\Phi_0 = \{\varphi_1, \varphi_2, \varphi_3, \varphi_4, \varphi_5, \varphi_6, \varphi_7, \varphi_8\}$.

We first take away from Φ_0 all the models which are incompatible with the application of a default rule δ in D for which $pre(\delta)$ is contained in all models and $jus(\delta)$ is contained in at least one model of Φ_0 (that is $jus(\delta)$ may consistently be assumed since $\neg jus(\delta)$ is not in all models). If we consider $\delta_1 = P:Q/Q$, this procedure eliminates $\varphi_1, ..., \varphi_4$ from Φ_0 to give $\Phi_1 = \{\varphi_5, \varphi_6, \varphi_7, \varphi_8\}$.

We may repeat this process for another default rule, $\delta_2 = Q:R/R$, say, to obtain Φ_2 from Φ_1, where $\Phi_2 = \{\varphi_5, \varphi_7\}$.

Repeating this procedure will produce a sequence of subsets of the class of all models of W". Their intersection is $\Phi = \bigcap_{i=0}^{\infty} \Phi_i = \{\varphi_5, \varphi_7\}$, in this case. There are no more default rules satisfying the condition described in the first step which could be used to reduce the class of models Φ further. That is, Φ is *stable* and represents the class of all models of some extension of Δ (in fact the only extension in this case, and P, Q, and R are true in this extension).

As we have mentioned, following Reiter's initial presentation of default logic, there was a period of several years before work on providing it with a semantics began to bear fruit. Now, most new versions of default logic are presented complete with semantics. However, there have still been some problems with the development of a completely general semantics for default logic. Besnard and Schaub (1993) have now managed to produce a general semantical framework for the various default logics.

6.3.17   Logic programming revisited.

In the early stages of this discussion on non-monotonic logics we introduced Prolog as one computer language which enabled a form of automated reasoning with incomplete information (the absence of negated information). We used some possible weaknesses of Prolog's negation as

failure as motivation for developing an alternative method of handling negated goals, which we termed default-negation. The primary purpose of
this was as a heuristic device to explain some of the motivation behind Reiter's formulation of default logic. However, it does also draw attention to
the fact that there may be close parallels between some of the formalisms
being developed in the logic programming community, and those being developed in the non-monotonic community.

It would be outside the scope of this book to go into details about logic
programming and its application to deductive database technology. Good
readable surveys of these fields can be found in (Gallaire et al, 1984) and
(Grant and Minker, 1989). Deductive databases are a development of the
widely used relational databases in which (implicit) information can be derived from the database, in addition to straightforward lookups of the facts
(explicitly) stored in the database. Since the things we do not know almost
always exceed in number the things we do know in a specific domain, there
are tremendous advantages in deductive databases in not explicitly storing
negated information. As a logic language, Prolog is designed for just such a
treatment of negated information. However, it does have some weaknesses
as we pointed out in Section 6.3.3. A great deal of work has been put into
developing alternative semantics for negation in logic programming (Shepherdson, 1988). In particular, the "perfect model" semantics (Przymusinski,
1988) produces our preferred answer to the graphical problem of Figure 6.1
(that vertex c is unreachable). In view of our treatment of this problem with
a pseudo-default logic, it should be no surprise that a logic programming
representation of this problem can be translated into a default logic theory
in such a way that the "perfect model" of the logic program and the minimal model of the extension of the default theory coincide (Bidoit and
Froidevaux, 1991).

The translation from logic program to default logic is helpful in that
representing a logic program as a default theory can help to clarify its semantics. However, the reverse translation may be of more interest. There is
a great deal of expertise in the actual implementation of logic programs in
existence. Consequently, if a default theory can be translated into a logic
program, it may be possible to provide an "off the shelf" theorem prover
for that theory. Such a translation does now exist for a certain class of theories in Reiter's default logic (Li and You, 1991), and this may be a significant step towards building efficient default logic theorem provers.

6.4   Discussion

This chapter has focused on the use of non-monotonic logics as models for reasoning in states of partial knowledge. We have included some fairly strong references to the properties of classical logic in order to emphasise the differences between deductive reasoning, where conclusions necessarily follow from their premises, and practical intuitive judgements, which lead to contingent context dependent conclusions.

Even though it has been studied and formalised for millennia, classical deductive reasoning still does not come naturally to most people. After years of training, logicians can still find certain logical deductions require a cold blooded conscious effort to perform correctly. For example, Johnson-Laird and Byrne (1991) provide a number of syntactically simple examples where subjects consistently failed to produce the correct inference. For example, if we have "all A are B" and "no A is C", what can we conclude about the relationship between B and C? The tendency may be to conclude quickly "no B is C". However, the correct inference is that "some B are not C", but it is very difficult to see this without drawing a simple Venn diagram. In contrast, people go about their daily lives making a constant stream of intuitive judgements, subconsciously, and with a high degree of confidence.

The irony is that the formal models of practical reasoning outlined in this chapter are more complex than classical logic; it is harder to grasp the intuitions that underlie them, and they are computationally intractable in the general case. Whilst (even with the "hard problems" of Johnson-Laird and Byrne) there are agreed correct solutions in the case of classical deductive reasoning, in the case of non-monotonic models of practical reasoning there is no general consensus as to which is the correct solution, as we have seen in many examples. One may justifiably begin to doubt that this is the right path to formalising practical reasoning at all:

> *The formal treatment (of reasoning) should be close to our mental patterns. The torture of truth tables, of model theory, is not only inelegant, it does not correspond to our informal way of thinking.* (Jean-Yves Girard).

One wonders whether there may not be an analogy with the development of chess playing programs. It soon became clear that chess Grand-Masters did not judge moves by searching through the consequences of *all* possible moves and picking that with the highest potential gain. Rather, they performed a rapid pattern matching over past similar situations to select a small number of models that best fitted the current situation, and so constrain their search space.

In a similar way, might not our intuitive judgements be based on matching against models derived from past experiences? From the cognitive science perspective, Johnson-Laird has been exploring similar ideas as a model of deduction (Johnson-Laird, 1983). From the computer science perspective, Bell (1992) has produced a model theoretic framework for non-monotonic reasoning (which also provides a general framework for comparing all the existing formalisms).

On a more conventional line, Pearl (1988) argues that non-monotonic logics can be given a cleaner semantics in terms of probability theory. Wilson (1992) provides a reinterpretation of default logic in terms of belief functions, which also has a slightly different behaviour to Reiter's default logic; Wilson argues that this behaviour should be preferred.

However, we do not wish to be too negative. There is much that is very appealing and stimulating about the work described in this chapter. Non-monotonic logics as models of reasoning are generating a great deal of interest, and their study has matured into an established discipline. In addition, as we shall see in the next section, they do have significant representational power.

6.4.1   Knowledge Representation.

With respect to our classification of uncertainty of Chapter 1 (Figure 1.2), non-monotonic logics address aspects of ignorance through partial knowledge. However, although notions of consistency are central to most presentations of non-monotonic logics, a default theory, for example, has the same strong requirements for global consistency that a theory in classical logic has. Consequently, there can be no representation of partial conflict; a default theory either has a consistent extension, or it does not.

Early forms of non-monotonic reasoning which have found widespread acceptance are the closed world assumption (cwa) and negation as failure (naf) (Clark, 1978). Generally, the things which are not true in any given problem representation far exceed in number those that are (when feeling hard-done-by, instead of thinking of all those things you *want* but have not got, try thinking of all those things you do *not* want and have not got). As we have seen, there are some difficulties with negation as failure as embodied in Prolog. However, many people find that the avoidance of needing to store negative information explicitly results in a concise and expressive knowledge representation language. Recent developments in alternative semantics for logic programs address many of the perceived semantic weaknesses of Prolog, and the connections with default, and other non-mo-

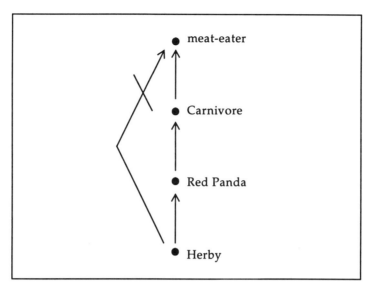

Fig 6.2   *Inheritance hierarchy for Carnivores. The plain arrows represent IS-A links (Herby IS-A Red Panda). The barred arrows represent negated IS-A links (Herby IS-NOT-A meat eater). The problem is to define notions of specificity whereby conflicts in the network may be resolved.*

notonic logics, means that they can be used to implement restricted fragments of those logics.

Non-monotonic systems are often discussed in connection with the representation of inheritance hierarchies (Touretzky, 1984; 1986). Inheritance systems are used to represent hierarchies of objects and classes. The hierarchy is used to pass information to subclasses of some general class, unless this information contradicts some more specific information. Again, this provides a concise way of representing knowledge. Attributes which are common to a class of entities need only be explicitly stated in the defining criteria for that class (or a superclass of that class).

We have seen an example of this in Section 6.3.13 in which subclasses of the general class *Carnivora* inherited properties of the carnivores (e.g. eating meat) unless this was overruled by more specific information (such as, Pandas eat herbs). Figure 6.2 shows an inheritance network representing Herby's possible eating habits. There are two contradictory conclusions which may be drawn from this network; Herby IS-A meat-eater, or Herby IS-NOT-A meat eater. We have seen how a notion of specificity may be expressed in default logic to resolve this conflict.

There is also an increasing interest in the use of non-monotonic logics to represent and process natural language. This again is exploiting the property that non-monotonic inferences are context dependent. For example, in the case of natural language, lexicographically identical words might have quite different semantics. Which semantics is relevant will depend on the context within which the word is being used. Poznanski (1992) gives the example of the word "nut", which may be used to denote: an idiot; a metal artefact usually associated with a "bolt"; a fruiting body which may be used as food. In an utterance such as "the squirrel found a nut" there would usually be little doubt as to which denotation was intended. The language processing system Crystal (Poznanski, 1992) uses a subset of autoepistemic logic as its deductive inference engine. Crystal can successfully provide interpretations for utterances obtained from fragments of children's stories.

A fairly obvious restriction of non-monotonic logics is that they do not offer any grading of belief or credibility; propositions are either believed true or false. In order to address this limitation, Froidevaux and Grossetête (1990) provide an extension of non-monotonic reasoning which allows graded levels of certainty. This is achieved by imposing a partial order on the default rules. There is quite a strong relationship between this approach and possibilistic logic, which we discussed in Chapter 5.

6.4.2   Knowledge Engineering.

The formalisms described in this chapter reflect very recent developments in the field of uncertain reasoning in AI. As yet, there have been few real attempts to produce large systems using, say, Reiter's default logic as the inference engine. Consequently, there is little to report with respect to knowledge engineering that is specific to non-monotonic logics.

However, there is a great deal of interest in validation, verification and knowledge elicitation with respect to rule-based systems which can be drawn on (e.g. Ayel and Laurent, 1991). Prolog is proving to be an expressive language for prototyping and implementing Expert Systems with some non-monotonic capability (Kazic et al, 1990), and the use of a logical representation language can allow checks to be made for consistency and coherence as the knowledge base is constructed. Fox et al (1990b) suggest that a high degree of integrity can be maintained if the knowledge base is structured as a small number of generic rules reasoning over domain knowledge expressed as simple facts and relations (see Chapter 7).

A higher degree of integrity can be ensured if abstract knowledge, or domain models are elicited prior to the construction of the knowledge-base. A knowledge editor may then be constructed which ensures that the knowledge elicited from the experts satisfies the constraints of the knowledge model (Glowinski et al, 1991). The KADS methodology, for example, provides a semi-formal framework for producing such knowledge models (Schreiber, 1992). Further advantages with respect to precision and integrity can be obtained if the abstract knowledge model is expressed in a formal language (van Harmelen and Balder, 1992; Krause et al, 1993c).

6.4.3   Computational Considerations.

Computation is really an overriding problem with non-monotonic logics at present. Even in the propositional case it is not possible to produce an algorithm to determine whether a given sentence is a member of an extension in anything less than exponential time (Kautz and Selman, 1991). In the first order case this task is undecidable (Section 6.2.5). But this is familiar territory; Bayesian probability and Belief functions also have serious computational problems in the general case.

Efficient computational procedures have been defined for specific fragments of non-monotonic logics. In the case of logic programming, many of the computational problems can be resolved by ensuring that the database is stratified (Grant and Minker, 1989); essentially ensuring the dependencies between items in the database are explicated and well-defined. One rather feels that if a non-monotonic logical representation of a problem can be structured in the right way then, as with the numerical calculi, efficient computations may be achievable.

Many early experiments in non-monotonic reasoning were carried out using truth maintenance, or perhaps more correctly, reason maintenance systems (Doyle, 1979). There is now a great deal of experience in developing efficient reason maintenance systems to implement restricted, but useful, fragments of non-monotonic logics (e.g. Junker, 1989; Hopkins and Clarke, 1992). We have given pointers to other approaches to developing efficient proof procedures for fragments of non-monotonic logics throughout the chapter (specifically, in Section 6.3.8).

6.5   Conclusion

This is by far the longest and technically most demanding chapter in this book. Many of the issues involved in, and intuitions underlying, the development of non-monotonic logics are quite intricate, and it does not seem possible to give a convincing account of them without introducing some degree of formality. By introducing default logic via the simplified notion of "default-negation", we have tried to satisfy two goals. Firstly, we wanted to make Reiter's definition as accessible as possible. Secondly we wanted to give the reader some feeling for the very strong connections between logic programming and non-monotonic reasoning, without going into the very high degree of technicality which is usual in papers on the subject.

We must confess to having taken the side of the angels in this chapter, and discussed the problems associated with developing a pure and rigorous formalisation of non-monotonic reasoning. That is the primary reason for the emphasis on the computational difficulties. There are many pragmatic implementations of non-monotonic reasoning systems which produce interesting results, although without such precisely understood behaviours. However, we feel that there has been, and continues to be, such progress in the development of formal approaches that this is where the focus of attention will remain.

7
Argumentation

An argument is not just contradiction ... an argument is a connected series of statements intended to establish a proposition. (The Argument Clinic, Monty Python's Flying Circus).

7.1   Introduction

It has long been acknowledged that a central component of intelligence is the ability to understand and engage in argumentation (see (Alvarado, 1992) for a review). The rationale for research on argumentation in the context of uncertainty management comes from at least two sources. On the one hand is the attempt to model competent patterns of human reasoning under uncertainty which do not fall naturally into any of the categories of reasoning discussed so far in this book. On the other hand is the attempt to produce models of uncertain reasoning which are in some respect more generic than the particular instances of uncertain reasoning subsumed by these formalisms. In these respects, research on argumentation is truly interdisciplinary.

Chapters 2 to 5 of this book were devoted to measure theoretic approaches to uncertainty management in AI systems. The sixth chapter provided an overview of non-monotonic and default logic approaches to uncertainty. In these, an attempt is made to augment classical logic in such a way as to produce a system with the power and syntactic simplicity of classical logic, but which is applicable to incompletely specified "everyday" situations. In this chapter we will review and critique a number of more recent symbolic systems; specifically, the heuristic models of Cohen and Fox, which draw inspiration from competent human uncertainty management and problem solving. These are based on heuristic reasoning rather than on classical logic. However, in the second part of this chapter, we will also look at some very recent work aimed at placing these models on a more formal logical basis.

Before describing these approaches, however, we invite the reader to engage in a thought experiment. We observe that very rarely do we have the opportunity to assess our certainty in an event by being able to sum equiprobable outcomes. Instead, degrees or states of uncertainty can be viewed as a synthesis of the outcome of reasoning processes (i.e. arguments) germane to the proposition in question.

7.2   Heuristic models of argumentation

Heuristic models of argumentation draw principally upon ideas from competent human reasoning.

7.2.1   Cohen's model of endorsements.

Cohen's theory of endorsements is motivated by the observation that states of uncertainty are composites of reasons to believe and disbelieve, and that the strength of evidence is a summary of the factors that pertain to certainty. An intelligent person may discriminate among these factors and use information about the type of uncertainty in selecting a strategy to resolve it. In consequence, summary representations of uncertainty, such as probabilities, are inadequate; it is necessary to know the sources of uncertainty, as well as its extent, to resolve it successfully. As Cohen puts it:

> We know much about uncertain situations besides our degree of belief: We discriminate among many kinds of uncertainty, and we know many approaches to resolving or discounting uncertainty. We recognise different kinds of evidence, we prefer some kinds to others, and we recognise that our certainty depends not only on evidence but also on the importance of the uncertain situation. We can judge the utility of evidence, and decide whether it is worth the effort to obtain it. Remarkably, in a world where almost nothing is certain, we use our knowledge about uncertainty to behave as if almost nothing is uncertain. (Cohen, 1985)

Cohen's argument is that it is necessary to represent explicitly different kinds of uncertainty in order to select an appropriate uncertainty resolution procedure. Furthermore, by so doing, it is possible to provide more intelligible explanations of conclusions and avoid many of the strong assumptions which are inherent in the quantitative approaches; evidence independence, hypothesis exhaustiveness, and so on.

The endorsements which Cohen introduced are data structures (or *support lists*) that summarise reasons for believing and disbelieving. Unlike the support lists which are sometimes used in implementing non-monotonic logics, however, which only distinguish between support based on absence and presence of information, endorsements classify the justifications according to whether evidence supports, or conflicts with a proposition, the possible actions required to resolve uncertainty and aspects of inferences that are relevant to reasoning about their certainty.

Cohen illustrates the use of endorsements to reason about uncertain evidence using an example based on a paper by Walker and Leakey (1978). This paper assesses the implications of three distinct types of fossil records for hypotheses about the number of species represented (one, two or three). For interest, the same article is analysed from a Bayesian and Dempster-Shafer theory perspective in (Shafer and Tversky, 1985). A more detailed example of the use of endorsements in portfolio management is given in (Cohen, 1985).

The fossils sets are named and described as:

Robustus: A form with very large jaws, molar and pre-molar teeth, wide fanning cheekbones, and a cranial capacity of about 500 cc. Also found in South Africa and East Asia. Classified as *Australopithecus robustus*.

Gracile: Smaller than *robustus*, but with similar cranial capacity and slightly smaller molars and pre-molars. Lacks wide fanning cheekbones.

Erectus: A form identified with *Homo erectus* specimens found in the Far East, namely, Java and northern China. This form has a smaller jaw and a large cranial capacity (~850 cc).

The five hypotheses are that the fossils represent:

H1. One single species (vague on sexual classification).

H2. Two species: *robustus* and *gracile* are male and female forms of *Australopithecus robustus* and the large brained fossil is *Homo erectus*.

H3. Two species: *robustus* is one species and *erectus* and *gracile* are male and female of a second.

H4. Two species: *gracile* is one species and *erectus* and *robustus* are another.

H5. Three separate species.

Evidence and argument is summarised as follows:

Culture argument (Pro H1, against rest): Once a hominid species acquires culture its ecological niche expands to crowd out other species (particularly hominid species without culture) so there cannot be two distinct hominid species with culture.

Adaptation Argument (Con H1 and H4, pro rest): Markedly different adaptations are not expected within the same species. *Robustus* and *erectus* have developed opposite adaptations (big teeth and a little brain versus smaller teeth and a larger brain) and therefore are different species.

Sexual Dimorphism Argument (Con H1, H2 and H3): Significant sexual dimorphism. Sexual dimorphism in excess of any observed in living hominid populations is unlikely to occur.

Location Argument 1 (Con H1 and H4): *erectus* form is abundant in Java and Northern China, but *robustus* is absent. So it is unlikely that *robustus* and *erectus* are the same species.

Location Argument 2 (Con H1 and H3): *gracile* form is absent from far east, so it is unlikely that *gracile* and *erectus* are the same species.

Walker and Leakey propose H5, since there are arguments against the other hypotheses and the degree of variability in brain size and dentition within the three fossil groups is not greater than that among living anthropoids. (This is deemed to be only a corroborating argument and is therefore not presented as *prima facie* evidence).

Cohen recasts some of the arguments as uncertain rules (Figure 7.1), with corresponding endorsements. For example, rule 2 is classified as 'maybe too general' because, before the excavation of the *erectus* fossil, Walker and Leakey considered the *robustus* and *gracile* fossils to be a single species. Thus the inference that different morphologies imply different species may be too general. Similarly conclusions from rule 3 may be spurious because the rule is based on lack of evidence. That is, there are no observations of X, therefore X does not exist. This kind of inference requires other factors to make it believable. For example, that physical anthropologists have looked for *robustus* in Java and China and that they would have found them had they existed.

Using these rules and the descriptions of the three fossil types described above it is possible to construct ledger book assessments of the various hypotheses as shown in Table 7.1.

This shows both the supporting arguments and their associated endorsements and demonstrates that the accounting of evidence is not a

```
rule 1: Culture Argument:
    if      hominid(Form_1)
    and     hominid(Form_2)
    and     not_equal(Form_1,Form_2)
    and     has_culture(Form_1)
    then    single_species(Form_1,Form_2)

rule 2: Morphology Argument:      (maybe too general)
    if      different_morphology(Form_1,Form_2)
    then    different_species(Form_1,Form_2)

rule 3: Location Argument:        (cwa not)
    if      found_at(Place_1,Form_1)
    and     not(found_at(Place_1,Form_2))
    then    different_species(Form_1,Form_2)
```

Fig 7.1   *Rule representation of arguments paraphrased from (Cohen, 1985). Capitalised atoms are variables.*

Single Species Hypothesis, H1.	
Evidence Pro	Evidence Against
(single species *erectus robustus*) **Endorsements**	**(different_species** *erectus robustus*) **Endorsements**
1. From rule 1, Figure 7.1	1. From rule 2, Figure 7.1
2. Rule 1 is a theoretical tenet (unproved and perhaps unprovable)	2. Premise is highly believable
	3. Conclusion of rule 2 is too general
	(different_species *erectus robustus*) **Endorsements**
	1. From rule 3, Figure 7.1
	2. Conclusion of rule 3 is based on absence of evidence

Table 7.1   *Ledger book for single species hypothesis. From (Cohen, 1985, p89).*

simple pooling process. As Cohen points out: "we do not have a 'one argument, one vote' setup, but rather, an accounting in which the credibility of the arguments determines their relative weight" (p88). Once such a ledger has been constructed, however, the question remains of determining whether the supporting evidence outweighs the conflicting evidence. Here, Cohen provides no comprehensive techniques for deriving composite measures of uncertainty from the constituent endorsements. A more detailed model of uncertainty reasoning with endorsements was, however, implemented in SOLOMON (Cohen, 1985). This was used to construct a financial portfolio management system called FOLIO.

SOLOMON uses first order predicate calculus for representing propositions and endorsements, and has a predominantly goal driven control strategy directed by a task agenda. When the goal driven strategy fails to produce a sufficiently well supported (endorsed) conclusion to satisfy a task goal, an impasse is reached. At this stage a task is generated which attempts to resolve or discount uncertainty (SOLOMON does not explicitly differentiate between these). Uncertainty can be resolved by obtaining missing information, corroborating conclusions endorsed by low data accuracy, or removing conflicts (e.g. by attempting to disprove the conflicting propositions or the positive endorsements they are based upon). Uncertainty may be discounted by selecting a course of action that effectively covers all outcomes.

Endorsements themselves are attached to data, rules, conclusions, tasks and resolution procedures: endorsements on data relate to the source, type and accuracy (low, medium and high); endorsements on conclusions denote whether they are corroborative, conflicting, potentially conflicting or redundant; endorsements on tasks indicate whether the outcome of the task is potentially corroborative, potentially conflicting, or potentially redundant. Some examples of endorsements on rules are shown in Table 7.2.

Endorsements are inherited in a straightforward manner. Essentially, if Q is inferred from P and $P \to Q$ and the endorsements of P are e_P and the endorsements of $P \to Q$ are $e_{P \to Q}$ then the endorsements of Q are the set of $\{e_P, e_{P \to Q}, e_O\}$, where e_O are any evidential relationships between Q and other conclusions in the database (Cohen, 1985, p62).

maybe-too-general:	more cases satisfy the condition than merit the conclusion.
maybe-too-specific:	fewer cases satisfy the condition than merit the conclusion.
exact:	neither too general nor too specific nor a negation.
supportive:	increase one's confidence if true, but does not cast doubt on conclusion if false.
necessary:	conceptually, the converse of supportive.
hard-not:	not(x) must be adequately endorsed.
cwa-not:	closed-world-assumption, not(x) appears in database or attempts to prove (x) fail.
ostrich-not:	(x) does not *currently* appear in the database.
flexible:	believable if a proposition is found that is approximately equal.
inflexible:	values must be precisely met.

Table 7.2   *Rule endorsements. From (Cohen, 1985, p89).*

7.2.2   Discussion of Cohen's endorsements.

Although it is clear that the endorsement approach is useful as a declarative representation of arguments and that it avoids some of the assumptions made by quantitative approaches, it has been most heavily criticised for the methods (or lack of methods) it employs for propagating, combining and ranking endorsements and hypotheses. The method of endorsement inheritance described above quickly leads to long lists of endorsements being attached to propositions, for example. Cohen has suggested some ways of combining endorsements, but not in sufficient number to cope with this potential explosion.

With respect to the combination of endorsements, Cohen does not provide a well developed apparatus, though he claims that (as with the Walker and Leakey analysis above) people almost never have to balance the credibility of one piece of evidence against another:

> *I suggest that one need weigh the evidence for conflicting hypotheses only very rarely, because if a state of the world is consistent, then it will provide inconsistent signals relatively rarely … weighing evidence to resolve conflicts may be necessary or desirable, but it is not the obvious method to use: indeed, it may be less useful than numerous least commitment approaches, such as hedging, worst-case analysis, taking a central value, deciding not to decide and so on* (p184).

A point that is often omitted in discussions of Cohen's work is that:

The model of endorsements does not preclude endorsements that include numerical measures such as degrees of belief (Cohen, 1985, p53).

This raises the possibility of conditional probabilities or other numerical measures of belief being treated as particular kinds of endorsements which can be propagated, combined and ranked according to the formal calculi described in earlier sections, thereby combining these quantitative measures within a wider, more general, qualitative framework. However, Cohen has not implemented such a procedure.

More recently, Cohen has focused on the importance of control in a system that manages uncertainty by reasoning about evidence and its current state of belief in an hypothesis. States of belief are classified as *disconfirmed, strongly detracted, detracted, unknown, supported, strongly supported,* or *confirmed,* and are assessed by the use of local evaluation functions implemented within a blackboard structure. This idea of identifying and formally defining states of uncertainty is central to Fox's work on semantic aspects of uncertainty discussed below. The reader is referred to (Cohen, 1987), (Cohen et al, 1987) and (Erman et al, 1980) for a description of how uncertainty and control are combined in a blackboard architecture.

7.2.3   Semantic symbolic systems.

In the following sections we discuss the development and application of a number of symbolic systems for uncertainty representation which are based on the assumption that aspects or states of uncertainty can be decomposed into a number of logically defined semantic categories. These systems derive from the initial ideas of Fox (1986a; 1986b) but also share ideas in common with the other symbolic systems discussed above.

Fox's pivotal claim was that there are qualitatively different aspects of uncertainty which can be formalized symbolically and used for reasoning about uncertainty. Fox (1986a; 1986b) identifies a number of different qualitative features of uncertainty, including the notions of possibility, plausibility, probability and definiteness, with further terms and productions defined (Table 7.3).

The argument is that with these qualitative distinctions, it is possible to write uncertain facts and rules in an intelligible manner (e.g. "gastric cancer is probably fatal" and "if weight loss is believed to be rapid and age is elderly then gastric cancer is possible"). In contrast to treating uncertainty as a quantitative object, Fox was attempting to provide a qualitative calculus that is broad in its applicability and cognitively realistic.

P is *possible*	if no conditions that are necessary for P are violated.
P is *plausible*	if P is possible, and there is an argument in support of P, or the balance of argument is for P.
P is *probable*	if P is possible, and there is at least one item of evidence in favour of P.
P is *certain*	if a sufficient condition for P is true.
P is *believed*	if it is reported by a credible source, or a reliable device or procedure, or if it is the most probable or plausible of the alternatives.
P is *likely*	if the summary of evidence and argument is in favour of P.
P is *suspected*	if it is not believed, but there is evidence or argument to support it.
P is *doubted*	if not-P is suspected or a competitor of P is suspected.
P is *assumed*	if it is asserted in domain knowledge (e.g. by default), or derived by general knowledge, and there is no evidence or argument to the contrary.

Table 7.3   *Fox's central uncertainty terms (Fox, 1986a; 1986b).*

Fox's proposals have been developed in two prototype systems. One is an Expert System to assist in medical image interpretation, Table 7.4 (Ellam and Maisey, 1987), and the other is a large knowledge-based decision support system for medical general practitioners, intended to cover most of general medicine (*The Oxford System of Medicine* (O'Neil et al, 1988; 1989; Fox et al, 1990b)), Table 7.5. For such large applications the data, expertise and time necessary for the derivation of quantitative parameters such as conditional probabilities may be unavailable. Under these circumstances, it is necessary to employ methods that employ weaker qualitative distinctions such as those proposed by Fox.

For the Ellam and Maisey system, evidence was constituted by features categorized as excluding, necessary for, sufficient for, evidence for and evidence against particular diagnostic categories. An example rule from the system is shown in Figure 7.2. The rule in Figure 7.2 states that if there is evidence for a particular kind of object, then look for evidence of subclasses of that object. This rule shows how the uncertainty categories defined by Ellam and Maisey are used to control inference (e.g. by looking for evidence associated with subclasses of an object for which evidence already exists). This approach is less extensive than that of Cohen's endorsements in terms of the kinds of information represented, but is an

P is *possible*	if no necessary conditions for P are violated.
P is *impossible*	if an excluding condition for P is present.
P is *suspected*	if P is possible, and at least one piece of evidence in favour of P is present.
P is *likely*	if P is possible, and the sum of evidence for P is greater than the sum of evidence against P.

Table 7.4   *Uncertainty categories employed by Ellam and Maisey (1987).*

P is *possible*	if P is considered and P is not excluded.
P is *excluded*	if P is considered and P is not inconsistent and reason excluding P.
P is *definite*	if P is considered and P is not inconsistent and reason sufficient for P.
P is *supported*	if P is possible and reason for P or reason sufficient for P.
P is *inconsistent*	if reason sufficient for P and reason excluding P.

Table 7.5   *Uncertainty categories employed by O'Neil et al (1988).*

---

if **Class** is *suspected*

    and **Subclass** is a type of **Class**

    and **Feature, Value** is evidence for **Subclass**

    and features include **Feature, Value**

    and **Subclass** is not *impossible*

then **Subclass** is *suspected.*

Fig 7.2   *Decision Rule employing symbolic uncertainty constructs (Ellam and Maisey, 1987). Expressions in bold are variables, expressions in italic are uncertainty terms defined in Table 7.4.*

improvement in terms of the ability to combine, rank and propagate evidence.

7.2.4   A symbolic model of decision making.

As stated in Chapter 1 of this book, a key facet in determining the most appropriate uncertainty management technique for a given application is the consideration of how uncertainty is to be used in that reasoning task. In previous chapters we have focused more on the uncertainty management itself than the specific reasoning task. Here, we change the emphasis somewhat, in order to illustrate how a weak symbolic uncertainty management technique can be used effectively in decision making in a challenging domain (though note that tasks other than decision making can also be potentially supported). Specifically, a symbolic model of decision making has been proposed which utilises the types of symbolic distinctions described by Fox (1986a, 1986b). The following summary presentation is based on (O'Neil et al, 1989; Clark et al, 1990) and other referenced papers. Readers are referred to these for a more detailed account. A deeper discussion of the relationship between uncertainty management and Decision Making is given in Chapter 8.

7.2.4.1   Decision making in a large unquantified domain.

In recent years many scientific and commercial computer-based decision support systems (including Expert Systems) have been developed which operate in highly circumscribed domains. In medicine, for example, most provide advice in restricted domains, such as the diagnosis of abdominal pain (De Dombal, 1975; Adams et al, 1986), or the interpretation of electromyograms (Jensen et al, 1987). For small domains which are characterised by extensive quantitative data, Bayesian systems combined with classical decision making techniques may provide an appropriate platform for the implementation of expert advice systems. However, for the construction of such systems in broad domains (such as general medicine) that are not extensively quantitatively parameterised, and where there are a vast number of potential tasks that may require assistance, Bayesian techniques in isolation will not be appropriate.

7.2.4.2   The Oxford System of Medicine.

The Oxford System of Medicine (OSM) project was established in 1986 with the long term aim of producing a large knowledge-based system providing; (a) a comprehensive medical information service covering most of general medicine, and (b) decision support to medical general

practitioners in the wide range of patient management tasks that characterise general medicine. These include diagnosis, problem refinement and
treatment, each of which may involve dealing with uncertain knowledge.
Various small scale experimental versions of the OSM have been implemented and described (Fox et al, 1987; O'Neil et al, 1989; Glowinski et al,
1989) and as a result of the issues raised, a symbolic theory of decision
making has been developed which augments classical approaches by explicitly addressing a number of issues not tackled by them. By a symbolic
theory, is meant that it is; (a) able to reason about the structure of the decision task itself, and (b) is not based solely on the evaluation of quantitative parameters. The medical examples given below are drawn from work
in the OSM project.

7.2.4.3 · Requirements of a Symbolic Model of Decision Making.

As noted in the conclusion of Chapter 2, it is frequently not the case in AI
that a probability structure will exist for a given problem. Rather, elicitation and construction of such a structure is a problem that has to be faced
by the system designers. Similarly in decision analysis, a large part of the
skill of the decision analyst is centred on the construction of a decision
framework. This includes the generation of mutually exclusive sets of decision options and the determination of the evidence for these decision options (Hill et al, 1978). Only when the structure of the decision has been
specified and the relevant parameters input to the model, can classical decision techniques be applied to select the decision with the highest expected utility (or minimum risk, etc). The symbolic theory of decision making
presented below (and elsewhere, O'Neil et al, 1989) is expressly conceived

1	Dynamically propose decision candidates[a].
2	Dynamically generate evidence relevant to the decision candidates.
3	Dynamically identify relationships among decision candidates relating to conjunctivity and exclusivity.
4	Operate in the absence of statistical parameters, but
5	Incorporate these when available.
6	Be generic and not limited to any particular decision task.

Table 7.6   *Requirements of a Symbolic Decision theory (Clark et al, 1990).*

a. Generally, the term decision candidates is given in preference to decision options.

with this task of decision structuring and evaluation in mind and attempts to move towards the criteria outlined in Table 7.6.

To do this, knowledge is represented at three different levels of abstraction corresponding to:

(1) domain facts,

(2) task specific knowledge, and

(3) generic decision procedures.

7.2.4.4   Domain Facts.

Domain facts are simple descriptive propositions about the field of interest which may express qualitative relations (about causes, associations, taxo-

QUALITATIVE RELATIONS:
causes of weight loss include cancer
causes of weight loss include peptic ulcer
positive associations of cancer include elderly patient
positive associations of gastric ulcer include elderly patient
kinds of diseases include ulcer
kinds of diseases include cancer
kinds of ulcer include peptic ulcer
kinds of peptic ulcer include gastric ulcer
kinds of peptic ulcer include duodenal ulcer
kinds of cancer include gastric cancer
kinds of cancer include colon cancer
investigations of acute breathlessness include chest x-ray
kinds of chest x-ray include lateral chest x-ray
cautions of x-ray include pregnancy
QUANTITATIVE PARAMETERS:
prior probability of cancer = 0.04
prior probability of peptic ulcer = 0.05
prior probability of weight loss = 0.1
conditional probability of weight loss given cancer = 0.4
conditional probability of weight loss given peptic ulcer = 0.5

Table 7.7   *Domain (medical) facts.*

nomic relations, etc) amongst entities, or quantitative parameters associated with these qualitative relations (such as the strength of an association). (See Table 7.7.) These simple structures form the majority of system knowledge and are typically propositions with three arguments, corresponding to an object (cancer, acute breathlessness, x-rays, disease, weight loss), attributes of that object (e.g. causes, kinds) and values of each attribute of that object (e.g. gastric cancer, lateral chest x-ray, pregnancy). The value of one fact may be the object in another, allowing networks of relations to be specified (Figure 7.3). Such structured sets of facts are sometimes termed frames (Minsky, 1975). This form of propositional representation has a number of advantages, as discussed in (Clark et al, 1990).

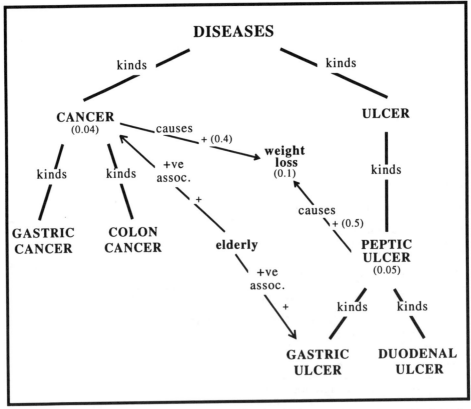

Fig   7.3   *Graphical representation of medical facts. Lines represent qualitative relationships (kinds, causes and positive associations) between facts. Numbers in brackets represent prior and conditional probabilities.*

7.2.4.5   Task Specific Knowledge.

Like domain facts, task specific knowledge is represented propositionally (Table 7.8). However, task specific knowledge is more general than domain facts, and is procedural in the sense that it specifies the function of domain facts (such as symptoms and causes of diseases) in reasoning processes (such as proposing decision candidates). The task specific knowledge relating to diagnosis, for example (Table 7.8), states that candidate diagnoses may be proposed by considering; (a) diseases causing diagnostic problems, (b) the immediate subclasses of diseases for which there is already evidence (kinds of supported diagnoses) or (c) diseases which themselves cause other diseases, for which there is already evidence (causes of supported diagnoses). By making this knowledge explicit it becomes possible for a symbolic procedure to 'reflect' on its knowledge of decision processes and therefore to reason about the decision process itself using meta-level arguments. The importance of meta-level reasoning for the development of autonomous decision making agents is not developed here, but is discussed in Chapter 8 and elsewhere (Fox et al, 1990a).

(a) For proposing decision candidates
proposal criteria of diagnoses include causes of diagnostic problems
proposal criteria of diagnoses include kinds of supported diagnosis
proposal criteria of diagnoses include causes of supported diagnosis
(b) For arguing about decision candidates
supporting arguments of diagnoses include positive signs
contradicting arguments of diagnoses include negative signs
eliminating arguments of diagnoses include excluding signs
confirming arguments of diagnoses include pathognomonic signs

Table 7.8   *Task specific knowledge for proposing and arguing about decision candidates*

7.2.4.6   Generic decision procedures.

Generic decision making knowledge is divided into five processes (Figure 7.4) each represented as a set of abstract, but generic, rules. These processes are inspired by aspects of competent human decision performance, though not based on empirical studies (Fox, 1989). For the purposes of presentation some simplification has been made. Each of these processes is represented as a set of generic rules and procedures as illustrated

Proposal: The dynamic proposal and augmentation of a set of decision candidates in a decision task.

Argumentation: Generation of arguments for and against proposed decision candidates (Evidence Collection).

Annotation: Logical evaluation of decision candidates and associated arguments to qualitatively annotate candidates as possible, eliminated, supported or definite, and so on.

Relation: Recording significant patterns of combination among decision candidates, such as subsumption and compatibility relations, to determine which sets of candidates should be evaluated separately.

Evaluation: The use of strong and/or weak quantitative methods to combine evidence for and against sets of decision candidates to produce total or partial orders, selections and other assessments.

Fig 7.4   *Stages in decision making (Fox et al, 1988; Clark et al, 1990). Each of these processes is represented as a set of generic rules and procedures.*

below. Figure 7.5 provides a schematic overview of the relations between them.

7.2.4.7   Proposal.

The process of proposal can be implemented as a rule (Figure 7.6) which uses the decision request, domain facts and task specific knowledge to infer decision candidates. Specifically, premise (a) of rule 8 matches on a decision specification supplied by a clinician ("diagnostic problems of Fred include weight loss"), premise (b) matches the task specific knowledge ("proposal criteria of diagnoses include causes of diagnostic problems") and premise (c) matches on the relevant domain facts ("causes of weight loss include cancer" and "causes of weight loss include peptic ulcer"), for the rule to infer immediately that "considered diagnoses of Fred include cancer" and "considered diagnoses of Fred include peptic ulcer". Further diagnostic candidates for the weight loss of Fred are proposed using the same rule with other task specific knowledge. Specifically once a diagnostic candidate (disease) is supported (there is at least one argument in favour, see annotation below) then diseases that cause that disease (proposition 6) are also considered, as are subclasses of that disease (proposition

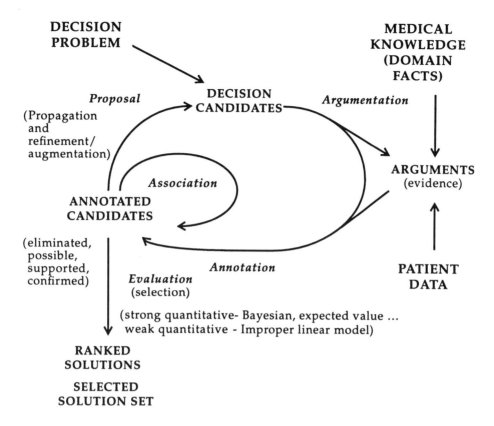

Fig 7.5   *A schematic representation of five generic decision processes and the role of the decision specification (problem), medical knowledge and patient data in their initiation. The five decision processes are shown in italics. All 5 make use of task specific knowledge, not shown here.*

7). Like proposition 5, propositions 6 and 7 both match on premise (b) of the general rule. In the example, this leads to the various types of cancer and ulcer becoming considered as diagnostic candidates. As the diagnosis proceeds and more symptoms are added to the patient record, the number of considered diagnoses increases. There are two things to note here:

- Firstly, the same generic rule can be used to make inferences about other tasks (such as treatments) when supplied with alternate sets of domain facts and task specific knowledge.

- Secondly, the appearance of the term "supported" in the task specific knowledge and the generic rule shows how uncertainty categories, in this case {supported, definite, excluded, possible, considered}, can be used to control the reasoning process.

required decision

  1 diagnostic problems of Fred include weight loss

domain facts

  2 causes of weight loss include cancer
  3 causes of weight loss include peptic ulcer
  4 kinds of cancer include gastric cancer

task specific knowledge

  5 proposal criteria of diagnoses include causes of diagnostic problems
  6 proposal criteria of diagnoses include causes of supported diagnoses
  7 proposal criteria of diagnoses include kinds of supported diagnoses

A generic rule for proposing decision candidates

  8 *if* Decision_class of Patient include Problems   (a)
       and proposal criteria of Decisions include Aspect of Decision_class (b)
       and Aspects of Problem include Candidate   (c)
     then considered Decisions of Patient include Candidate

immediate inferences

       considered diagnoses of Fred include cancer
       considered diagnoses of Fred include peptic ulcer

Fig 7.6   *Proposing Diagnostic Candidates for weight loss of Fred: In the rule,
variables begin with an upper case letter. The term considered is used to
indicate candidates that have been proposed. The rule uses the information in
the decision requirement, together with domain facts relating to weight loss
and task specific knowledge concerning the proposal of diagnostic candidates
to infer that both cancer and peptic ulcer should be considered immediately.*

For reasons of space we do not provide detailed worked examples of all
the decision processes. However, the interested reader is referred to (Clark
et al, 1990) for a more detailed presentation.

7.2.5   Discussion of symbolic systems.

There are a number of things to be emphasised about the symbolic systems discussed above. These weak uncertainty representation schemes
have arisen in response to the need to build systems that can operate in
large domains where there is little chance of collecting all the necessary

quantitative parameters required for some of the stronger uncertainty management formalism discussed above[1].

With respect to the precise sets of terms used, an empirical analysis of some of the terms proposed by Fox was conducted by Clark (1988a). In this study, measures of pairwise similarity between expressions were generated on the basis of nominal scaling procedures, and then analysed using multivariate statistical techniques. The results supported the idea of qualitatively different aspects of uncertainty (see Figure 8.2) but found few of the specific definitions proposed by Fox to be empirically validated by subjects. Only definitions for the expression "assumed" reflected people's interpretation of the expression. Furthermore the fact that equiplausible sets can be proposed (contrast Tables 7.3, 7.4 and 7.5) suggests that more detailed experimental analysis needs to be conducted to ensure that the particular set both has the widest coverage and matches people's intuitions about the meanings of the expressions. What should be emphasised, however, is that these are not fundamental flaws, but areas of the theory that need deeper analysis.

Fox's approach is less extensive than that of Cohen's endorsements in terms of the kinds of information represented. However, this loss of specificity provides the basis for more sophisticated aggregation techniques. Specifically by assigning uniform weight to each supporting argument (as in improper linear modelling; Dawes, 1979) it is possible to use weak quantitative methods to combine, rank and propagate evidence. Furthermore the kinds of symbolic distinctions in Tables 7.3, 7.4 and 7.5 are expressly aimed at addressing the issue of representing the various aspects of uncertainty as outlined in Figure 1.2.

With respect to meta-level reasoning, the facts that

- inconsistencies are explicitly marked, and
- task specific knowledge is represented declaratively

means that

- user preferences can potentially be accommodated in methods of argumentation and assessment, by selecting from options in the task specific knowledge, and more generally,
- it is possible to reason about current inconsistencies in the data and determine procedures for their resolution.

---

1. Weak in the sense of making few assumptions.

Not all the criteria of Table 7.6 are met adequately. However the following is a reasonable summary:

- Decision options can be dynamically constructed or retracted (rather than being stated in advance, see Figure 7.6).

- Combination procedures can identify and reason about inconsistencies.

- It is possible to reason about sets of decision options (e.g. which are alternative and which are complementary) rather than options in isolation.

- Furthermore, meta-level decisions can be made about the decision process itself, e.g. reasoning about when is it necessary to make a decision and what methods of argumentation and assessment should be used.

- With respect to dealing with quantified domain facts, (Clark et al, 1990) give a highly simplified example of how quantitative and qualitative data might be combined based on the assessment of posterior probabilities. However, the problem has not been dealt with in any great depth and certainly not solved for the general case (see also Parsons, 1993).

This presentation has been more to do with decision making that about uncertainty management. However, it illustrates one of the key points made in the introduction, namely that in discussing how to represent uncertainty, it is important to consider how that uncertainty is to be used.

Attempts to put some of these symbolic ideas on a more formal basis are discussed below.

7.3   Logical models of argumentation

The division of this chapter into two distinct sections reflects one of the central tensions of AI. How do we model the range and expressiveness of human reasoning without being open to charges of ad-hocery? To put it another way, to what extent must we be constrained by the development of formal models of the behaviours we are trying to capture? In the foregoing section of this chapter, we discussed a number of approaches to the handling of uncertainty which were intended to capture more fully the richness of human reasoning. Yet they were (perhaps refreshingly) informal in character. In this section, we will review some of the recent work in developing more formal models of argumentation.

Both Cohen and Fox agree that the arguments concerning propositions have structure which is important. That in reasoning under uncertainty, it is not just the establishment of claims which is important, but also the reasoning *about* the arguments for and against those claims. In this sense, uncertainty is a meta-level concept obtained from the evaluation and appraisal of arguments; we are uncertain about a claim because the arguments which support it may fail to convince.

This brings us back again to the historical discussion at the beginning of Chapter 4 in which we reviewed the philosophical background to the view of probability as an epistemic notion. This should be borne in mind whilst reading the remainder of this chapter.

7.3.1   Toulmin's model of argumentation.

Further insight into probability as derived from the analysis and appraisal of arguments may be gained from considering the work of Toulmin (1958). In "The Uses of Argument" Toulmin explored the question of why traditional formal logical models of reasoning have apparently little relevance to everyday dispute and debate. He discussed how arguments may be used to establish and to counter claims, and so induce a degree of conviction in a claim. Although his work was not formal in a mathematical sense, he did provide a useful decomposition of the structure of an argument. In general terms, an argument supporting a *claim*, he said, consists of: *data* to which we appeal as foundation for the claim; a *warrant* justifying the step from the data to the claim; the *backing* which establishes the authority of the claim; the conditions of *rebuttal* indicating the circumstances under which the authority of the warrant would have to be set aside; a *qualifier* for the claim indicating the degree of force which the data confer on the claim by virtue of the warrant. The interrelationships of these components are more clearly presented as a "schema", which we reproduce here in Figure 7.7.

Toulmin used the following example to illustrate this: "in support of the claim that Harry is a British subject, we appeal to the datum that he was born in Bermuda," given the warrant "'A man born in Bermuda may be taken to be a British subject': ... we shall have to insert a qualifying 'presumably' in front of the conclusion, and note the possibility that our conclusion may be rebutted in case it turns out that both his parents were

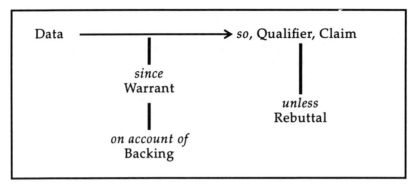

Fig 7.7   *Toulmin's argument schema.*

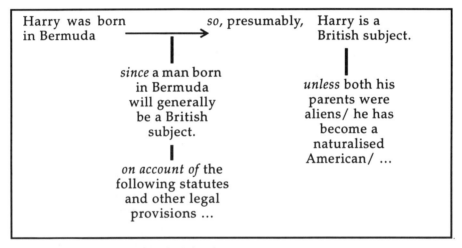

Fig 7.8   *An instance of Toulmin's schema.*

aliens or he has since become a naturalised American". This produces the instance of the argument schema shown in Figure 7.8.

Notice that the claim of an argument will rarely be categoric. The presence of a non-categoric qualifier will indicate that we allow the possibility that the argument may be challenged in some way (for a more detailed discussion of the semantics of such verbal uncertainty expressions see Section 8.3). Although the schema only explicitly refers to rebuttal, we would like to draw a distinction between two different ways in which an argument may be challenged. We may attempt to *defeat* the argument by attacking the warrant (the relevant Act of Parliament may not apply in specific circumstances, perhaps). Alternatively, we may *rebut* the claim by directly contradicting it (we *know* this person is a naturalised American). In general, whether these defeating or rebutting arguments will cause the claim to be retracted, or merely weaken the qualifier, will depend on the relative force of the appropriate arguments. Note that in this particular scheme there is no mechanism for expressing doubt in the data upon which the argument is founded.

Notions of defeat among arguments have been quite widely discussed in the AI literature. Jon Doyle, for example, included a section on dialectical argumentation in his original paper on truth maintenance systems (Doyle, 1979). More recently, Loui (1987), Nute (1988) and Pollock (1992) have each produced descriptions of reasoning systems which are augmented with defeasible arguments. Indeed, we have already seen how default rules can be viewed as arguments and how defeat and rebuttal are modelled in default logic (Section 6.3.10). In the remainder of this chapter we will briefly review some recent progress in the development of logical models of argumentation.

7.3.2   A "Logic of Argumentation".

Many have found the work reported in Section 7.2 to be intuitively appealing. However, it was felt that an attempt should be made to place some aspects of this work into a more mathematically rigorous framework. In (Fox and Clarke, 1991) an extended form of inference was introduced in which propositions, P, were labelled with a qualifier, Q, and appropriate grounds, G: KB $\vdash$ (G, Q, P). The grounds would be a set of propositions which would include the basic data from which the proposition was derived, but may also include information about the inference rules used, the authorities who sanctioned the data, and so on. The qualifier would be taken from one of a number of possible "dictionaries" depending on the format of the available uncertainty information. The dictionaries considered included: {eliminated, opposed, supported, confirmed}; the natural numbers, $\mathbf{N}$, ("counting of arguments"); the unit interval [0,1].

This idea was developed into a logic of argumentation, LA (Fox, Krause and Ambler, 1992; Krause, Ambler and Fox, 1993a). In LA, the arguments are represented in a precise mathematical notation; as "terms in the typed λ-calculus". This representation was chosen because of an equivalence well known to mathematical logicians between logical proofs and the λ-terms. So, in this formalism, the term labelling a proposition provides a faithful and concise summary of the information used to derive a proof, or argument, supporting that proposition.

As a simple example, a medical database used by LA might include the inference rule "r1: elderly ⊃ cancer". That is, when an elderly patient presents, the possibility of their suffering from cancer is at least supported (along with several other possibilities, of course). Note the reading of this primitive argument; "if *elderly*, this argues for *cancer*". The force of this argument is weaker than certainty. Given the additional fact "f1: elderly", LA would infer "apply(r1, f1): cancer". That is, there is an argument "apply(r1, f1)" ("apply the rule labelled r1 to the fact labelled f1") supporting the patient suffering from cancer. (If it seems a bit implausible that a doctor should hypothesise 'cancer' as soon as he or she sees an elderly patient, then think of this along the lines of establishing the 'priors' for a given patient context).

In its basic form, the arguments generated by LA are unqualified. They merely either support a proposition, or oppose a proposition (support its negation). However, primitive to the logic is a notion of *aggregation*. Arguments supporting a proposition may be collected together to obtain more information about the potential validity of that proposition. The notion of aggregation is actually embedded in the semantics of LA, and we really need to say a little bit about the semantics before explaining the practical impact of aggregation.

7.3.3   The semantics of LA.

In Chapter 6 we mentioned that a standard approach to developing a semantics for a logic is to use model theory, whereby a meaning is ascribed in terms of possible interpretations of the sentences in the logic. In this case we ascribe a semantics to the logic by saying what the sentences in the logic *denote*. Denotations for a logic are normally either *t* (true) or *f* (false). This is the Tarskian tradition in semantics.

An alternative approach is not to ask "when is a sentence P *true*?" (*à la* Tarskian semantics), but to ask "what is a *proof* of A?". We ascribe a meaning to the proofs in the logic, and not to the sentences themselves. In terms of LA, the idea was to ascribe a formal meaning to the arguments in LA. LA was given such a *proof theoretic* semantics in terms of a relatively recent branch of mathematics called category theory (Pierce, 1991).

Once again, a "meaning" is given to the logic LA in terms of a formal mathematical structure. We will not go into the details here as they are, as with model theory, quite technical. However, an important feature of the category theoretic semantics of LA is that this formal structure is augmented with some primitive ordering information on the representation of sets of arguments. An aggregation operation is then defined in terms of a least upper bound, or *supremum*, which says that if f and g are (the representation of) two sets of arguments supporting a proposition, then the aggregation $f \vee g$ (read "f sup g") contains at least as much information as either of the two sets of arguments on their own. The aggregation $f \vee g$ has the basic properties of set union. In particular, $f \leq f \vee g$ and $g \leq f \vee g$.

7.3.4   The aggregation of arguments.

One benefit of using a formal framework to define this notion of aggregation is that it ensures that as arguments are combined and composed, the aggregation operation behaves in a coherent way. But this is still a very abstract notion, and a further step is required to map aggregations of arguments into some meaningful representation which a human user can interpret. The general strategy is that a meaning is ascribed to (sets of) arguments using the very abstract framework of category theory. A meaning is then assigned to the propositions themselves by defining *strength mappings* from sets of arguments to one of a number of possible dictionaries (as earlier). *These* meanings are more easily interpreted by a human user. A variety of alternative qualitative, semi-qualitative and numerical uncertainty calculi may be modelled by the use of different strength mappings. For example, if f is a set of arguments supporting a proposition P, we may have:

$$s(f) \in \left\{ \begin{array}{l} \{0, +, ++\} \\ \mathbf{N}^{\infty} \\ [0,1] \end{array} \right.$$

In the first case, we have confirmation or proof (++), support (+), or the vacuous argument supporting a proposition (0). Note the last does *not* correspond to the falsity of the proposition; a proposition is false if its negation is confirmed, whereas the vacuous argument merely says we have no information.

The second case, the natural numbers augmented with infinity, corresponds to a slight refinement of the improper linear model with uniform weights (Dawes, 1979); basically the counting of arguments, but here no matter how many supporting arguments we have, they will not outweigh a logical proof (mapped to infinity).

In the third case, there are several alternative approaches to defining a mapping to the unit interval (M1 to M3), which we will outline below. However, before we do this, we need to explain a little notation.

Axioms in a database used by the Argumentation Theorem Prover (henceforth ATP) are labelled with atomic labels. These may follow a simple naming convention, which perhaps allows some typing of the information to which they refer. For example, pathologies may be labelled "pN: Pathology", where N is a natural number, or symptoms labelled "sN: Symptom". An argument may be of the form *apply(r1, pair(a1, a2))* (*pair(a1, a2)* is an argument for a conjunction P ∧ Q, where *a1* is an argument for P and *a2* is an argument for Q). The *assumptions* used in constructing this argument are the labels {r1, a1, a2}.

The axioms in a database may have some associated confidence value. For example, we might have:

> r1: *elderly ⊃ cancer*   (0.1)
> r2: *elderly ⊃ arthritis*   (0.2)

This allows a mapping to be defined from assumptions to confidence values (e.g. r1→ 0.1, r2 → 0.2). We may now describe the strength mappings to the [0, 1] interval:

(M1)   Evaluate the confidence in an argument as the minimum of the confidences in the assumptions it uses. The confidence in a proposition is then the maximum of the confidences of the arguments which support it. (A "weakest link" approach.)

(M2)   Evaluate the confidence in an argument by multiplying together the confidences in the assumptions it uses. The confidence in a proposition is then the maximum of the confidences of the arguments which support it. (A "shortest path" approach.)

(M3)   First map individual arguments to the sets of assumptions used in their construction (e.g. *apply (r1, pair(a1, a2))* → {r1, a1, a2}). Then the confidence conferred on a proposition by the aggregation of two arguments is given in terms of the probability valuation of sets of assumptions by the formula

$$p(x \lor y) = p(x) + p(y) - p(x \land y)$$

p(x) is obtained by multiplying together the confidences of all the assumptions in x. x ∧ y can be thought of as the intersection of the set x and the set y. Note that the value of p(x ∧ y) will increase towards a maximum of p(x) (or p(y)) as the number of assumptions shared between x and y increases.

The first two aggregation schemes will only assign a confidence to a proposition on the basis of the strongest argument supporting it. Additional, weaker, arguments will not reinforce our confidence in the argument, no matter how many of them there are. This is a cautious approach, given that one may not know what the dependencies between the arguments are. The third aggregation scheme does, however, allow for reinforcement of confidence. The term $p(x \wedge y)$ ensures that the axioms common to two arguments are taken into account as their confidence values are aggregated. It should be emphasised that this is a syntactic notion of independence, and not a semantic notion of independence.

Krause, Ambler and Fox (1993a) summarise their approach by saying that this is a proof theoretic model of reasoning under uncertainty in which subjective estimates of confidence are assigned to the proofs of LA in a coherent way.

7.3.5   Discussion of LA.

LA provides, subject to some limitations, a uniform framework for implementing a variety of uncertainty calculi. With respect to the mappings to the [0, 1] interval, mapping (M1) returns a value which can be interpreted as the greatest lower bound of a necessity measure (see Section 5.15), whilst mapping (M3) is a generalisation of Dempster-Shafer belief (Wilson, 1989). In addition, LA provides some alternative strategies which can be used in the absence of numerical data. The limitations are that it does not handle the set-theoretic aspects of vagueness and imprecision, and that it employs a weaker notion of negation than most of the uncertainty calculi discussed so far in this book. The latter was a conscious design decision (Krause, Ambler and Fox, 1993a), but is not uncontroversial. The former is, perhaps, a more serious limitation.

A theorem prover, ATP, which is sound and complete with respect to the semantics of LA has been implemented. However, this is very much of the nature of a prototype, and efficiency issues have not been seriously addressed so far. For example, as currently implemented, when using the min-max aggregation scheme, all proofs are evaluated and then the confidence in the strongest is returned. Contrast this with possibilistic logic in which a search strategy is used to trace only the strongest proof (Section 5.4).

The representation of arguments used to label propositions is more succinct than Cohen's endorsement scheme. It does not explicitly contain as much information as Cohen's endorsements. However, the representation is machine readable and it is straightforward to write programs which will recurse down through an argument and use the axiom labels to cross-reference to any additional information which is known about specific axioms (both facts and rules). The intent is for this to provide a sound framework for meta-level reasoning about arguments. This is the subject of continuing work.

7.3.6   Poole's theory preference model.

In this section we will gain a slightly different perspective on default reasoning and argumentation by looking at the work of David Poole. This work takes some inspiration from the way in which people reason with and construct scientific theories. Poole's hypothesis is that practical reasoning need not be modelled by changing the logical system, as in non-monotonic logics, but rather by changing the way we use logic.

Poole's work resulted in the development of a logic programming based system called Theorist which used a uniform deductive reasoning mechanism to construct explanations of observations in terms of facts and hypotheses (Poole et al, 1987). This system provided a uniform framework for diagnosis, default-reasoning and learning. However, we will only focus on the model of reasoning which was developed by Poole (1988), look at some of the problems with it, and briefly discuss how these have been addressed by Prakken's more recent argumentation framework (Prakken, 1993).

In this model, a database is partitioned into three components. This database represents a world model for some problem solving context. The components are:

F - The set of formulae which we know to be true in the world. This set is assumed consistent.

Δ - The set of possible hypotheses. These are data which we are prepared to accept as part of an explanation of the state of the world. The set Δ as a whole may be inconsistent. There will, however, be subsets of Δ which are consistent.

G - The set of observations to be explained.

Poole's original idea was that a set of observations G was *explainable* if a consistent set, D, of hypotheses could be selected from Δ so that all the observations in G could be derived from D and the facts F. That is:

Definition 7.1   (Poole, 1985)

G is explainable iff $\exists D \subseteq \Delta$ such that
$$F \cup D \vdash G$$
and $F \cup D$ is consistent.

D can be regarded as the theory which explains G (in the context of F).

7.3.7   Poole's model as a system of argumentation.

Of more interest here is that the idea can be refined to give a slightly different notion of an argument to that discussed in Section 7.3.2. Instead of looking at sets of observations to be explained, we will consider just a single proposition φ. As before, F is a set of facts about the world, and Δ a set of hypotheses. If we can collect together a consistent set of data from the pair of databases (F, Δ) which entails φ, then we have an argument for φ.

Definition 7.2

If $D \subseteq \Delta$, then $A = F \cup D$ is an argument for φ (in the context F) iff:
$$A \vdash \varphi$$
and   A is consistent.

Note that the condition that A is consistent is needed to ensure that arguments are non-trivial. That is, if A is inconsistent, then we can conclude anything. So, of course we have an argument for φ, and for ¬φ, and for anything else we might care to mention.

This is a very generous definition of an argument, as there may be data in A which has no relevance to the derivation of φ. We will see later, that there are alternative definitions which have a requirement for the "minimality" of A.

Let us set up an example. We have some general facts about birds which we know to be true. For example, penguins are birds: F_n = {penguin(X) ⊃ bird(X)}. We also have some case specific data: tweety is a penguin, F_c = {penguin(tweety)}. Let $F = F_n \cup F_c$. Now we also have a set of data which may be appropriate to use in a given context, or it may not.

We might choose to use some, or all, of this data to argue for a specific claim with reasonable confidence. But we might be open to contradiction when we do so. Here are some hypotheses:

$$\Delta = \{\text{penguin}(X) \supset \neg\text{fly}(X), \text{bird}(X) \supset \text{fly}(X)\}.$$

Then $A_i = F \cup \{\text{penguin}(X) \supset \neg\text{fly}(X)\}$ is an argument for $\neg\text{fly(tweety)}$.

But $A_j = F \cup \{\text{bird}(X) \supset \text{fly}(X)\}$ is an argument for fly(tweety). So, which conclusion should we prefer? Given no other grounds to prefer arguments, Poole defined a notion of specificity to resolve such conflicts.

Generally, an argument A_i is more specific than A_j if there is a possible scenario in which *only* A_j applies (the cases where A_i applies are more specialised). Poole wanted this notion of specificity to be generic, and not dependent on case specific data. That is why he, as did we in the Tweety example, divided the facts F into case specific data F_c (contingent facts) and data which always hold, F_n (necessary facts). In defining the notion of specificity, the contingent facts F_c are replaced by any set of possible facts which may be used to establish that one argument is more specific than another. Here is Poole's definition:

Definition 7.3   after (Poole, 1985)
Consider a general theory (F, Δ) where $F = F_n \cup F_c$. Let $A_i = (F_n \cup F_c \cup D_i)$ be an argument for φ, and $A_j = (F_n \cup F_c \cup D_j)$ be an argument for $\neg\varphi$, where $D_i, D_j \subseteq D$. Then A_i is *more specific than* A_j with respect to φ iff there is a fact f_p s.t.

$$F_n \cup \{f_p\} \cup D_j \vdash \neg\varphi$$
and   *neither* $F_n \cup \{f_p\} \cup D_i \vdash \varphi$ *nor* $F_n \cup \{f_p\} \cup D_i \vdash \neg\varphi$ hold.

A_i is *strictly more specific than* A_j if A_i is more specific than A_j, but A_j is not more specific than A_i.

Basically, what we are saying is that if we can replace F_c by a scenario in which A_j rebuts A_i without A_i being able to defend itself, then A_i must be applicable in more specific circumstances than A_j.

Here is our example again:
$A_i = F_n \cup F_c \cup D_i$, where $D_i = \{\text{penguin}(X) \supset \neg\text{fly}(X)\}$,
$A_j = F_n \cup F_c \cup D_j$, where $D_j = \{\text{bird}(X) \supset \text{fly}(X)\}$,
and $F_n = \{\text{penguin}(X) \supset \text{bird}(X)\}$, $F_c = \{\text{penguin(tweety)}\}$.

We have $A_i \vdash \neg fly(tweety)$, and

$A_j \vdash fly(tweety)$.

Consider now the scenario in which we just know that tweety is a bird; $f_p = bird(tweety)$. Now:

$A_j' = F_n \cup \{f_p\} \cup D_j \vdash fly(tweety)$.

But we do not have either $A_i' \vdash \neg fly(tweety)$ or $A_i' \vdash fly(tweety)$, where $A_i' = F_n \cup \{f_p\} \cup D_i$.

On the other hand, whatever fact $\{f_p'\}$ we substitute for F_c in A_i must also entail penguin(tweety) if we are still to be able to conclude $\neg fly(tweety)$. So in this case, we will be able to conclude fly(tweety) from $A_j' = F_n \cup \{f_p'\} \cup D_j$. That is, there is no scenario in which A_i is applicable without A_j being applicable. So A_i is strictly more specific than A_j. Hence we prefer A_i and conclude that tweety does not fly.

This defines some grounds for preferring arguments just based on the structure of those arguments. Of course, if some preference or priority ordering can be placed on the data in the knowledge base, then this will also give us grounds upon which to base a preference in the case of conflicting arguments. These preference criteria have good clear formal definitions, and in that respect they have more credibility in the theoretical AI community than the heuristic models of argumentation which we opened the chapter with. But two questions still arise. Are they reasonable definitions? And on what grounds can we judge whether they are reasonable?

7.3.8   Some problems with Poole's model.

At the moment there does not seem to be any agreed axiomatisation of common sense or pragmatic reasoning, and there are not really any general agreed standards by which to judge a model such as Poole's. Often it is just a matter of throwing specific examples at a model until it breaks in some way, and then patching it up so that it behaves in a more acceptable way again. This seems to be the case with Poole's model of argumentation. Prakken (1993) identified a number of examples in which Poole's model behaved in a possibly counter-intuitive way. We will briefly outline Prakken's criticisms and his proposed solution. Full details can be found in (Prakken, 1993).

The first problem is that arguments are not just the theories which support the claim. They also have some structure (Poole himself recognises this, but does not deal with it as strongly as Prakken would wish). Essentially, for an argument to be preferred, it is not only the final claim which should be preferred. All the intermediate conclusions should be preferred too.

The second problem is a little trickier to get the mind around. It is a matter of *contraposition*. In classical logic, an inference rule may not only be used in a 'forward' direction (modus ponens); from p and p ⊃ q, conclude q. It may also be used in a 'reverse' sense. If the conclusion of the rule p ⊃ q is known to be false, ¬q, then it must be the case that the premise is also false, ¬p. Otherwise the theory would be inconsistent (if p were true we would have {p, ¬q, p ⊃ q} ⊢ ⊥). Prakken argues that if the hypotheses in Δ allow contraposition, then this may lead to some arguments for claims being preferred, when those arguments seem unintuitive.

This problem has often been discussed in the context of modelling commonsense reasoning. Basically, whilst a rule such as bird(X) ⊃ fly(X), "birds typically fly", seems reasonable as a hypothesis, the contraposition ¬fly(X) ⊃ ¬bird(X), "non-flying things are typically not birds", is not particularly helpful. Nic Wilson, who seems to have an inexhaustible ability to dream up pertinent examples and counter examples, came up with the following. Typically people who are of this planet *do not* know about non-monotonic reasoning. That seems a reasonable hypothesis. The contraposition is; people who *do* know about non-monotonic reasoning are typically not of this planet. There are no recorded instances of this second rule, as yet!

Prakken suggests using rules which do not allow contraposition in the hypothesis set Δ. He reformulates Poole's system using default rules (which do not allow contraposition) in Δ, and using a more complex notion of preference which incorporates notions of *sub-arguments* and *final conclusions* to enable a preference on the basis of specificity of all intermediate conclusions to be expressed.

7.3.9   Discussion of Prakken's revised model.

A critique of Poole's system can also be found in (Brewka, 1991a). He describes his own preferred sub-theories approach, which also uses default logic as a basis. Prakken, however, believes that this approach is open to similar criticisms. Who is right? At the moment there are really no absolute grounds for a judgement. We must reiterate what we said in the discussion section of Chapter 6; the time is ripe to validate these models against real world applications. In a sense, this is where Prakken comes from as his motivation was to develop a model of the adversarial aspect of legal reasoning. A number of his examples are taken from aspects of behaviour he would expect to see in the legal field, so his work is a step in that direction.

On the less positive side, it has to be said that these models do seem to become increasingly baroque as they are further refined. It becomes much harder to see what the underlying intuitions are behind their formal definition. It does seem a curious paradox that the aspects of reasoning which people seem to manage so easily are proving to be the most complex to formalise.

7.3.10   Logical uncertainty?

The final models of argumentation which we will look at in this chapter take their inspiration from recent work in inconsistency tolerant reasoning. This is very recent work indeed, and is still in its formative stages. However, we include it here to give a flavour for some of the current directions of research in the uncertainty in AI community.

Classically, the detection of an inconsistency in a logical theory has been regarded as pathological; everything follows from a deduction of *falsum*, $\perp$. This property of classical, intuitionistic and most modal logics is not, however, a feature which is reflected in everyday reasoning. People generally have an ability to localise inconsistency, and may suspend resolution of a contradiction if it does not involve information which is directly relevant to the action at hand (Gabbay and Hunter, 1991). There has been a steady interest in developing models for reasoning in the presence of inconsistent data in both the AI (Dubois, Lang and Prade, 1992; Fox et al, 1992; Perlis, 1990) and philosophical logic (Nelson, 1949; Priest, 1989; Priest et al, 1988) communities. From a more pragmatic perspective, the sheer impracticality of ensuring consistency in large scale deductive databases has also lead the logic programming community to consider consequence relations which are tolerant of varying levels of inconsistency (Wagner, 1991). In this section we will describe a system which actually encourages the use of inconsistency to provide a logical model of a form of dialectical argumentation.

Dubois and Prade's research group have recently expanded on their work on possibilistic logic (see Chapter 5) to consider how argumentative inference may be used in uncertain and inconsistent knowledge bases (Benferhat et al, 1993a; 1993b). They have defined a number of different consequence relations on an inconsistent knowledge base which employ differing degrees of scepticism in the conclusions they allow. This, together with the definition of priority levels on the database based on the framework of possibility theory has allowed them to identify preferred conclusions in the presence of inconsistency.

The basic idea is very similar to Poole's argumentation framework. Given an inconsistent knowledge-base Δ (such as $\{p, \neg p, p \supset q\}$ we may select consistent sub-bases ($\{\neg p\}$ or $\{p, p \supset q\}$) from which meaningful conclusions may be drawn in the context of those sub-bases. Benferhat, Dubois and Prade give the following definition of an argument:

Definition 7.4

A sub-base δ of Δ is said to be an argument for a formula φ if:

i) δ is consistent

ii) $\delta \vdash \varphi$

iii) $\forall p \in \delta, \delta\text{-}\{p\} \nvdash \varphi$

The third criterion of this definition ensures that the argument is minimal. That is, does not include any information which is irrelevant to the conclusion of φ.

So, with the database Δ above, $\delta_1 = \{p, p \supset q\}$ is an argument for q, whilst $\delta_2 = \{\neg p\}$ is an argument for $\neg p$.

It is then possible to define a notion of an argumentative consequence, whereby a proposition is an argumentative consequence of a database if it is not possible to rebut the argument supporting it:

Definition 7.5   (Benferhat et al, 1993a)

A formula φ is said to be an argumentative consequence of Δ iff:

i)   there exists an argument for φ in Δ, and

ii)   there is no argument for $\neg\varphi$ in Δ.

In the previous example, we see that whilst q is an argumentative consequence of Δ, p is not.

Independently of this work, Elvang-Gøransson, Krause and Fox (1993) have also explored ideas from inconsistency tolerant reasoning to formalise the linguistic terms discussed in Section 7.2.3. In keeping with the work on LA (Section 7.3.2), the arguments are structures incorporating the claim of the argument, together with the information used to derive the claim. That is, an argument is a pair (δ, p), where δ is the set of facts in the database from which the conclusion, p, is derived. Their primitive notion of an argument does *not* require that the facts δ are consistent:

Definition 7.6

If $\delta \subseteq \Delta$ is minimal such that $\delta \vdash p$, then (δ, p) is an argument from Δ *supporting* p.

Then there are two specific forms of arguments, the first corresponding to Benferhat et al's definition:

Definition 7.7

An argument (δ, p) is a *consistent argument* if δ is consistent.

Definition 7.8

An argument (δ, p) is a *tautological argument* if $\delta = \emptyset$.

Definition 7.8 merely says that the proposition p must be a tautology of the logic.

Now, we come back to the two ways in which an argument may be challenged which we discussed in connection with Toulmin's schema. Firstly, an argument (δ, p) can *rebut* an argument (γ, q) if and only if p is a direct contradiction of q (p is "logically equivalent" to $\neg$q). Secondly, an argument (δ, p) can *defeat* an argument (γ, q) if and only if, for some r $\in$ γ, p is a direct contradiction of r.

Once more using $\Delta = \{p, \neg p, p \supset q\}$, we see that the argument ($\{\neg p\}$, $\neg$p) rebuts the argument ($\{p\}$, p), whilst the argument ($\{\neg p\}$, $\neg$p) defeats the argument ($\{p, p \supset q\}$, q).

"Acceptability" classes may then be defined using these notions of defeat and rebuttal. These classes can be arranged into a hierarchy in which arguments have to pay a successively higher price of membership to be accepted into successive classes. The basic class allows all possible arguments as members. The second class only allows consistent arguments as members. The third class only allows those arguments which are not open to rebuttal as members, whilst the fourth class allows only those arguments which are not open to rebuttal and defeat. The final class consists of the tautological arguments.

Let Δ be any, possibly inconsistent, database. Then the following classes reflect increasing degrees of acceptability:

$A_1(\Delta) = \{(\delta, p) \mid (\delta, p) \text{ is any argument from } \Delta\}$

$A_2(\Delta) = \{(\delta, p) \in A_1(\Delta) \mid (\delta, p) \text{ is a consistent argument from } \Delta\}$

$A_3(\Delta) = \{(\delta, p) \in A_2(\Delta) \mid \neg(\exists\delta') ((\delta', \neg p) \in A_2(\Delta))\}$

$A_4(\Delta) = \{(\delta, p) \in A_3(\Delta) \mid (\forall q \in \delta) (\neg(\exists\delta')((\delta', \neg q) \in A_2(\Delta)))\}$

$A_5(\Delta) = \{(\delta, p) \in A_4(\Delta) \mid (\delta, p) \text{ is a tautological argument from } \Delta\}$

It can be seen that in the case of $\Delta = \{p, \neg p, p \supset q\}$, $(\{p, p \supset q\}, q) \in A_3(\Delta)$ since it cannot be rebutted. However, it is *not* the case that $(\{p, p \supset q\}, q) \in A_4(\Delta)$ since this argument is open to defeat from the consistent argument $(\{\neg p\}, \neg p)$.

Elvang-Gøransson et al then go on to suggest that this hierarchy could be used to assign linguistic "measures" of uncertainty to formulae. Let $\mathcal{L}$ be the set of well-formed formulae in propositional logic. Then *confidence classes* associated with a database Δ may be defined as:

$$C_{ce}(\Delta) = \{p \mid (\exists\delta) ((\delta, p) \in A_5(\Delta))\}$$
$$C_{co}(\Delta) = \{p \mid (\exists\delta) ((\delta, p) \in A_4(\Delta))\}$$
$$C_{pr}(\Delta) = \{p \mid (\exists\delta) ((\delta, p) \in A_3(\Delta))\}$$
$$C_{pl}(\Delta) = \{p \mid (\exists\delta) ((\delta, p) \in A_2(\Delta))\}$$
$$C_{su}(\Delta) = \{p \mid (\exists\delta) ((\delta, p) \in A_1(\Delta))\}$$
$$C_{op}(\Delta) = \mathcal{L}$$

The subscripts may be read as: *c*ertain; *co*nfirmed; *p*robable; *su*pported; *op*en. By "open", we mean that the proposition is a meaningful sentence, but we have no information upon which to base a judgement about its certainty.

An ordering is induced over these classes by the property of the acceptability classes that for $i < j$, $A_i(\Delta) \supseteq A_j(\Delta)$ for any Δ. We have that for any Δ:

$$C_{ce}(\Delta) \subseteq C_{co}(\Delta) \subseteq C_{pr}(\Delta) \subseteq C_{pl}(\Delta) \subseteq C_{su}(\Delta) \subseteq C_{op}(\Delta).$$

This ordering induces a candidate for a confidence measure. The following function is defined:

Definition 7.9

Let $\Delta \subseteq L$ be any set of propositions. Let $g_\Delta: L \rightarrow \{ce, co, pr, pl, su, op\}$ be defined by:

$$g_\Delta(p) = \max(\{x \mid p \in C_x(\Delta)\}).$$

"max" is defined over the order $ce \geq co \geq pr \geq pl \geq su \geq op$.

Returning again to our example database, $\Delta = \{p, \neg p, p \supset q\}$. It should be clear that $g_\Delta(p) = g_\Delta(\neg p) = pl$. That is, both p and $\neg$p are "plausible". Consistent arguments can be constructed which support them, but each argument is open to rebuttal by the other. However, $g_\Delta(q) = pr$; q is "probable". No argument can be constructed which rebuts the argument supporting q, as we have seen. Nevertheless, q cannot be confirmed as its supporting argument is open to defeat by ($\{\neg p\}, \neg p$).

7.3.11   Discussion of "logical uncertainty".

The motivation for wanting to pursue this line of research is not without foundation. It is very much in keeping with the view, expressed in the historical section of Chapter 4, that epistemic probability is derived from an appraisal of arguments and need not necessarily be numerical.

The definitions of arguments and of the various alternative consequence relations do seem to reflect a convergence of many trains of thought. In addition, further work suggests that the confidence "measure" g_Δ has some quite reasonable properties. However, whether the ordering on confidence values induced by the set inclusion ordering of acceptability classes reflects a "natural cognitive ordering" is currently open to question. The results obtained from simple examples seem intuitive, but the technique still awaits validation on larger scale examples. Nevertheless, we do feel that this work provides an exciting insight into current research into argumentation.

7.4   Discussion

By comparison with the previous six chapters of this book, where the variants of the formalisms discussed were sufficiently similar to permit general statements to be made, all the schemes presented in this chapter have been accompanied by individual discussions. The following thus makes some key points and picks out generic features of all the systems.

7.4.1   Knowledge representation.

With respect to the heuristic systems:

- Cohen's theory of endorsements is useful as a declarative representation of uncertainty and avoids some of the assumptions made by quantitative approaches. However, the major problems are that mechanisms for propagation, combination (evaluation) and resolution of endorsements are under-specified.

- The Symbolic Semantic Systems of Fox and others are also weak. However, with a generic decision theory they can be used to combine and compare decision candidates using a weak quantitative scheme in which all supporting arguments are assumed to have equal weights. It can be used for explicitly representing different states of uncertainty (rather than degrees) and provides a useful tool for uncertain and meta-level reasoning in broad domains.

A number of other systems have attempted to place some of these ideas on a more formal basis:

- LA for example, attempts to provide a formal vehicle for argument based reasoning which categorises evidence according to one of a number of alternate, non-simultaneous dictionaries. LA also provides, subject to some limitations, a uniform framework for implementing a variety of uncertainty calculi. The argument systems of Poole and Prakken deal with inference using contingent, possibly inconsistent, data. They allow only notions of truth and falsity. The work of Benferhat et al enables some ordinal relationship on propositions (in terms of possibility theory) to be incorporated. In contrast, the system of Elvang-Gøransson et al allows a finer grading of belief to be expressed purely symbolically, using notions of defeat and rebuttal amongst arguments.

7.4.2   Knowledge engineering.

The purposes of the heuristic approaches was partly to allow expression of uncertain facts and rules in an intelligible manner. However, other than Clark's (1988a) analysis of Fox's semantic terms, there is not yet a body of evidence against which the ease or otherwise of knowledge engineering can be assessed.

7.4.3   Computational considerations.

Most of the systems (both heuristically based and logically based) could run into serious computational problems. However, being relatively new, there are as yet few formal studies documenting the precise computational complexities.

It should be emphasised, however, that Poole's model of argumentation was incorporated into a practical implementation, using conventional logic programming techniques. The proposals of Benferhat et al, are also thought to be computationally feasible.

7.5   Conclusions

We began this chapter with the observation that argumentation is an important process in reasoning under uncertainty, and then went on to describe two sets of heuristically based approaches and several logically based approaches aimed at formalising some of the processes of argumentation. Of the heuristic approaches Cohen's approach is highly declarative but underspecified. In contrast, the Symbolic Systems of Fox and others is ontologically less expressive (i.e. there are simply less types of things), but gains as a result in terms of combination and propagation procedures, employing weak quantitative methods where possible. The final chapter of this book discusses the more general prospects for an integrated combination of symbolic and quantitative approaches.

The logical approaches described in this chapter take some inspiration from intuitive ideas of argumentation. Much of this work is very recent and provides a clear demonstration that the field of uncertain reasoning is still very much a rich and fertile research area.

8
Overview

If you only have a hammer, you tend to see every problem as a nail. (Maslow).

Not all problems of uncertainty in AI lend themselves to probability. Other approaches are often required. (Shafer and Pearl, 1990).

8.1   Introduction

We start this chapter with two quotations. The intention behind the quotation from Maslow is to emphasise that problem solving (in this case managing uncertainty) should be driven by the requirements of the problem and not by the most immediate solution tool. Extending the metaphor, we view the field of uncertainty management as one in which there are many different types of problems and a variety of tools from which one may select for a solution.

In some respects the history of uncertainty management in AI up to the 1970s can be seen as one in which probability theory was the hammer and all problems were seen as nails. However, as the quotation from Pearl and Shafer suggests, this characterisation has begun to subside with greater tacit admission of the challenges of the field and limitations of particular techniques.

We began this book with an overview of the requirements of AI uncertainty management techniques in terms of the various levels of information that must be represented, and other issues relating to system construction. Chapters 2 to 7 then explored in detail six distinct families of techniques that have been employed or proposed to this end. This chapter first provides a resumé of the relative rationales, merits and disadvantages of each technique. It then explores four more general issues: verbal uncertainty expressions, decision making with uncertainty management techniques, uncertainty and meta-level reasoning and, finally, the convergence of uncertainty management techniques.

The first concerns how the various formalisms described map onto human representations of uncertainty as mediated by verbal uncertainty expressions. This is very distinct from the more formal discussions at the end of each of the preceding chapters. However, it is also complementary in the sense that, as pointed out in the introduction, when considering the net effectiveness of an uncertainty management system, the appropriate level of analysis must cover the user interaction with the system; the system should not just be considered in isolation, a point made clear in the work of de Dombal et al (1992) discussed at the end of Chapter 2. In this respect, verbal uncertainty expressions are not the only factor to consider, but they are in some respects representative of the required level of analysis.

Finally, we discuss future trends in terms of those unsolved problems that await solution and steps being taken to integrate the respective merits of the various systems.

8.2   Resumé

The following sections provide a brief resumé of the approaches to uncertainty that have been described in this book. We will stress the key points on how they may be exploited before moving on to some more general themes.

8.2.1   Bayesian approaches.

The discussion in Chapter 2 emphasised that the Bayesian calculus both imposes a strict discipline on knowledge engineering, and provides a useful tool for representing and updating subjective probabilities under certain well defined conditions. If these conditions are not met, however, applying the Bayesian scheme may impose some difficulties (Section 2.7). Probability theory is generally centred on the notion of uncertainty as it applies to atomic or conditional propositions. Therefore, concepts such as inconsistency, incompleteness and irrelevance are not permitted, and are not formally part of the Bayesian model. Thus, for example, with respect to incompleteness in the (set theoretic) sense of gaps in relevant knowledge, the Bayesian formulation makes the strong assumption that all the relevant knowledge is encoded in the model. Should subsequent knowledge be identified as relevant then the dependency network may have to be revised, the new relevant parameters determined and the appropriate values assessed. This can be a costly business if restructuring is required and therefore the model should be as complete as possible prior to the elicitation of marginal probabilities (although adding additional cliques in isolation is relatively straight forward).

This raises an important point about the Bayesian approach. As we have stressed, work on Bayesian inference nets is fundamentally concerned with the structure of reasoning; not merely with the numerical coefficients themselves. That this is a critical and very general point is illustrated by the following:

- The emphasis on the structure of reasoning is important because in AI the initial problem is usually the construction of an appropriate model of the universe of discourse.

- A number of generalisations of the Bayesian approach exist which deal with coefficients other than probabilities (e.g. Shenoy and Shafer, 1986; 1990). There are, for example, some systems which employ essentially Bayesian methods to propagate non-numerical coefficients (e.g. MUM; Cohen, 1989). Note, however, that the set of axioms that such measures must satisfy are not satisfied by every proposed uncertainty measure.

8.2.2   The certainty factor model.

The CF formalism was at one time very popular with Expert System designers. It appeared to provide a method for both formalising heuristic reasoning as deductive rules, and simultaneously allowing uncertainty to be quantified and combined within a "formal", but syntactically simple calculus. It thus apparently provided a simple way to get the best of both worlds; the power of deductive logic, with the sensitivity of quantitative uncertainty measures. Furthermore, the formalism has indeed been employed successfully in some systems.

The CF formalism makes a modular closed world assumption in which it is assumed that any unknown knowledge is not necessarily relevant, but can be added to the existing knowledge base if it becomes needed. However, in Section 3.4.5 it was demonstrated that the assumption of semantic modularity (locality and detachment criteria) is untenable. This makes the formalism fundamentally limited in its expressiveness, and means it can only be used under highly circumscribed situations, namely;

(a) when all rules are predictive or all rules are diagnostic, but not a mixture of both, and

(b) when all non-independent evidence is chunked together in single rules.

The latter reduces to a large conditional probability-like table in which a separate rule may be required for each truth functional state of the non independent antecedents. This gives the formalism an operational semantics vastly different from that which was originally intended.

It should also be emphasised, however, that the work of the Mycin team was pivotal in the development of Expert System research. They identified a number of phenomena apparently not formally represented in probabilistic systems which anticipated the development of subsequent formalisms. In particular, the CF formalism shared some of the intuitions underlying the Dempster-Shafer theory. The latter, for example, does permit an argument to support an hypothesis without having any direct bearing on the negation or complement of that hypothesis.

8.2.3   Belief functions.

The Dempster-Shafer theory of evidence provides the first really coherent attempt at a generalisation of the Bayesian model. This satisfies a slight weakening of the axioms of probability theory, whereby: beliefs need not be additive; beliefs can be assigned to sets of propositions, rather than of necessity to each individual proposition, and as a consequence, it is possible to pool evidence with respect to hierarchically nested hypothesis sets.

In the sense that it is more general than Bayesian probability, it naturally allows greater representational flexibility. For example, it permits explicit statements of ignorance and can provide a measure of the partial inconsistency of evidence sources. Being more general, however, may also have its down side; exact combinations of belief functions are computationally exponential in the general case. However, as discussed in Section 4.6.3, a number of recent approximation techniques have been developed which avoid some of these problems. Overall, Dempster-Shafer theory has rapidly evolved into a mature discipline with many supporters, a good understanding of its strengths and limitations and a number of large scale applications are beginning to emerge.

8.2.4   Possibility theory.

Possibility theory and fuzzy logic provide the principal formal systems explicitly devoted to the representation and manipulation of incomplete knowledge manifested as vagueness. There is an underlying numerical calculus which represents partial knowledge (confidence, propensity), upon which is superimposed a set theoretic component to represent indeterminate knowledge (vagueness). Information expressed in terms of fuzzy sets also allows some representation of ambiguity; there may be some overlap between the membership functions of different concepts. Additionally, some accommodation of partial degrees of inconsistency can occur.

As a whole, possibility theory is weaker than some of the other formalisms discussed in this book (in the sense of being less tightly constrained). This means that the resulting uncertainty distributions are necessarily less precise, but it does confer computational advantages. However, given that possibility distributions typically extend across a range of values, the elicitation of possibilistic functions from human sources may be more complex than the elicitation of probabilities.

Overall, possibility theory continues to be a rich area of research which has spawned many applications and has a clear role in the domain of uncertain reasoning.

8.2.5   Non-monotonic logics.

Non-monotonic and default logics, as discussed here, are concerned with the development of formal frameworks for understanding the nature and form of inference patterns which attempt to deal with incompleteness by making assumptions. In assessing such issues it was pointed out that it is useful to distinguish between two groups of systems.

The first group are the pragmatic special purpose systems developed in mainstream AI, which include: databases relying upon assumptions such as closed domain and closed world (there are no more instances of a relation than those deducible from the database), (Reiter, 1984); inheritance networks, where in general classes are assumed to inherit the properties of their superclass unless this conflicts with more specific information, (Touretzky, 1986); truth/reason maintenance systems; and logic programs employing negation as failure (in which negative literals hold by default, Clark, 1978).

Such systems can deal moderately well with highly circumscribed kinds of default inference, provide an important set of requirements for more general theories, and are in widespread use in research applications. However, they mostly fall short of providing a complete formal system.

The second type of system is the more general system which relies more for its motivation on the idea of extending classical logic. Chapter 6 focused specifically on this kind of system, though with inspiration drawn from challenging examples from the special purpose systems. The conclusion was that no comprehensive satisfactory formalism has yet been developed and that, perhaps in consequence, none have been successfully demonstrated in a large real domain.

8.2.6   Argumentation.

Of all the approaches described in this book, models of argumentation have the shortest AI pedigree; though, of course, studies of rhetoric have their origins in classical Greek literature. The motivation for wanting to pursue this line of research is not without foundation, however. It is very much in keeping with the view, expressed in the historical section of Chapter 4, that epistemic probability is derived from an appraisal of arguments and need not necessarily be numerical.

The heuristic approaches to argumentation that were reviewed are driven by the twin desires to both deal with uncertainty in unquantified domains and also to interleave uncertainty and control. The symbolic system developed by researchers at the Imperial Cancer Research Fund (Section 7.2.4) meets these criteria to some extent, allowing the combination of symbolic methods with weak quantitative methods in evaluation.

The more axiomatically based presentations are an attempt to represent a formal convergence of several trains of thought. The results obtained from simple examples seem intuitive, but the technique still awaits validation on larger scale examples.

Overall, this work provides an exciting insight into an approach to uncertainty management that at first sight appears antithetical to the more established probabilistic methods, yet is directly concerned with many of the issues that are now emerging as research directions for the established community.

8.2.7 Formalisms not covered in this book.

Because of the breadth of the field, the coverage of any book must be incomplete and there are many formal systems that we have not covered in this book (e.g. RUM-PRIMO, (Bonissone, 1992); upper and lower probability bounds (Dubois and Prade, 1982); qualitative uncertainty (Parsons, 1992; Parsons and Mamdani, 1993; Wellman, 1990)). Such systems are excluded not because we think they are inadequate, but because they share elements in common with the formalism described in the preceding chapters.

8.3 Verbal uncertainty expressions

Sometimes the parameters necessary for the various formalisms described throughout this book may be assessed directly from data. However, frequently they can only be elicited from domain specialists. Therefore the manner in which humans represent and express uncertainty must be taken into account. In general, this provides a potential source of insight into the requirements of computer systems intended both to reason about uncertainty and to communicate to users the results of that reasoning.

The manner in which people most frequently communicate uncertainty is through verbal uncertainty expressions (such as likely, probable, etc). An understanding of the nature of the types of uncertainty manifested by these expressions is an important consideration in how they are modelled. Throughout the book references have been made to the modelling of the use of verbal uncertainty expression by the various formalisms (e.g. Sections 5.2, 5.5.2 and 7.2.3). In this section we review these attempts, make some general statements about verbal uncertainty expressions and report on some empirical studies conducted by Clark (1988a) which shed light upon their role in human uncertain reasoning.

8.3.1 What are verbal uncertainty expressions?

In uncertain reasoning people frequently quantify or qualify the degree or nature of the belief using an expression such as possible, probable, very likely, consistent etc.

> "....There is also an unusual shadow seen in the right side representing, *very likely*, an anomalously coursing pulmonary vein..."... ".... A diagnosis outside of total anomalous connection is *unlikely*, even though the AV canal is a *remote possibility*."... "...this pulse rate is *highly unlikely* if that patient had conges-

*tive heart failure..." "It's **unlikely** that this is a total anomalous pulmonary venous connection below the diaphragm to the inferior vena cava, as is seen with the Scimitar syndrome; and is **extremely unlikely** that its a total anomalous connection to the portal venous system."... ".... This is **most likely** a prominent tricuspid closure sound suggesting the **possibility** of right ventricular hypertension."... "The second hunch is an atrial septal defect of the primum type, with a small right-to-left shunt, which is either due to an anomaly to the AV canal, or, **even less likely**, due to pulmonary vascular disease."... "My hunches at this point are a total anomalous pulmonary venous connection either to the vertical vein or to the azygous vein. **Much less likely** is a total anomalous pulmonary venous connection to the inferior vena cava with Scimitar syndrome."* (Johnson et al, 1981, emphasis added).

All the uncertainty management systems discussed in this book can be used to give an interpretation of such expressions.

Recently the importance of verbal uncertainty expressions for communicating uncertainty has been highlighted by a number of Expert Systems which have employed verbal uncertainty expressions to communicate aspects or degrees of belief to the user (Fox, 1986a; Bonissone et al, 1987). With the exception of Fox (1986a), these treat verbal uncertainty expressions either as probability values, probability ranges, fuzzy probability intervals, or simply as nominal annotations. RUM (Bonissone et al, 1987), for example, communicates uncertainty to the user using sets of linguistic uncertainty terms defined as trapezoidal (highly regular) fuzzy membership functions on the unit probability interval. One such set (based on the results of Beyth-Marom, 1982) and the associated fuzzy parameters is shown in Table 5.1.

In the context of decision technologies such as Expert Systems, the frequency and naturalness of verbal uncertainty expressions suggests that they may provide a graceful interface for communicating uncertainty to system users. However, the question of their appropriateness in interface design is dependent upon a clear account of their use, particularly factors such as within-subject variability, between-subject variability and context specificity of meaning.

If people are not internally consistent in the meanings they assign to verbal uncertainty expressions, or if between-subject variability is high (at the appropriate level of resolution), then attempts to incorporate verbal uncertainty expressions into an interface will be unsuccessful. Moreover, if the meaning of verbal uncertainty terms is found to be dependent upon contextual factors, a successful system must incorporate the relevant contextual knowledge and a model of how it affects the meaning of verbal uncertainty expressions in order to use them appropriately. Finally, if verbal uncertainty expressions are to be modelled as probability values, ranges or fuzzy subsets of the unit probability interval, then it must be established that the semantics of the expressions employed permit unidimensional mapping. Treating non-unidimensional objects as unidimensional would clearly force them into a semantic straight-jacket that may both ignore the richness of the information they convey and lead to communication error.

In short, a comprehensive account of the use of verbal uncertainty expressions is a prerequisite for their successful application in Expert Systems and other technologies.

Attempts to model verbal uncertainty expression using the formalisms described in this book usually, and laudably, draw inspiration from the attempt to make the user interface more graceful; applications certainly abound. However, as argued by Clark (1988a; 1990b), the attempt to employ verbal uncertainty expression in Expert System interfaces is doomed if designers attempt to force verbal uncertainty expressions into an inappropriate semantic straight-jacket.

As illustrations of how verbal uncertainty expression have been used: the MUM system (Cohen, 1989) employed them as probability points, RUM and many other systems have given them a possibilistic interpretation over the unit probability interval, while many modal terms such as *possibility* and *necessity* derive from natural language. Conversely, Fox (1986a) and others have attempted to define these terms in terms of logical categories (Section 7.2).

As we will argue in the following sections, there are a great many misunderstandings about verbal uncertainty expressions. These partially derive from the very attempt to model them within specific calculi.

8.3.2   Empirical studies of verbal uncertainty expressions.

Partly as a result of the dominance of the Bayesian paradigm in the behaviour decision theory field, most studies of verbal uncertainty expressions have been conducted within a unidimensional probabilistic framework. Clark (1990b) critically reviewed empirical studies of verbal uncertainty expressions, spanning two decades of research between 1967 and 1987, with the principal conclusions that:

- People are highly internally consistent in their use of verbal uncertainty expressions, though few studies have made a serious attempt to control for simple replication of performance effects, the time between replications being generally too small;

- No conclusions about between-subject variability are justified principally because, (a) there is currently no consensus as to what is to count as consistent or inconsistent use, and (b) there are several factors that confound purported analyses of between-subject consistency such as the composition of the stimulus set and the scaling tasks themselves;

- One study suggested that assessments of the meaning of verbal uncertainty expressions may be conditioned by the prior perceived probabilities of the events they describe. However, other interpretations of this study are open.

Overall, Clark (1990b) concluded that there was little evidence to suggest that verbal uncertainty expressions are inappropriate for communicating uncertainties in Expert Systems and other decision technologies. However a clear model of their semantics (i.e. scaling characteristics) was essential to this end.

In a separate series of experimental studies, Clark (1988a) investigated the psychological scaling properties of a number of verbal uncertainty expressions in great detail. The experimental details are complex and therefore not reported here. However, the principal results were that following extensive piloting:

- some sets of verbal uncertainty expressions were identified that could be treated as points or regions on a unidimensional scale consistent with a probabilistic or possibilistic interpretation. An example is the set shown in Figure 8.1.

> definite
> highly likely
> very likely
> quite likely
> quite possible
> quite unlikely
> very unlikely
> highly unlikely
> impossible

Fig 8.1   *9 verbal uncertainty expression that do scale unidimensionality. Note that 9 was generally the largest number of uncertainty categories that were reliably distinguished.*

It is noted that sets of expression such as those in Figure 8.1 provide a natural basis for modelling unidimensional uncertainty measures such as probabilities, or fuzzy sets.

- Some sets of verbal uncertainty expressions had decidedly non-unidimensional properties. The most extreme set being {ambiguous, equivocal, indefinite, uncertain, unsure, unknown, doubted, denied, disbelieved, unexpected, unsuspected, unlikely, improbable, implausible, infeasible, inconceivable, impossible}, Figure 8.2. Indeed because this set of terms had no clear unidimensional (or bidimensional) semantics, as assessed by a Multidimensional Scaling analysis, their empirical similarity was represented in a dendrogram produced by cluster analysis of pairwise similarity measures.

While the clear unidimensional properties of the expressions in Figure 8.1 endorse the cognitive validity of some attempts to adopt a unidimensional framework for uncertainty modelling, the expression in Figure 8.2 also emphasises the wider aspects of uncertainty as embodied in Figure 1.2. We do not view Figure 8.2 as definitive evidence for the typology in Figure 1.2 and acknowledge that different typologies serve difference purposes. However, we do view the data underlying Figure 8.2 as supporting the notion that not all aspects of uncertainty can be squeezed into a unidimensional semantics.

8.4   Uncertainty and decision making

A key point raised in the introduction was that an important criteria in assessing the utility of an uncertainty management system was to consider how the representation of uncertainty was to be used in reasoning. In this section, we briefly discuss the potential use of all the representation schemes in one type of reasoning task; decision making.

Although uncertainty is an important aspect of decision making, decisions can be made on the basis of very different types of uncertainty measure as a function of the information measure. At one extreme are the precise probabilities attached to all propositions, along with utility measures. At the opposite end of the spectrum, we may simply have a set of propositions currently believed.

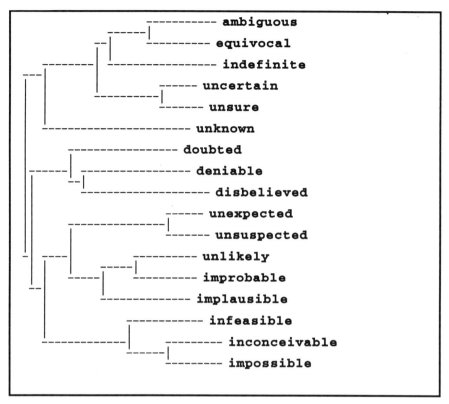

Fig 8.2   *Empirical similarity of non unidimensional verbal uncertainty expressions represented as a tree (from Clark, 1988a). In this "ADDTREE" representation (Corter, 1982), the dissimilarity between any pair of expression is modelled as the sum of the horizontal arc lengths between them.*

8.4.1   Bayesian systems.

Decision making in Bayesian systems can be based on a number of models. We may for example wish to maximise (subjective) expected utility, a strategy that is expected to give the highest return in the long term over many decisions. Alternatively, we may decide that the possible losses are too great and decide to be risk averse and minimise our possible loss (what is sometimes encapsulated by the term insurance or in a medical context preventative care (e.g. vaccination)). Yet again, we may decide to attempt to maximise our possible gain without incurring a large possible loss (e.g. betting in a national lottery). Or we may adopt some more complex strategy.

8.4.2   Certainty factors.

In Mycin, decisions were typically made on the basis of covering (pre-scribing for) all hypotheses with CFs above a given threshold. This would not work with probabilities, since there are many diseases whose proba-bility is low, but tangible, for which the possible outcomes are catastroph-ic (i.e. death to the patient or in the longer term to a whole community). However, the CF formalism coped with this by assigning higher CFs to diseases with worse outcomes via recursive rules, which essentially stat-ed that if there was evidence for a serious condition then boost the CF of that condition to ensure that it is treated. This confounding of uncertainty and utility information is, however, inadvisable.

8.4.3   Belief functions.

A detailed discussion of how to act upon a belief was given in Section 4.4. Assuming utilities exist as in the Bayesian discussion above, then the pig-nistic approach of Smets reduces to the Bayesian case. However as noted in Section 4.4, converting beliefs and plausibilities into a point value probability may be to disregard some of the potential of the Dempster-Shafer formalism. Therefore it is arguable that maintaining the plausibili-ty and belief measures may in fact be more useful in risk averse or risk se-lective decisions. Not only can we employ utilities in this respect, as in the Bayesian case, but these can be combined with the plausibility and be-lief measures. Decisions can then be made either on the basis of the plau-sibilities of the least favourable outcomes (risk averse) or by comparing the beliefs of the favourable outcomes (risk selective). Other strategies are also possible. Decisions about which strategy to use can be taken at a meta-level.

8.4.4   Possibility theory.

With probabilities we have point values, with belief functions we have plausibility and belief measures, with possibility theory we have a mem-bership function for the value of a variable over the domain of interest. Therefore in a manner analogous to belief functions, we can either reduce the distribution to a measure of central tendency (usually the median val-ue) or exploit the information about possible values to make risk averse or risk selective decisions; again the choice possibly determined by meta-level control.

8.4.5   Non-monotonic logics.

In most of the non monotonic logics we discussed, the set of propositions held to be true usually exists as one or more sets of valid extensions. If we have simply one valid extension, then all the propositions it contains can be treated as true and decisions made on the basis of those propositions, i.e. uncertainty has in one sense disappeared. If various alternate extensions are possible, where the propositions relevant to the decision have different truth conditions in the different extensions, then no such unequivocal decision procedure can be used. However, in such circumstances it may be possible to take a least commitment approach in which decisions are made on the basis of propositions that are true in every extension. A risk averse strategy would involve covering for all possibilities. The converse would be risk selective where the desired outcome is only valid in one extension. Allowing graded default rules as in Froidevaux and Grossetête (1990) clearly extends the kinds of decisions that can be made.

8.4.6   Symbolic argumentation systems.

In the symbolic systems discussed, the uncertainty attached to a proposition is based on the supporting and conflicting arguments. Decision making can therefore be facilitated by either providing some simple weighting scheme (such as uniform weights) across all arguments, or by being risk selective or risk averse as a function of the number of arguments. In a medical context, being risk averse might involve treating or investigating all severe diseases which are supported by arguments. Conversely, for a patient with a very bad prognosis, it might be appropriate to try a (possibly experimental) treatment for which there is tangible but only weak support.

Another important aspect of decision making is sensitivity analysis (i.e. determining to what extend the proposed decision would change as a result of changes to the particular context). In this respect all the formalisms discussed have their own method of sensitivity measures that can be applied.

8.5   Meta-level reasoning and control

A theme of Chapters 6 and 7 of this book was the need for explicit meta-level reasoning to augment various aspects of the formalisms discussed, in order to extend or more fully utilise potential for representing and reasoning about a larger variety of sources of uncertainty. This is particularly acute in the context of contradictions. These have to be engineered out, a priori, in Bayesian approaches, lead to problems of normalisation for the Dempster-Shafer formalism and can lead to unresolvable mutually exclusive extensions for non-monotonic reasoning schemes.

Essentially whenever there are a number of ways of achieving a goal, or some inconsistency cannot be resolved at the object theory level, then some meta-level component is required to decide among them or resolve that inconsistency. As pointed out in the discussion above, meta-level control can be used productively in determining the most appropriate basis for selecting between decision candidates.

8.6   Future trends: the convergence of symbolic and quantitative methods?

Throughout this book, we have taken trouble to highlight the differences between the various approaches to uncertainty management. This is important for apprehending their respective merits. In this final section we would like to stress possible complementarities.

In Chapter 2, we presented a detailed overview of Bayesian probabilistic approaches to uncertainty management in AI systems. We concluded that Bayesian reasoning is as much about the qualitative structure of reasoning as it is about the numbers themselves. This was demonstrated by Shafer and Shenoy who, using the formal structure of belief networks, showed it is possible to pass around parameters other than probabilities. As noted by Shafer and Pearl (1990), two individuals whose influence on the field of uncertainty management has been instrumental:

In the long run, the most important contribution of AI to probability should be in forcing more serious consideration of the problem of model construction. Discussions of probability theory have traditionally started with the assumption that we have a probability structure, even probability numbers. This is not the starting point for AI, and as we learn more from attempts to implement probability in AI, it cannot remain the starting point for probability theory in general.

Conversely, in Chapter 7 we presented some systems, both heuristic and axiomatic, whose aim is to explicitly represent the structure of argumentation and employ numerical uncertainty measures attached to arguments when available. The two systems have very different starting points. However, the potential complementarity and convergence is clear. By the very nature of its operation, the result of using the OSM Symbolic System (Section 7.2.4.) in a decision task is to construct a low order network of interrelated entities relevant to the specific decision task. Weak quantitative aggregation methods can then be applied to this structure to produce partial orders on hypothesis sets. Thus, starting from a vast network of possible dependencies, a small decision specific subset is produced which can be used as the basis for evaluation. Conversely, it is such a representation that usually provides the starting point for the application of knowledge elicitation and the application of the more formal aspects of the Bayesian formalism as described in Chapter 2. It is very much the case therefore that the two approaches meet, raising the potential for the judicious combination of the two.

As we began this chapter with a quotation from Pearl and Shafer, we end with another:

> [the different formalisms]... point to a possible consensus, in which qualitative relationships can be seen as abstractions from probability ideas [including belief functions] and numerical probabilities can be seen as supplementary to traditional symbolic systems. (Shafer and Pearl, 1990).

At the end of the day, what we would like to do is to harness the power of the Bayesian propagation algorithms with the organising principals and opportunities for meta-level control afforded by the more recent work on symbolic aspects of uncertainty management and argumentation. Viewing numerical uncertainty measures as concomitants to symbolic representations does appear to provide the leverage necessary both to represent the various types of uncertainty described in Figure 1.2 and to meet most of the requirements with respect to control and meta-level capabilities. Yet, as shown in Chapters 6 and 7, such symbolic systems are far from operationally complete. Our own view is that the next decade will see a further heightening of the importance of symbolic relations between quantitative data structures on the one hand, and increasing axiomatic specification of symbolic systems on the other.

References

Adams, J. B. (1984) Probabilistic Reasoning and Certainty Factors. In (eds Buchanan, B. G. and Shortliffe, E. H.) *Rule-Based Expert Systems: The MYCIN experiments of the Stanford Heuristic Programming Project*. Reading, Massachusetts, Addison-Wesley.

Adams, I. D., Chan, M., Clifford, P. C., Cooke, W. M., Dallos, V., de Dombal, F. T., Edwards, M. H., Hancock, D. M., Hewett, D. J., McIntyre, N., Somerville, P. G., Spiegelhalter, D. J., Wellwood, J. and Wilson, D. H. (1986) Computer aided diagnosis of acute abdominal pain: a multicentre study. *British Medical Journal*, **293**, 800-804.

Alvarado, S. J. (1992) Argument Comprehension. In (ed Shapiro, S. C.) *Encyclopedia of Artificial Intelligence*. Second Edition. New York, John Wiley.

Andreassen, S., Woldbye, M., Falck, B. and Andersen, S. K. (1987) MUNIN - A Causal Probabilistic Network for Interpretation of Electromyographic findings. *Proc. IJCAI '87*, Milan, Italy, 366-372.

Andress, K. M. and Kak, A. C. (1988) Evidence Accumulation & Flow of Control in a Hierarchical Spatial Reasoning System. *AI Magazine*, **9**, 75-94.

Andress, K. M. and Kak, A. C. (1989) *The PSIEKI Report - Version 3*. Technical Report TR-EE 89-35, School of Electrical Engineering, Purdue University.

Arrow, K. J. (1963) *Social Choice and Individual Values*. New York, John Wiley.

Ayel, M. and Laurent, J-P. (1991) *Validation, Verification and Test of Knowledge-Based Systems*. Chichester, John Wiley.

Barnett, J. A. (1981) Computational methods for a mathematical theory of evidence. *Proc. IJCAI '81*, Vancouver, BC, 868-875.

Bell, J. (1992) *Pragmatic Logics*. Department of Computer Science Technical Report, Queen Mary and Westfield College, London.

Benferhat, S., Dubois, D. and Prade, H. (1993a) *Argumentative inference in uncertain and inconsistent knowledge bases*. IRIT Research Report, Université Paul Sabatier, France.

Benferhat, S., Cayrol, C., Dubois, D., Lang, J. and Prade, H. (1993b) Inconsistency management and prioritized syntax-based entailment. *Proc. IJCAI '93*, Chambery, France.

Bernoulli, J. (1713) *Ars Conjectandi*. Basel.

Besnard, P. (1989) *An Introduction to Default Logic*. Berlin, Springer-Verlag.

Besnard, P. and Schaub, T. (1993) Possible Worlds Semantics for Default Logics. *Proc. AAAI '93*, Washington DC, USA.

Beyth-Marom, R. (1982) How Probable is Probable: A Numerical Translation of Verbal Probability Expressions. *Journal of Forecasting*, **1**, 257-269.

Bezdek, J. C. (1976) Feature Selection for Binary Data - Medical Diagnosis with Fuzzy Sets. *Proc. AFIPS*, **45**, 1057-1068.

Bidoit, N. and Froidevaux, C. (1991) General Logical Databases and Programs: Default Logic Semantics and Stratification. *Information and Computing*, **91**, 15-54.

Black, M. (1937) Vagueness: An exercise in logical analysis. *Philosophy of Science*, **4**, 427-455.

Bonissone, P. P. (1987) Reasoning, Plausible. In (ed Shapiro, S. C.) *Encyclopedia of Artificial Intelligence*. New York, John Wiley.

Bonissone, P. P. (1992) Reasoning, Plausible. In (ed Shapiro, S. C.) *Encyclopedia of Artificial Intelligence*. Second Edition. New York, John Wiley.

Bonissone, P. P., Gans, S. S. and Decker, K. S. (1987) RUM: A Layered Architecture for Reasoning with Uncertainty. *Proc. IJCAI '87*, Milan, Italy, 373-379.

Bonté, E. and Lévy, F. (1989) *Une procédure complete de calculi des extensions pour les théories de defauts en reseau*. Technical Report, LIPN, Université de Paris Nord.

Brewka, G. (1991a) *Nonmonotonic Reasoning: Logical Foundations of Commonsense*. London, Cambridge University Press.

Brewka, G. (1991b) Cumulative Default Logic - In Defense of Nonmonotonic Inference Rules. *Artificial Intelligence*, **50**, 183-206.

Brouwer, L. E. J. (1976) *Collected Works, Vol. 1, Philosophy and Foundations of Mathematics*, Amsterdam, North-Holland.

Buchanan, B. G. and Shortliffe, E. H. (1984) *Rule-Based Expert Systems: The Mycin experiments of the Stanford Heuristic Programming Project*. Reading, Massachusetts, Addison-Wesley.

Buchanan, B. G. and Smith, R. G. (1988) Fundamentals of Expert Systems. *Annual Review Computer Science*, **3**, 23-58.

Buisson, J. C., Farreny, H., Prade, H., Turin, M. C., Tauber, J. P. and Bayard, F. (1987) TOULMED, an inference engine which deals with imprecise and uncertain aspects of medical knowledge. In (eds Reicherte, P. L. and Lindberg, D. A. B.) *Lecture notes in Medical Informatics: Proceedings AIME '87*, Marseilles.

Chang, C. L. and Lee, R. C. T. (1973) *Symbolic Logic and Mechanical Theorem Proving*. New York, Academic Press.

Cheeseman, P. (1985) In Defense of Probability. In *Proc. IJCAI '85*, Los Angeles, 1002-1009.

Cheeseman, P. (1986) Probabilistic vs. Fuzzy Reasoning. In (eds Kanal, J. F. and

Lemmer, L. N.) *Uncertainty in Artificial Intelligence*. Elsevier Science Publishers (North-Holland).

Cheeseman, P. (1988) An Inquiry into Computer Understanding. *Computational Intelligence*, **4**(1), 58-66.

Church, A. (1936) A note on the Entscheidungsproblem. *The Journal of Symbolic Logic*, **1**, 40-41.

Clark, D. A. (1988a) *Psychological Aspects of Uncertainty and their Implications for Artificial Intelligence*. PhD Thesis, University of Wales.

Clark, D. A. (1988b) AI and the Management of Uncertainty. *Knowledge Engineering Review*, **3**(1), 59-63.

Clark, D. A. (1990a) Numerical and Symbolic approaches to Uncertainty Management in AI: A Review and Discussion. *Artificial Intelligence Review*, **4**(2), 109-146.

Clark, D. A. (1990b) Verbal Uncertainty Expressions: A Review of two decades of Research. *Current Psychology: Research and Reviews*, **9**(3), 203-235.

Clark, D. A. (1992) Human Expertise, Statistical Models and Knowledge-Based Systems. In (eds Wright, G. and Bolger, F.) *Expertise and Decision Support*. New York, Plenum Press, 227-250.

Clark, D. A., Fox, J., Glowinski, A. J. and O'Neil, M. (1990) Symbolic Reasoning for Decision Making. In (eds Borcherding, K., Larichev, O. I. and Messick, D. M.) *Contemporary Issues in Decision Making*. Elsevier Science Publishers (North-Holland).

Clark, K. (1978) Negation as Failure. In (eds Gallaire, H. and Minker, J.) *Logic and Databases*. New York, Plenum Press.

Clarke, M. R. B. (1988) Discussion to "Belief Functions" by Smets, P. In (eds Smets, P., Mamdani, E. H., Dubois, D. and Prade, H.) *Non-Standard Logics for Automated Reasoning*, London, Academic Press.

Cohen, P. (1985) *Heuristic Reasoning about Uncertainty: An Artificial Intelligence Approach*. London, Pitman.

Cohen, P. (1987) The control of Reasoning under Uncertainty: A discussion of some programs. *The Knowledge Engineering Review*, **2**(1), 5-25.

Cohen, P. (1989) Steps Towards Programs that Manage Uncertainty. In (eds Kanal, J. F., Levitt, T. S. and Lemmer, L. N.) *Uncertainty in Artificial Intelligence 3*. Elsevier Science Publishers (North-Holland).

Cohen, P., Day, D. S., de Lisio, J., Greenberg, M., Kjeldsen, R., Suther, D. and Berman, P. (1987) Management of Uncertainty in Medicine. *Int. J. of Approximate Reasoning*, **1**, 103-116.

Cooper, G. F. (1990) The computational complexity of probabilistic inference using Bayesian belief networks. *Artificial Intelligence*, **42**, 393-405.

Corter, J. E. (1982) ADDTREE/P: A PASCAL program for fitting additive trees based on Sattath and Tversky's ADDTREE algorithm. *Behavior Research and Instrumentation*, **14**(3), 353-354.

Cox, R. (1946) Probability, frequency and reasonable expectation. *American Journal of Physics*, **14**, 1-13.

Dawes, R. M. (1971) A Case Study of Graduate Admissions: Application of three principles of Human Decision Making. *American Psychologist*, **26**, 180-188.

Dawes, R. M. (1979) The robust beauty of improper linear models in decision making. *American Psychologist*, **34**, 571-582.

de Dombal, F. T. (1975) Computer Assisted Diagnosis of Abdominal Pain. In (eds Rose, J. and Mitchell, J.) *Advances in Medical Computing*. New York, Churchill Livingston.

de Dombal, F. T., Barnes, S., Dallos, V., Kumar, P. S., Sloan, J., Chan, M., Stapleton, C. and Wardle, K. S. (1992) How should computer-aided decision-support systems present their predictions to the practising surgeon? *Theor. Surg*, **7**, 111-116.

de Finetti, B. (1937) La prevision: See lois logiques, ses sources objectives. *Annales de l'Institut Henri Poincare*, **7**, 1-68. Translated in: Kyberg, H. and Smokler, H. (1964) *Studies in Subjective Probability*. New York, John Wiley.

Delgrande, J. P. and Jackson, W. K. (1991) Default logic revisited. *Proc. of the Conference on Knowledge Representation '91*, San Mateo, Morgan Kaufmann.

de Mántaras, R. L. (1990) *Approximate Reasoning Models*. Chichester, Ellis Horwood.

Dempster, A. P. (1967) Upper and Lower Probabilities Induced by a Multi-valued Mapping. *Annals of Mathematical Statistics*, **38**, 325-339.

Dempster, A. P. (1968) A Generalisation of Bayesian Inference (with discussion). *J. Roy. Statistical Soc.*, **B30**, 205-247.

Deville, Y. (1990) *Logic Programming - Systematic Program Development*. Reading, Massachusetts, Addison-Wesley.

Dodd, T. (1990) *Prolog - A Logical Approach*. Oxford Science Publishers.

Doyle, J. (1979) A Truth Maintenance System. *Artificial Intelligence*, **12**, 231-272.

Dressler, O. (1988) Extending the Basic ATMS. *Proc. ECAI '88*, München.

Dubois, D. and Koning, J.-L. (1991) Social choice axioms for fuzzy set aggregation. *Fuzzy Sets and Systems*, **44**, 1-18.

Dubois, D. and Prade, H. (1982) On several representations of an uncertain body of evidence. In (eds Gupta, M. M. and Sanchez, E.) *Fuzzy information and decision processes*, Amsterdam, North-Holland, 167-181.

Dubois, D. and Prade, H. (1987) Necessity measures and the resolution principle. *IEEE Trans. on Systems, Man and Cybernetics*, **17**, 474-478.

Dubois, D. and Prade, H. (1988a) (with the collaboration of Farreny, H., Martin-Clouaire, R. and Testamale, C.) *Possibility Theory: An Approach to Computerised Processing of Uncertainty*, New York, Plenum Press.

Dubois, D. and Prade, H. (1988b) An Introduction to Possibilistic and Fuzzy Logics. In (eds Smets, P., Mamdani, E. H., Dubois, D. and Prade, H.) *Non-Standard Logics for Automated Reasoning*. London, Academic Press.

Dubois, D. and Prade, H. (1991a) Fuzzy sets in approximate reasoning, Part I; Inference with possibility distributions. *Fuzzy Sets and Systems*, **40**, 143-202.

Dubois, D. and Prade, H. (1991b) Epistemic entrenchment and possibilistic logic. *Artificial Intelligence*, **50**, 223-239.

Dubois, D. and Prade, H. (1992) Belief Change and Possibility Theory. In (ed Gärdenfors, P.) *Belief Revision*. London, Cambridge University Press, 142-182.

Dubois, D., Lang, J. and Prade, H. (1987) Theorem proving under uncertainty - A Possibility Theory Based Approach. *Proc. IJCAI '87*, Milan, Italy, 984-986.

Dubois, D., Lang, J. and Prade, H. (1992) Inconsistency in possibilistic knowledge-bases - to live with it or not live with it. In (eds Zadeh, L. and Kacprzyk, J.) *Fuzzy Logic for the Management of Uncertainty.* Chichester, John Wiley.

Dubois, D., Lang, J. and Prade, H. (1993) Automated reasoning using possibilistic logic: semantics, belief revision and variable certainty weights. *IEEE Trans. on Data and Knowledge Engineering* (to appear).

Duda, R., Gashnig, J. and Hart, P. (1979) Model design in the Prospector consultant system for mineral exploitation. In (ed. Michie, D.) *Expert Systems in the Microelectronic age*. Edinburgh, Edinburgh University Press.

Duda, R. O. and Shortliffe, E. H. (1983) Expert Systems Research. *Science*, **220**, 261-268.

Ellam, S. and Maisey, M. N. (1987) A Knowledge-Based System to assist in Medical Image Interpretation: Design and Evaluation Methodology. In (ed Bramer, M. A.) *Research and Development in Expert Systems III*. London, Cambridge University Press.

Elvang-Gøransson, M., Krause, P. J. and Fox, J. (1993) Logic and linguistic uncertainty terms. *Proc. 9th Conference on Uncertainty in Artificial Intelligence*, Washington DC, USA.

Erman, L. D., Hayes-Roth, F., Lesser, V. R. and Reddy, D. R. (1980) The Hearsay-II Speech-Understanding System: Integrating Knowledge to resolve Uncertainty. *Computing Surveys*, **12**(2), 213-253.

Etherington, D. W. (1987a) A Semantics for Default Logic. *Proc. IJCAI '87*, Milan, Italy, 495-498.

Etherington, D. W. (1987b) Formalizing Nonmonotonic Reasoning Systems. *Artificial Intelligence*, **31**, 41-85.

Fox, J. (1986a) Knowledge, Decision Making and Uncertainty. In (ed Gale, W. A.) *Artificial Intelligence and Statistics*, Reading, Massachusetts, Addison-Wesley.

Fox, J. (1986b) Three Arguments for Extending the Framework of Probability. In (eds Kanal, L. N. and Lemmer, J. F.) *Uncertainty in Artificial Intelligence*. Elsevier Science Publishers, (North-Holland).

Fox, J. (1989) Automating assistance for safety critical decisions. *Phil. Trans. R. Soc. Lond.*, B**327**, 555-567.

Fox, J. and Clarke, M. (1991) Towards a formalisation of arguments in decision making. *Proc. Stanford Symposium on Argumentation and Belief*, AAAI Spring Symposium Series, 92-99.

Fox, J., Barber, D., and Bardhan, K. D. (1980) Alternatives to Bayes. *Methods of Information in Medicine*, **19**, 210-215.

Fox, J., Glowinski, A. J. and O'Neil, M. O. (1987) The Oxford System of Medicine: A Prototype Information System for Primary Care. *Lecture Notes in Medical Informatics*, **33**, 213-226.

Fox, J., O'Neil, M., Glowinski, A. J. and Clark, D. A. (1988) Decision Making as A Logical Process. In (eds Kelly, B. and Rector, A.) *Research and Development in Expert Systems V*. London, Cambridge University Press.

Fox, J., Clark, D. A., Glowinski, A. J. and O'Neil, M. (1990a) Using Predicate Logic to Integrate Qualitative Reasoning and Classical Decision Theory. *IEEE Trans. Systems, Man and Cybernetics*, **20**, 347-357.

Fox, J., Glowinski, A. J., Gordon, C., Hajnal, S. J. and O'Neil, M. J. (1990b) Logic engineering for knowledge engineering. *Artificial Intelligence in Medicine*, **2**, 323-339.

Fox, J., Krause, P. J. and Ambler, S. J. (1992) Arguments, contradictions and practical reasoning. *Proc. ECAI '92*, Vienna, Austria, 623-627.

Froidevaux, C. (1986) Taxonomic Default Theory. *Proc. ECAI '86*, Brighton, England, 123-129.

Froidevaux, C. and Grossetête, C. (1990) Graded default theories for uncertainty. *Proc. ECAI '90*, 283-288.

Froidevaux, C. and Mengin, J. (1992) *A Framework for Default Logics*. LRI Technical Report, Université Paris Sud.

Gabbay, D. (1985) Theoretical Foundations for Non-Monotonic Reasoning in Expert Systems. In (ed Apt, K. R.) *Logics and Models of Concurrent Systems*, Berlin, Springer-Verlag, 439-457.

Gabbay, D. (1990) *Labelled Deductive Systems*. CIS Technical Report 90-22, University of Munich.

Gabbay, D. and Hunter A. (1991) Making Inconsistency Respectable: a logical framework for inconsistent reasoning. *Proceedings of the International*

Workshop on Fundamentals of Artificial Intelligence Research, Bratislava.

Gallier, J. H. (1987) *Logic for Computer Science - Foundations of Automatic Theorem Proving*. Chichester, John Wiley.

Gallaire, H., Minker, J. and Nicolas, J-M. (1984) Logic and Databases: A Deductive Approach. *Computing Surveys*, **16**, 153-185

Gärdenfors, P. (1988) *Knowledge in Flux - Modelling the Dynamic of Epistemic States*. Cambridge, Mass., MIT Press.

Gashnig, J. (1982) PROSPECTOR: an expert system for mineral exploration. In (ed Michie, D.) *Expert Systems in the Microelectronic age*. Edinburgh, Edinburgh University Press, 153-167.

Gebhart, J. and Kruse, R. (1993) The Context Model: An Integrating View of Uncertainty and Vagueness. *Int. J. Approximate Reasoning*, Special Issue on Fuzzy Expert Systems (to appear).

Geiger, D. and Pearl, J. (1988) On the logic of causal models. *Proc. Fourth Workshop on Uncertainty in Artificial Intelligence*, Minneapolis, MN, 136-147.

Ginsberg, M. (1984) Non-monotonic reasoning using Dempster's rule. *Proc. AAAI '84*, Austin, Texas, 126-129.

Glowinski, A. J., O'Neil, M. and Fox, J. (1989) Design of a generic information system and its application to primary care. In *Lecture Notes in Medical Informatics vol. 38, Proc. of European Conference on AI in Medicine*. Berlin, Springer-Verlag, 1989.

Glowinski, A. J., Coiera, E. and O'Neil, M. (1991) The role of domain models in maintaining consistency of large medical knowledge bases. *Proc. AIME '91*, Maastricht.

Gödel, K. (1931) Über formal unentscheidbare Sätze der Principia Mathematica und verwandter Systeme I. *Monatshefte für Mathematik und Physik*, **38**, 173-198. English translation in: ed. van Heijenoort, J. (1967) *From Frege to Gödel A Source Book in Mathematical Logic, 1879-1931*. Cambridge, Mass., Harvard University Press, 596-616.

Gordon, J. and Shortliffe, E. H. (1984) The Dempster-Shafer Theory of Evidence. In (eds Buchanan, B. G. and Shortliffe, E. H.) *Rule-based Expert Systems: The MYCIN experiments of the Stanford Heuristic Programming Project*. Reading, Massachusetts, Addison-Wesley.

Grant, J. and Minker, J. (1989) Deductive database theories. *The Knowledge Engineering Review*, **4**, 267-304.

Guerreiro, R. A. de T., Casanova, M. A. and Hemerly, A. S. (1990) Contribution to proof theory for generic defaults. *Proc. ECAI '90*, 213-218.

Guinan, D., Streicher, K. and Kerre, E. (1990) *Set-theoretic properties of the class of fuzzy sets endowed with the bounded sum and the bold intersection*. University of Nebraska-Lincoln, Dept. of Computer Science and Engineering Report no. 114.

Hacking, I. (1975) *The emergence of probability.* London, Cambridge University Press.

Heckerman, D. (1986) Probabilistic Interpretation of Mycin's Certainty Factors. In (eds Kanal, L. N. and Lemmer, J. F.) *Uncertainty in Artificial Intelligence.* Elsevier Science Publishers (North-Holland).

Heckerman, D. (1991) *Probabilistic Similarity Networks.* Cambridge, Mass., MIT Press.

Heckerman, D. (1992) Certainty Factor Model. In (ed Shapiro, S. C.) *Encyclopedia of Artificial Intelligence. Second Edition.* New York, John Wiley.

Heckerman, D. and Horvitz, E. (1988) The Myth of Modularity in Rule-Based Systems for reasoning with Uncertainty. In (eds Lemmer, J. F. and Kanal, L. N.) *Uncertainty in Artificial Intelligence 2.* Elsevier Science Publishers (North-Holland).

Henrion, M. (1986) Should we use Probability in Uncertain Inference Systems? *Proc. Cognitive Science Society Meeting,* Amherst, Penn.

Hill, P. H., Bedau, H. A., Chechile, R. A., Crochetiere, W. J., Kellerman, B. L. and Ounjian, D. (1978) *Decisions: A Multidisciplinary Introduction.* Reading, Massachusetts, Addison-Wesley.

Hopkins, M. and Clarke, M. (1992) *Multiple Extension Calculations for a Useful Fragment of Default Logic.* Department of Computer Science Technical Report, Queen Mary and Westfield College, London.

Horvitz, E. and Heckerman, D. (1986) The inconsistent use of measures of certainty in artificial intelligence research. In (eds Kanal, L. N. and Lemmer, J. F.) *Uncertainty in Artificial Intelligence.* Elsevier Science Publishers (North-Holland).

Horvitz, E. J., Heckerman, D. E. and Langlotz, C. P. (1986) A Framework for Comparing Alternative Formalisms for Plausible Reasoning. *Proc. AAAI '86,* 210-214.

Hsia, Y.-T. and Shenoy, P. P. (1989) A Visual Environment for Constructing and Evaluating Evidential Systems. Working Paper No. 211, School of Business, University of Kansas, USA.

Hughes, G. E. and Cresswell, M. J. (1984) *A Companion to Modal Logic.* London, Methuen.

Ishizuka, M., Fu, K. S. and Yao, J. T. P. (1981) Inexact inference for rule based damage assessment of existing structures. *Proc. IJCAI '81,* Vancouver, BC, 837-842.

Jensen, F. V., Andersen, S. K., Kjaerulff, U. and Andreassen, S. (1987) MUNIN - On the case for Probabilities in Medical Expert Systems - A Practical Exercise. In *Lecture Notes in Medical Informatics, vol. 33.* Berlin, Springer-Verlag.

Johnson, P. E., Duran, A. S., Hassebrock, F., Moller, J., Prietula, M., Feltovich, P. J. and Swanson, D. B. (1981) Expertise and Error in Diagnostic Reasoning. *Cognitive Science*, **5**, 235-283.

Johnson-Laird, P. N. (1983) *Mental Models*. London, Cambridge University Press.

Johnson-Laird, P. N. and Byrne, R. M. J. (1991) *Deduction*. London, Lawrence Earlebaum Associates.

Johnstone, P. T. (1987) *Notes on logic and set theory*. London, Cambridge University Press.

Junker, U. (1989) A Correct Non-Monotonic ATMS. *Proc. IJCAI '89*, Detroit, USA, 1049-1053.

Kahneman, D., Slovic, P. and Tversky, A. (1982) *Judgement under uncertainty: heuristics and biases*. London, Cambridge University Press.

Kak, A. C., Andress, K. M., Lopez-Abadia, C., Caroll, M. S. and Lewis, J. R. (1990) Hierarchical Evidence Accumulation in the PSEIKI system. In (eds Henrion, M., Schachter, R. D., Kanal, L. N. and Lemmer, J. F.) *Uncertainty in Artificial Intelligence 5*, Elsevier Science Publishers (North-Holland).

Kautz, H. A. and Selman, B. (1991) Hard problems for simple default logics. *Artificial Intelligence*, **49**, 243-279.

Kazic, T., Lusk, E., Olson, R., Overbeek, R. and Tuecke, S. (1990) Prototyping Databases in Prolog. In (ed Sterling, L.) *The Practice of Prolog*. Cambridge, Mass., MIT Press.

Kennes, R. and Smets, P. (1990) Computational Aspects of the Möbius Transformation. In (eds Bonissone, P. P., Henrion, M., Kanal, L. N. and Lemmer, J. F.) *Uncertainty in Artificial Intelligence 6*, Elsevier Science Publishers (North-Holland).

Krause, P. J., Ambler, S. J. and Fox, J. (1993a) The development of a "Logic of Argumentation". In (eds Bouchon-Meunier, B., Valverde, L. and Yager, R.) *Advanced Methods in Artificial Intelligence*. Berlin, Springer-Verlag.

Krause, P. J., Byers, P. and Hajnal, S. J. (1993b) Formal Specifications and Decision Support Systems. *Decision Support Systems*, to appear.

Krause, P. J., Fox, J., O'Neil, M. and Glowinski, A. J. (1993c) Can We Formally Specify a Medical Decision Support System? *IEEE Expert*, to appear.

Kruse, R., Schwecke, E. and Heinsohn, J. (1991) *Uncertainty and Vagueness in Knowledge Based Systems*. Berlin, Springer-Verlag.

Lambert, J. H. (1764) *Neues Organon, oder Gedanken über die Erforschung und Bezeichnung des Wahren und dessen Unterscheidung Von Irrtum und Schein*. Leipzig. Reprinted in 1965 by Olms of Hildesheim as the first two volumes of Lambert's *Philosophische Schriften*.

Lang, J. (1991) Semantic Evaluation in Possibilistic Logic. In (eds Bouchon-Meunier, B., Yager, R.R. and Zadeh, L. A.) *Lecture Notes in Computer Science No*

521. Berlin, Springer-Verlag.

Lang, J., Dubois, D. and Prade, H. (1991) A Logic of Graded Possibility and Certainty Coping with Partial Inconsistency. *Proc. 7th Conference on Uncertainty in Artificial Intelligence*, San Mateo, Morgan Kaufmann, 188-196.

Lauritzen, S. L. and Spiegelhalter, D. J. (1988) Local Computations with probabilities on graphical structures and their application to expert systems (with discussion). *Proc. Royal Statistical Society*, **B.50**, 157-224.

Lebailly, J., Martin-Clouaire, R. and Prade, H. (1987) Use of fuzzy logic in rule-based systems in petroleum geology. In (eds Sanchez, E. and Zadeh, L. A.) *Approximate Reasoning in Intelligent Systems, Decision and Control*. Oxford, Pergamon Press, 125-144.

Lemmer, J. F. and Kanal, L. N. (1988) *Uncertainty in Artificial Intelligence 2*. Elsevier Science Publishers (North-Holland).

Leung, K. S., Wong, W. S. F. and Lam, W. (1989) Applications of a novel fuzzy expert system shell. *Expert Systems*, **6**(1), 2-10.

Lévy, F. (1991) Computing Extensions of Default Theories. In (eds Kruse, R. and Siegel, P.) *Symbolic and Quantitative Approaches to Uncertainty*. Berlin, Springer-Verlag, 219-226.

Li, L. and You, J-H. (1991) Making default inferences from logic programs. *Computational Intelligence*, **7**, 142-153.

Lindley, D. V. (1985) *Making Decisions*. Chichester, John Wiley.

Lindley, D. V. (1987) The Probability Approach to the Treatment of Uncertainty in Artificial Intelligence and Expert Systems. *Statistical Science*, **2**, 3-44.

Lloyd, J. W. (1984) *Logic Programming*. Berlin, Springer-Verlag.

Locke, J. (1671) See: *An early draft of Locke's Essay*, (1936) (eds Aaron, R. I. and Gibb, J.), Oxford University Press.

Locke, J. (1690) *An Essay Concerning Human Understanding*. London.

Lohmann, G. (1991) An Evidential Reasoning Approach to the Classification of Satellite Images. In (eds Kruse, R. and Siegel, P.) *Symbolic and Quantitative Approaches to Uncertainty*, Berlin, Springer-Verlag, 227-231.

Loui, R. P. (1987) Defeat among arguments: a system of defeasible inference. *Computational Intelligence*, **3**, 100-106.

Lukaszewicz, W. (1985) Two Results on Default Logic. *Proc. IJCAI '85*, Los Angeles, USA, 459-461.

Lukaszewicz, W. (1988) Considerations on Default Logic. *Computational Intelligence*, **4**, 1-16.

Lukaszewicz, W. (1990) *Non-Monotonic Reasoning - Formalization of Commonsense Reasoning*. Chichester, Ellis Horwood.

Makinson, D. (1989) General theory of cumulative inference. In *Proc. 2nd Interna-*

tional Workshop on Non-monotonic reasoning, Grasseau, Germany, Lecture Notes in Artificial Intelligence, **346**, Berlin, Springer-Verlag, 1-18.

Mamdani, E. H. (1983) Process Control Using Fuzzy Logic. In (eds Sime, M. E. and Coombs, M. J.) *Designing for human-computer communication*, London, Academic Press.

Mamdani, E. H. and Gaines, B. R. (1981) *Fuzzy Reasoning and its Applications*. London, Academic Press.

Mamdani, E. H. and Efstathiou, H. J. (1985) Higher-order logics for handling uncertainty in expert systems. *International Journal of Man Machine Studies*, **22**, 283-293.

Martin-Clouaire, R. and Prade, H. (1986) SPII-1: a simple inference engine capable of accommodating both imprecision and uncertainty. In (ed Mitra, G.) *Computer-Assisted Decision Making*. Amsterdam, North-Holland, 117-131.

McDermott, D. (1982) Nonmonotonic Logic II: Nonmonotonic Modal Theories. *JACM*, **29**, 33-57.

McDermott, D. and Doyle, J. (1980) Nonmonotonic logic I. *Artificial Intelligence*, **13**, 41-72.

Mendelson, E. (1964) *Introduction to Mathematical Logic*. Princeton NJ, Van Nostrand.

Minsky, M. (1975) A Framework for Representing Knowledge. In (ed Winston, P.) *The Psychology of Computer Vision*. New York, McGraw-Hill.

Moinard, Y. (1990) *Preference by Specificity in Default Logic*. IRISA Technical Report, Campus de Beaulieu, France.

Moinard, Y. (1992) Unifying various approaches to default logic. *Proc. IPMU '92*, Mallorca, Spain, 61-64.

Moore, R. C. (1985) Semantical Considerations on Nonmonotonic Logic, *Artificial Intelligence*, **25**, 75-94.

Neapolitan, R. (1990) *Probabilistic Reasoning in Expert Systems*. Chichester, John Wiley.

Nelson, D. (1949) Constructible falsity. *Journal of Symbolic Logic*, **14**, 16-26.

Nute, D. (1988) Defeasible Reasoning and Decision Support Systems. *Decision Support Systems*, **4**, 97-110.

O'Neil, M., Glowinski, A. J. and Fox, J. (1988) Decision Making in the Oxford System of Medicine. *Proc. Expert Systems and their Applications*, Avignon, 1988.

O'Neil, M., Glowinski, A. J. and Fox, J. (1989) A Symbolic Theory of Decision Making applied to several medical tasks. In *Lecture Notes in Medical Informatics, 38: Proc. European Conference in AI in Medicine*. Berlin, Springer-Verlag.

Orponen, P. (1990) Dempster's Rule is #P-complete. *Artificial Intelligence*, **44**, 245-

253.

Paass, G. (1988) Discussion to "Belief Functions" by Smets, P. In (eds Smets, P., Mamdani, E. H., Dubois, D. and Prade, H.) *Non-Standard Logics for Automated Reasoning*. London, Academic Press.

Parsons, S. (1992) Qualitative belief networks. *Proc. ECAI '92*, Vienna, Austria, 48-50.

Parsons, S. (1993) *Qualitative methods for reasoning under uncertainty*. PhD Thesis, Department of Electronic Engineering, Queen Mary and Westfield College, London (in preparation).

Parsons, S. and Mamdani, E. H. (1993) On reasoning in networks with qualitative uncertainty. *Proc. 9th Conference on Uncertainty in Artificial Intelligence*, Washington DC, USA.

Pearl, J. (1986) A Constraint-Propagation Approach to Probabilistic Reasoning. In (eds Kanal, J. F. and Lemmer, L. N.) *Uncertainty in Artificial Intelligence*. Elsevier Science Publishers (North-Holland).

Pearl, J. (1988) *Probabilistic Reasoning in Intelligent Systems: networks of plausible inference*. San Mateo, Morgan Kaufmann.

Pearl, J. (1990) Bayesian and Belief-Function Formalisms for Evidential Reasoning: a Conceptual Analysis. In (eds Shafer, G. and Pearl, J.) *Readings in Uncertain Reasoning*. San Mateo, Morgan Kaufmann, 540-574.

Pearl, J. (1992) *Bayesian Inference Methods*. In (ed Shapiro, S. C.) *Encyclopedia of Artificial Intelligence*. Second Edition. New York, John Wiley.

Perlis, D. (1990) Truth and Meaning. *Artificial Intelligence*, **39**, 245-250.

Pierce, B. C. (1991) *Basic Category Theory for Computer Scientists*. Cambridge, Mass., MIT Press.

Pollock, J. L. (1992) How to reason defeasibly. *Artificial Intelligence*, **57**, 1-42.

Poole, D. L. (1985) On the comparison of theories: preferring the most specific explanation. *Proc. IJCAI '85*, Los Angeles, USA, 144-147.

Poole, D. L. (1988) A logical framework for default reasoning. *Artificial Intelligence*, **36**, 27-47.

Poole, D. L., Goebel, R. and Aleliunas, R. (1987) Theorist: A Logical Reasoning System for Defaults and Diagnosis. In (eds Cercone, N. and McCalla, G.) *The Knowledge Frontier: Essays in the Representation of Knowledge*. Berlin, Springer-Verlag, 331-352.

Poznanski, V. (1992) Defaults for Language Understanding. *Proc. IPMU '92*, Mallorca, Spain, 225-230.

Prade, H. (1983) Databases with fuzzy information and approximate reasoning in expert systems. *Proc. IFAC International Symposium on Artificial Intelligence*, Leningrad, 113-120.

Prakken, H. (1993) An argumentation framework in default logic. *Annals of Mathematics and Artificial Intelligence*, (to appear).

Preece, A. D., Shinghal, R. and Batarekh, A. (1992) Principles and practice in verifying rule-based systems. *The Knowledge Engineering Review*, **7**, 115-142.

Priest, G. (1989) Reasoning about Truth. *Artificial Intelligence*, **39**, 231-244.

Priest, G., Routley, R. and Norman, J. (eds.) (1988) *Paraconsistent Logics*. Philosophia Verlag.

Przymusinska, H. and Przymusinski, T. (1990) Semantic Issues in Deductive Databases and Logic Programs. In (ed Banerjii, R. B.) *Formal Techniques in Artificial Intelligence - A Sourcebook*. Amsterdam, North-Holland.

Przymusinski, T. (1988) On the declarative semantics of deductive databases and logic programs. In (ed Minker, J.) *Foundations of Deductive Databases and Logic Programming*, San Mateo, Morgan Kaufmann.

Quinlan, R. (1983) Consistency and Plausible Reasoning. *Proc. IJCAI '83*, Karlsruhe, Germany, 137-144.

Reddy, D. R. (1988) Foundations and Grand Challenges of Artificial Intelligence. *AI Magazine*, Winter 1988, 9-21.

Reichenbach, H. (1949) *Theory of probability*. Berkeley, University of California Press.

Reiter, R. (1980) A Logic for Default Reasoning. *Artificial Intelligence*, **13**, 81-132.

Reiter, R. (1984) Towards a Logical Reconstruction of Relational Database Theory. In (eds Brodie, M., Myopoulos, J. and Schmidt, J. W.) *On Conceptual Modelling*, New York, Springer-Verlag, 163-189.

Reiter, R. and Criscuolo, G. (1981) On Interacting Defaults. *Proc. IJCAI '81*, Vancouver, BC, Canada, 270-276.

Rychlik, P. (1991) Some Variations on Default Logic. *Proc. AAAI '91*, 373-378.

Saffiotti, A. and Umkehrer, E. (1991) PULCINELLA: A General Tool for Propagating Uncertainty in Valuation Networks. In (eds D'Ambrosio, B., Smets, P. and Bonissone, P.) *Proc. 7th Conference on Uncertainty in AI*, San Mateo, Morgan Kaufmann, 323-331.

Schaub, T. (1991) On commitment and cumulativity in default logic. In (eds Kruse, R. and Siegel, P.) *Symbolic and Quantitative Approaches to Uncertainty*, Berlin, Springer-Verlag, 305-309.

Schreiber, G. ed (1992) *Knowledge Acquisition*, **4**(1), Special issue on the KADS approach to knowledge engineering.

Schrödinger, E. (1947) The foundation of the theory of probability-I, II. *Proc. Roy. Irish Academy*, Series A, **51**, 51-66, 141-146.

Shackle, G. L. S. (1961) *Decision, Order and Time in Human Affairs*. London, Cambridge University Press.

Shafer, G. (1976) *A Mathematical Theory of Evidence.* Princeton University Press.

Shafer, G. (1978) Non-additive probabilities in the work of Bernoulli and Lambert. *Archive for History of Exact Sciences*, **19**, 309-370.

Shafer, G. (1981) Constructive Probability. *Synthese*, **48**, 1-60.

Shafer, G. (1987) Probability Judgement in Artificial Intelligence and Expert Systems. *Statistical Science*, **2**(1), 3-16.

Shafer, G. and Tversky, A. (1985) Languages and Designs for Probability Judgment. *Cognitive Science*, **9**, 309-339.

Shafer, G., Shenoy, P. P. and Mellouli, K. (1987) Propagating Belief Functions in Qualitative Markov Trees. *Int. J. Approximate Reasoning*, **1**, 349-400.

Shafer, G. and Pearl, J. eds (1990) *Readings in Uncertain Reasoning.* San Mateo, Morgan Kaufmann.

Shenoy, P. P. and Shafer, G. (1986) Propagating Belief Functions with Local Computations. *IEEE Expert*, **1**, 43-52.

Shenoy, P. P. and Shafer, G. (1990) Axioms for Probability and Belief Function Propagation. In (eds Shachter, R., Levitt, T., Kanal, J. and Lemmer, J.) *Uncertainty in Artificial Intelligence 4*, Elsevier Science Publishers (North-Holland).

Shepherdson, I. C. (1988) Negation in Logic Programming. In (ed Minker, J.) *Foundations of Deductive Databases and Logic Programming*, San Mateo, Morgan Kaufmann.

Shortliffe, E. H. (1976) *Computer-Based Medical Consultations: Mycin.* American Elsevier.

Shortliffe, E. H. and Buchanan, B. G. (1975) A Model of Inexact Reasoning in Medicine. *Mathematical Biosciences*, **23**, 351-379.

Smets, P. (1990a) The Combination of Evidence in the Transferable Belief Model. *IEEE Trans. PAMI.*, **12**, 447-458.

Smets, P. (1990b) Constructing the pignistic probability function in the context of uncertainty. In (eds Henrion, M., Schachter, R. D., Kanal, L. N. and Lemmer, J. F.) *Uncertainty in Artificial Intelligence 5*, Elsevier Science Publishers (North-Holland).

Smets, P. and Kennes, R. (1989) *The Transferable Belief Model: comparison with Bayesian models.* Technical Report TR/IRIDIA/89-1, Université Libre de Bruxelles, Belgique.

Smith, C. A. B. (1965) Personal Probability and Statistical Analysis (with discussion). *J. Roy. Statistical Soc.*, **A128**, 469-499.

Smithson, M. (1989) *Ignorance and Uncertainty*, Berlin, Springer-Verlag.

Spiegelhalter, D. J. (1986a) A Statistical View of Uncertainty in Expert Systems. In (ed Gale, W. A.) *Artificial Intelligence and Statistics.* Reading, Massachusetts, Addison-Wesley.

Spiegelhalter, D. J. (1986b) Probabilistic Reasoning in Predictive Expert Systems. In (eds Kanal, L. N. and Lemmer, J. F.) *Uncertainty in Artificial Intelligence.* Elsevier Science Publishers (North-Holland).

Spiegelhalter, D. J., Franklin, R. C. G. and Bull, K. (1989) Assessment, criticism and improvement of imprecise subjective probabilities for a medical Expert System. In (eds Henrion, M., Schachter, R. D., Kanal, L. N. and Lemmer, J. F.) *Uncertainty in Artificial Intelligence 5,* Elsevier Science Publishers (North-Holland).

Spiegelhalter, D. J. and Lauritzen, S. (1990) Sequential updating of conditional probabilities on directed graphical structures. *Networks,* **20,** 579-605.

Spiegelhalter, D. J. and Cowell, R. (1991) Learning in Probabilistic Expert Systems. *Proc. Fourth International Meeting on Bayesian Statistics,* Peniscola, Spain.

Spiegelhalter, D. J., Harris, N., Bull, K. and Franklin, R. (1991) *Empirical evaluation of prior beliefs about frequencies: methodology and a case study in congenital heart disease.* BAIES Report BR-24, MRC Biostatistics Unit, Cambridge, England.

Sterling, L. and Shapiro, E. (1986) *The Art of Prolog.* Cambridge, Mass., MIT Press.

Tan, Y. H. and Treur, J. (1991) *Constructive Default Logic and the Control of Defeasible Reasoning.* Artificial Intelligence Group Technical Report 280, Free University of Amsterdam.

Teach, R. L. and Shortliffe, E. H. (1981) An Analysis Of Physician Attitudes Regarding Computer-Based Clinical Consultation Systems. *Computers in Biomedical Research,* **14,** 542-558. Reprinted in eds Buchanan, B. G. and Shortliffe, E. (1984) *Rule-Based Expert Systems: The Mycin experiments of the Stanford Heuristic Programming Project.* Reading, Massachusetts, Addison-Wesley.

Toulmin, S. (1958) *The Uses of Argument.* London, Cambridge University Press.

Touretzky, D. S. (1984) Implicit Ordering of Defaults in Inheritance Systems. *Proc. AAAI '84,* Austin, Texas, 322-325.

Touretzky, D. S. (1986) *The Mathematics of Inheritance.* London, Pitman.

Tribus, M. (1969) What do we mean by rational? In *Rational Descriptions, Decisions and Designs.* New York, Pergamon Press.

Van Gelder, A. (1989) Negation as failure using tight derivations for general logic programs. *Journal of Logic Programming,* **6,** 109-133.

van Harmelen, F. and Balder, J. (1992) (ML)^2: A formal language for KADS models of expertise. *Knowledge Acquisition,* **4,** 127-161.

van Melle, W., Shortliffe, E. H. and Buchanan, B. G. (1984) EMYCIN: A Knowledge Engineer's Tool for Constructing Rule-Based Expert Systems. In (eds

Buchanan, B. G. and Shortliffe, E. H.) *Rule-Based Expert Systems: The MY-CIN experiments of the Stanford Heuristic Programming Project.* Reading, Massachusetts, Addison-Wesley.

Verma, T. and Pearl, J. (1988) Causal Networks: Semantics and Expressiveness. In (eds Shachter, R., Levitt, T., Kanal, J. and Lemmer, J.) *Uncertainty in Artificial Intelligence 4*, Elsevier Science Publishers (North-Holland).

von Neumann, J. and Morgenstern, O. (1947) *Theory of Games and Economic Behaviour.* Princeton University Press.

von Winterfeldt, D. and Edwards, W. (1988) *Decision Analysis and Behavioural Research.* London, Cambridge University Press.

Wagner, G. (1991) Ex contradictione nihil sequitur. *Proc. IJCAI '91.* San Mateo, Morgan-Kaufmann.

Walker, A. and Leakey, R. E. F. (1978) The Hominids of East Turkana. *Scientific American*, August, 54-66.

Walker, T. C. and Miller, R. K. (1986) *Expert Systems 1986.* Madison, SEAI Tech. Publ.

Walley, P. (1991) *Statistical Reasoning with Imprecise Probabilities.* London, Chapman and Hall.

Wallsten, T. S., Budescu, D. V., Rapoport, A., Zwick, R. and Forsyth, B. (1986a) Measuring the Vague Meanings of Probability Terms. *J. of Experimental Psychology: General.* **115**(4), 348-365.

Wallsten, T. S., Fillenbaum, S. and Cox, J. A. (1986b) Base Rate Effects on the Interpretations of Probability and Frequency Expressions. *J. Mem. and Lang.* **25**, 571-587.

Wellman, M. P. (1990) Fundamental Concepts of Qualitative Probabilistic Networks. *Artificial Intelligence*, **44**, 257-303.

Wermuth, N. and Lauritzen, S. (1983) Graphical and Recursive Models for Contingency Tables. *Biometrika*, **70**, 537-552.

Williams, P. (1974) Indeterminate Probabilities. In (eds Przelecki, M., Szaniawski, K. and Wojcicki, R.) *Formal Methods in the Methodology of Empirical Sciences*, Dortrecht, Reidel, 229-246.

Williams, P. (1982) Discussion of Shafer, G. Belief Functions and parametric models. *J. Roy. Statist. Soc.* **B44**, 342.

Wilson, P. N. (1989) *Justification, computational efficiency and generalisation of the Dempster-Shafer Theory.* Research Report no. 15, Dept. of Computing and Math. Sciences, Oxford Polytechnic (also to appear in *Artificial Intelligence*).

Wilson, P. N. (1991) A Monte-Carlo Algorithm for Dempster-Shafer Belief. In (eds D'Ambrosio, B., Smets, P. and Bonissone, P.) *Proc. 7th Conference on Uncertainty in AI*, San Mateo, Morgan Kaufmann, 414-417.

Wilson, P. N. (1992) Some Theoretical Aspects of the Dempster-Shafer Theory. PhD Thesis, Dept. of Computing and Mathematical Sciences and Dept. of Hotel and Catering Management, Oxford Polytechnic.

Wyatt, J. and Spiegelhalter, D. J. (1989) Evaluating Medical Expert Systems: what to test and how? In (eds Talmon, J. and Fox, J.) *Systems Engineering in Medicine*. Berlin, Springer-Verlag.

Wyatt, J. and Spiegelhalter, D. J. (1990) Evaluating Medical Expert Systems. *Proc. AAAI Spring Symposium on AI in Medicine*, 211-215.

Xu, H. (1991) An Efficient Implementation of Belief Function Propagation. In (eds D'Ambrosio, B., Smets, P. and Bonissone, P.) *Proc. 7th Conference on Uncertainty in AI*, San Mateo, Morgan Kaufmann, 425-432.

Yager, R. R., Ovchinnikov, S., Tang, R. M. and Nguyen, H. T. (1987) *Fuzzy Sets and Applications: Selected papers by L. A. Zadeh*. Chichester, John Wiley.

Yu, V. L., Fagan, M. L., Bennett, S. W., Clancey, W. J., Scott, A. C., Hannigan, J. F., Blum, R. L., Buchanan, B. G. and Cohen, S. N. (1979) An Evaluation of Mycin's Advice. *Journal of the American Medical Association*, **242**, 1279-1282. Reprinted in eds Buchanan, B. G. and Shortliffe, E. (1984) *Rule-Based Expert Systems: The Mycin experiments of the Stanford Heuristic Programming Project*. Reading, Massachusetts, Addison-Wesley.

Zadeh, L. A. (1965) Fuzzy Sets. *Information and Control*, **8**, 338-353.

Zadeh, L. A. (1968) Probability Measures of Fuzzy Events. *J. Math. Analysis and Appl.*, **10**, 421-427.

Zadeh, L. A. (1971) Similarity Relations and Fuzzy Orderings. *Information Sciences*, **3**, 177-200.

Zadeh, L. A. (1978) Fuzzy Sets as a Basis for a Theory of Possibility. *Fuzzy Sets and Systems*, **1**, 3-28.

Zadeh, L. A. (1984) Review of Shafer's 'A Mathematical Theory of Evidence'. *AI Magazine*, **5**, 81-83.

Zadeh, L. A. (1986a) Is Probability Theory Sufficient for Dealing with Uncertainty in AI: A negative view. In (eds Kanal, L. N. and Lemmer, J. F.) *Uncertainty in Artificial Intelligence*. Elsevier Science Publishers (North-Holland).

Zadeh, L. A. (1986b) A Simple View of the Dempster-Shafer Theory of Evidence and its Implication for the Rule of Combination. *AI Magazine*, **7**, 85-90.

Zadeh, L. A. and Kacprzyk, J. (1992) *Fuzzy Logic for the Management of Uncertainty*. Chichester, John Wiley.

Zarley, D., Hsia, Y.-T. and Shafer, G. (1988) Evidential Reasoning using DELIEF. *Proc. AAAI '88*, Minnesota, USA, 205-209.

Zimmer, A. C. (1986) What Uncertainty Judgements can tell about the Underlying Subjective Probabilities. In (eds Kanal, J. F. and Lemmer, L. N.) *Uncertainty in Artificial Intelligence*. Elsevier Science Publishers (North-Holland).

Subject Index

Author Index